TOMCAT! • THE GRUMMAN F-14 STORY

TOMCAT!
THE GRUMMAN F-14 STORY

PAUL T. GILLCRIST
REAR ADMIRAL, (USN, RET.)

Schiffer Military/Aviation History
Atglen, PA

Acknowledgements

In writing this book, so many debts were incurred to so many people that I doubt, in this lifetime, ever could be repaid. I hope that each of the contributors will experience some sense of satisfaction that their assistance, rendered so generously, was perhaps worth it after all.

First, and foremost, my deepest appreciation goes to the youngsters in the fleet who taught me so much while I was trying to learn, first hand, about the Tomcat. The youngsters include, not just the aircrews, but all the young men and women . . . the bluejackets, the supply and maintenance officers . . . the whole team whose efforts were necessary to make the Tomcat the finest fighter plane in the world.

Second, in order of importance, are all the naval officers, retired and active duty, and civilian experts whom I sought out and interviewed. Details of the principal interviews are contained at the rear of the book under sources, but many more occurred which space and time do not permit me to single out.

Most of the photographs in this volume came from the fleet! I solicited photographic inputs from all F-14 squadrons in the Navy, many of which have some very talented photographers flying Tomcats. Some of the photographs are from official Navy sources and are so labelled. But, several of them came from the voluminous files of Commander Chuck "Heater" Heatley, Commander J.J. Quinn, Lieutenant Commander Dave Parsons, Jan Jacobs, Bob Lawson and Lieutenant Steve Umekubo, all of them talented photographers of naval aviation subjects. But, a great number of the photographs came from the collection of Lieutenant Commander Tom "Tumor" Twomey, Fighter Squadron FIFTY-ONE. He, more than any other person, is responsible for the wonderful collection of F-14 photography which appears in this book. "Tumor" willingly gave of his own personal time and photo resources to enhance the quality of the photography which appears within these pages.

I especially want to single out two gentlemen who volunteered to do the thankless task of technical review of the first draft of the manuscript. Mr. George Duffy, Director, Warfare Analysis of the Advanced Programs Branch of the Grumman Aircraft Systems Division devoted his own time and energy to ensure that this book is technically correct in all respects. George was assisted in this effort by Joseph H. Wilkers, a former F-14 radar intercept officer, now working for Grumman. Joe was particularly helpful in reconstructing the sequence of events in Chapter 28. The able assistance of these two gentlemen, without which this book never would have been published, have made its writing an absolute delight . . . no, a labor of love!

A special acknowledgement is appropriate to a gentleman whose name is not ordinarily connected to the F-14. He is one of the finest gentlemen ever to wear a pair of Navy wings. Vice Admiral Bill Schoech held just about every command a senior naval aviator could hope to achieve. His last assignment before he retired was as Chief of Naval Materiel. Although he retired before the real problems appeared in the development of the F-14, he was called back to serve as a special consultant to the Chief of Naval Materiel to help solve some of them. I was privileged to conduct a telephone interview with Admiral Schoech during his terminal illness and shortly before his death. He is truly one of the unsung heroes of the F-14 story. This volume would probably never have been written had it not been for the sage advice and enormous support he gave unstintingly to the program over the years.

The final three chapters contain my own views on the F-14; where it should fit into the overall scheme of Naval Aviation and some observations which are somewhat at variance with current thinking among the Navy's leadership. None of the contributors had any part in the writing of these chapters and should not be held accountable for views which are mine and mine alone.

Book Design by Robert Biondi.

Copyright © 1994 by Paul T. Gillcrist.
Library of Congress Catalog Number: 94-66977

All rights reserved. No part of this work may be reproduced or used in any forms or by any means – graphic, electronic or mechanical, including photocopying or information storage and retrieval systems – without written permission from the copyright holder.

Printed in China.
ISBN: 0-88740-664-5

We are interested in hearing from authors with book ideas on related topics.

Published by Schiffer Publishing Ltd.
77 Lower Valley Road
Atglen, PA 19310
Please write for a free catalog.
This book may be purchased from the publisher.
Please include $2.95 postage.
Try your bookstore first.

VF-41
BLACK ACES

VF-51
SCREAMING EAGLES

VF-74
BE-DEVILERS

VF-84
JOLLY ROGERS

VF-101
GRIM REAPERS

VF-102
DIAMONDBACKS

VF-103
SLUGGERS

VF-111
SUN DOWNERS

VF-114
AARDVARKS

FOREWORD

Dedication
In memory of "Hank" Kleeman, Captain, U.S.Navy, the first man to take the Tomcat into aerial combat ... the first F-14 pilot to down a MiG ... and he did it with such class!

The senior tower petty officer received the first radio call at 8:48 AM on a warm winter morning. The date was 3 December 1985. He was the duty tower operator at Naval Air Station, Miramar, California, also known as "Fightertown, U.S.A." There was a duty crew of five on his watch team. He was the senior person in the tower. Miramar approach control had called him moments earlier on the squawk box alerting him to the hand-off of a flight of two F/A-18 Hornets inbound from the naval facility at San Clemente Island, California. The flight had filed a "pop-up" clearance for an approach to Miramar. San Clemente is a single runway on the island of San Clemente about sixty-five miles east of San Diego. It is used by the Navy to train for carrier qualification flights. The petty officer recognized the Vandy flight call sign as that of Air Test and Evaluation Squadron Four, home stationed at NAS Point Mugu, California. That was where the flight had originated with a stop-over at San Clemente. The voice of the flight leader when they called for a visual approach was crisp but slightly casual ... professionally casual.

"Roger, 620 you are cleared to continue. Miramar is VFR. Duty runway is two four. There is standing water on the runway. Call the break, over." The petty officer's quick response was equally professional. He looked out the glass enclosure to the northeast to see if he could see them. No luck! There was still a little of the morning haze under the overcast and visibility wasn't that good. Atlas was the VFR (good weather) entry point for visual approaches to Miramar. Approaching aircraft were required to pass over the old Atlas missile testing site exactly four thousand feet above sea level and headed directly for the field. The Miramar course rules further stipulated that jet aircraft fly at three hundred knots from Atlas on in to the break. Moments later he spotted the two sets of running lights of the section of Hornets and expertly judged them to be complying fairly closely to the course rules. As the flight neared the break, a point twelve hundred feet over the landing end of runway two four, the casual voice came up. "Miramar Tower, this is 620 in the break, over."

"Roger, 620 take it around. We are checking the condition of standing water on runway two four. It will take a few minutes for crash vehicles to clear the runway. Call re-entering the break, over." The casual voice wilcoed for the directions and the flight began a three hundred sixty degree circle to the left.

Standing water on a runway has particular significance for carrier airplanes especially when their tires are pumped up for carrier landings. The problem is a phenomenon called "hydroplaning." In effect, an airplane mainmount when braking on a wet surface will capture a small wedge of water under the tire and ride up on it. When this occurs friction decreases dramatically and the mount slides along as on an icy surface. The higher the tire pressure, the greater is the tendency to hydroplane. Obviously, when hydroplaning, all braking is lost along with directional control. It is standard operating procedure at Miramar to arrest airplanes at the mid-field arresting gear on the alternate runway two eight any time there is standing water on the runway. Also, the heavier the airplane, the greater is the tendency to run into difficulties simply because the speed at touch down is higher and the problem of energy absorption more daunting. The flight leader's fuel quantity was significantly higher than his wingman's so he elected to circle again and follow his wingman in the landing sequence. This he did.

The leader seemed to flare ever so slightly on an approach that was slightly fast then the main mounts touched down. After rolling a thousand feet or so the nose wheel was lowered onto the runway. The rest of the landing was normal until about three thousand feet down the runway when braking apparently was initiated and hydroplaning ensued immediately. The airplane began a right drift, departed the runway at a speed of about 72 knots whereupon the right mainmount settled into the soft, wet earth. The airplane began to swerve farther to the right as the left mainmount entered the earth and the right wingtip dug in to the ground. The airplane flipped inverted and came to a halt upside down and headed in a direction roughly 320 degrees with the engines running and the canopy separated from the fuselage. All of this occurred very rapidly, and the tower operator immediately went into action issuing the warnings over the radio and telephone and rolling the crash trucks. The first crash truck arrived at the airplane at 9:11. They found the pilot's helmeted head jammed into the soft earth with a mixture of rainwater and jet fuel filling up the depression it had made. There were several serious concerns which the crash crew needed to consider. There was the presence of leaking jet fuel and two engines still running, an ejection seat which had been arrested in mid ejection sequence and still ready to explode as well as an injured pilot whom they had to extricate from an airplane which was crushing him into the earth. But, they determined that the pilot was alive after the ambulance reached the scene at 9:22. The crane arrived at 9:30 to lift the airplane and extricate the pilot. Meanwhile, being unable to reach the engine throttles, the crash crew extinguished the engines with water. By 10:00 the seat was safetied by an escape system technician. Six minutes later the airplane was lifted clear of the ground and the pilot removed. At 10:31 the pilot was pronounced dead. Cause of death was determined to be a transected spinal chord which occurred at impact with the ground.

And so ended a legend. The pilot was "Hank" Kleeman, Captain, USN, Commanding Officer of Test and Evaluation Squadron Four (VX-4), the hero of the Gulf of Sidra, the first U.S. pilot to shoot down a Libyan fighter and the first pilot to take the Tomcat into combat and come out a winner. But, "Hank" Kleeman was a winner in every meaning of the word.

And, that is what this book is all about. It is the story of the Tomcat; how and why it was conceived, how it was designed and tested, put into production and finally introduced into the fleet. There is also some operational history leading up to "Hank" Kleeman's blooding; and finally, how the airplane has evolved today into the most lethal fighter plane in the world!

CONTENTS

Acknowledgements 4
Dedication 5
Foreword 5

PART I: Design For Maritime Air Superiority 10
Chapter 1: The Blooding 14
Chapter 2: The Admiral's Revolt 18
Chapter 3: The Requirement 22
Chapter 4: The Concept 25

PART II: Development Of A Navy Fighter 32
Chapter 5: The Acid Test 36
Chapter 6: The Great Rebate 44
Chapter 7: Selling The Shah 46
Chapter 8: Khatami 52
Chapter 9: The Little Engine That Couldn't 57
Chapter 10: NASA 62

PART III: In The Fleet 66
Chapter 11: The First Tomcat Deployment 81
Chapter 12: "Fightertown, U.S.A." 84
Chapter 13: AIM/ACEVAL 91
Chapter 14: Television Camera System 96
Chapter 15: Fleet Aerial Reconnaissance 99
Chapter 16: The Gunfighter 103
Chapter 17: The F-14B 109

PART IV: Fixing The Tomcat 112
Chapter 18: The Future Of The F-14 116
Chapter 19: The Blue Room 121
Chapter 20: The A-Plus 123
Chapter 21: Electronic Countermeasures 127
Chapter 22: The Reserves 130

PART V: Battle Group Operations 134
Chapter 23: Off Lebanon 138
Chapter 24: Indian Ocean 139
Chapter 25: The Achille Lauro Incident 142
Chapter 26: Norwegian Sea 145
Chapter 27: Northwestern Pacific 148
Chapter 28: "Navy Four, Libya Zero" 153

PART VI: The Persian Gulf War 160
Chapter 29: Persian Gulf 164
Chapter 30: Red Sea 168

PART VII: The Multi-Mission Fighter 170
Chapter 31: F-14D "Super Tomcat" 174
Chapter 32: "Tomcat 21" 178
Chapter 33: The Advanced Strike Fighter 182
Chapter 34: The Little Fighter That Can't 190

Part VIII: "Quo Vadis?, Naval Aviation" 190

Appendixes
Appendix I: F-14 Technical Data 193
Appendix II: F-14 Milestone Dates 194
Appendix III: Glossary 196
Appendix IV: U.S. Carrier Force Levels 197
Appendix V: F-14 Model Numbers 198

Sources 204

PART I
DESIGN FOR MARITIME AIR SUPERIORITY

For the last three years of my naval career I tried to get people, military and civilians, to stop using the phrase fleet air defense. It is the wrong way to describe the mission which navy fighter airplanes do . . . for any navy. The phrase has so often been used against the United States Navy that one would think that thoughtful naval officers would eschew it like the plague! One could infer, from use of the expression, the carrier battle group's fighter squadrons had only one function, that of defending it from the grave threat posed by the Soviet anti-ship missile threat. This is far from the case. The battle group's main purpose is to prowl the oceans of the world protecting the interests of the United States. A principal one of those interests is the protection of the freedom of the seas, the precious sea lines of communication over which flows the steady stream of materials critical to America's existence as an island nation.

Should those interests require, the battle group is fully prepared to project naval power over land in support of freedom of the seas, or in a larger land campaign in which deep interdiction targets can be reached by naval power. In any of the above cases an essential element of success is air superiority either over water or land. The F-14 design was intended to provide that air superiority. It could involve the escort of strike groups to deep interdiction targets, or it could be patrolling over an amphibious operation, or it could be over "blue water." Built into the F-14 design there has always been the nascent capability for air-to-surface strike warfare. For a variety of reasons the F-14 fighter community never took their strike capabilities seriously. It was not until the late 1980s that forward thinking members of the community realized the tremendous potential the F-14 possessed as a multi-mission strike fighter. The arrival in the fleet of the F-14A Plus and the F-14D were the catalysts for the return of this U.S. Navy fighter to its proper role.

Certainly, the ability to defend the carrier battle force is important. It is also a very challenging mission. So challenging has it been, in fact, that every so often some one thinks up the idea of the missileer. That is a real turkey, but one that keeps coming back. Put the capability into the missile is the thinking behind it, and not into the fighter. If this thesis is accepted the missileer would be a large, sub-sonic airplane carrying a large load of missile firepower. But, it also defies the laws of physics and common sense. Several instances come to mind to illustrate why this statement is true. In the first instance, an aerial target is vulnerable to a missile in a zone depicted on an F-14's tactical information display (TID) as a launch acceptable region (LAR). Depending on its velocity, altitude, and distance from the fighter to the target the size and shape of the LAR changes. As an example, the fighter aircrew objective is to maneuver their aircraft so that the LAR overlays the predicted target flight path. This ensures optimum missile employment. In the case of a high altitude, high speed target in a head-on situation the LAR becomes a sector emanating from the nose of the target. As the target speed increases the sector described by the LAR narrows. In order for the F-14 to get off a successful Phoenix missile shot the aircrew must position their airplane inside the LAR. As the sector narrows, the positioning limits of the missile launch airplane begin to become constraining. When confronting a high mach bomber like the Soviet "Backfire" the LAR sector becomes very narrow. A simple "jinking" maneuver by the bomber could actually take the fighter outside the LAR requiring it to move laterally to put itself back into a firing position. At such high closure rates the time available to do such a repositioning maneuver becomes critical. Therefore, cross sector agility is an important requirement of the fighter. High acceleration and high speed are the two factors which provide that capability.

In the second instance, survival in the outer air battle requires a combination of many things including, especially, speed and agility. The missileer has neither and would be the prime target for enemy escort fighters. With the large number of outer air battle missiles loaded on just a few airplanes, successfully taking them out would leave a battle force extremely vulnerable.

The specter of the missileer rose again in the midst of the battle to force the U.S. Air Force's F-111 down the Navy's throat as a platform carrying the long range Eagle missile. Had the apostles of commonality been successful the resultant diminution of the tactical effectiveness of the carrier air wing would have been horrible to behold.

F-14 escorting Russian Tu-95 Bear bomber.

1

THE BLOODING

The Tomcat roared down the number 1 catapult in full afterburner. Moments earlier, as the catapult officer of the *U.S.S. Nimitz* had touched his extended left hand to the flight deck (the signal for the launch) he notice the name stencilled on the forward left canopy rail. It had read Commander "Hank" Kleeman, Commanding Officer, Fighter Squadron FORTY-ONE. The airplane's side number was 102. The time was 0615 on 19 August 1981. Seconds later another of the Black Aces' F-14As roared down catapult number 2. *Nimitz*, at the time was steaming off the coast of Libya conducting the second day of an air-to-air live missile firing exercise. In the back seat of Kleeman's airplane was his radar intercept officer (RIO) Lieutenant Dave Venlet. The second F-14, piloted by Lieutenant Larry "Music" Muczynski with Lieutenant Dave Anderson in his back seat bore the side number 107. About an hour after launch Kleeman's RIO picked up a radar contact on the inbound leg of their combat air patrol (CAP) station race track pattern. The CAP was assigned an altitude of twenty thousand feet and the two F-14s were in a combat spread with Kleeman, the flight leader on the left. A good abeam position for a combat spread at that altitude was about one and one-half miles.

The radar contact became a "down the nose" intercept with the contact climbing to their altitude, leveling off and accelerating to 540 knots. Kleeman called his wingman for an offset turn to the right thirty degrees followed by a return to base course. This was intended to give the F-14s a little angle off their bogeys and therefore a bit of advantage. There was an almost immediate matching maneuver by the radar contact which put them again nose-to-nose. Obviously either the bogey's radar was as good as theirs or the Libyan ground controllers observed the F-14s maneuver, correctly assessed it and countered with the necessary directions to the bogeys.

Years later in the Pentagon Hank described the engagement and opined that in earlier incidents between Libyan fighters and F-14s from the *U.S.S. Forrestal* similar initial maneuvers had been successful. "I guess those Libyan air controllers have a pretty good learning curve, because I don't believe their airplanes' radars were that good." Convinced that another offset attempt would not work, Hank ran the throttles to full afterburner (zone five) and directed his wingman to step up. Muczynski climbed about five thousand feet higher than his flight leader and dropped back slightly in the process. If they had to "meet them at the pass" (head-on) Kleeman wanted to have his wingman with an altitude advantage. Venlet locked up the contact and with the help of the tracking diamond in the heads up display (HUD), Kleeman was able to visually acquire the radar contact and identified them at eight miles as Sukoi SU-22 Fitters in a very close formation. They were almost "at the pass" in a classic left to left passing situation when Kleeman started a left roll intended to keep the planes in sight as they passed down his left side.

At that moment his airplane was about one thousand feet from the Fitter flight leader and slightly higher closing fast he saw a flash as a missile was fired by the flight leader. Kleeman, call sign Fast Eagle 102, called on the radio for his wingman to execute a hard left break climbing turn. Just before the two Fitters flashed past and momentarily out of sight both F-14 pilots observed them start what looked like a splitting maneuver. About twenty-five degrees into the turn (two or three seconds) Kleeman saw the defensive splitting maneuver developing and directed his wingman to "take the one on the left."

They rolled out after essentially a one hundred eighty degree turn in trail of the Fitters (at their six o'clock position) with Kleeman's wingman, Muczynski in a firing position on the Fitter which had fired. For some reason the leader reversed his turn back toward his wingman who was now being pursued by Kleeman in a hard nose-down turn. Muczynski, now closing fast on the lead Fitter fired an AIM-9L Sidewinder heat-seeking missile which made a direct hit in the tailpipe.

CHAPTER 1: THE BLOODING

TOMCATS 2 – FITTERS 0 - The Gulf of Sidra Incident
by Jerry Crandall
See text for mission description. (Artwork courtesy of Eagle Editions Ltd.)

Muczynski executed a high-speed yo-yo maneuver up and back toward Kleeman's airplane. As he did so he saw an explosion and pieces of airplane coming off the lead Fitter. Kleeman's quarry continued the hard right turn pulling up into the sun. Knowing the sun would decoy his own heat seeking Sidewinder, Kleeman held his shooting position until his own missile guidance tone told him the sun was no longer a factor, and fired. Kleeman's missile struck the Fitter in the tailpipe. The airplane went out of control and the pilot ejected almost immediately. The entire engagement lasted between forty and fifty seconds from the first firing until the third missile struck its target.

Only four years later "Hank" Kleeman walked down the fourth floor E-ring of the Pentagon with me to the Blue Room to get the Secretary of the Navy's approval for the F-14D program. He came out victorious in both engagements. He will always be known in my "book" as the first man to fight the F-14 and the man who also got it fixed.

But there was more to the event than a single four plane encounter. It was a two carrier exercise in the Gulf of Sidra during which *Nimitz*'s air wing exercised their weapons systems, and there had been other incidents. Just the previous day the air wing commander, Commander "Bad Fred" Lewis had mixed it up with a pair of Libyan F-1 fighters and ended up with both of his F-14s sitting "in the saddle"; each in trail of his opponent. The opponents departed the scene. On the day of the shoot down two F-14s from *U.S.S. Forrestal* (also in the area)

Left to right: #107 crew, Lt. Jim Anderson and Lt. Larry Muczynski; #102 crew, Cdr. Hank Kleeman and Lt. Dave Venlet, of VF-41 on board U.S.S. NIMITZ, August 19, 1981, after the MiG kill mission.

were mixing it up with two Libyan MiG-25s. CAG Lewis was in the combat information center listening to both events which were on the same ultra-high frequency (UHF) radio channel. He heard "Music" ask excited over the radio (when he was in the saddle), "Skipper, what should I do?"

The F-14 pilot from *Forrestal*, who was maneuvering with the MiG-25 must have heard the question because he came up on the air with, "Shoot him, shoot him, shoot him!" "Music" shot him!

The return to the carrier after a shoot down is traditionally a triumphant event with a fly by victory roll and a smart recovery. Hank must have a little too much adrenalin pumping through his veins because, there before the watchful eyes of the battle group commander, Rear Admiral Jim Service, the ship's Captain, Jack Batzler and his own CAG, he boltered (missed a wire and went around for another landing attempt).

CHAPTER 1: THE BLOODING

Section of VF-41 Tomcats.

2

THE ADMIRAL'S REVOLT

The three men sat silently in the rear of the black limousine as it sped across the fourteenth street bridge spanning the Potomac River. Two of the men wore the blue uniforms of senior naval officers. The one wearing the three stripes of a Vice Admiral, US Navy said nothing and seemed to be overly interested in the passing scenery of a brisk spring afternoon. The second naval officer wore the stripes of a four star admiral and was engaged in a desultory conversation with the civilian about trivialities. They seemed to be carefully avoiding any mention of the event they were about to participate in, as principal actors. They were the top two men in the Navy; the Chief of Naval Operations and his civilian boss, the Secretary of the Navy. The date was 4 March 1968. The civilian, wearing a gray business suit, periodically detached himself from the conversation and absorbed himself in a document he held. For Vice Admiral Thomas Connolly, Deputy Chief of Naval Operations (Air Warfare), this particular trip to Capitol Hill had very foreboding possibilities. As the limousine threaded its way through the heavy traffic he had ample time to review the terrible sequence of events which had led him inexorably down the path of imminent self destruction.

It had all begun, he remembered vividly, with the presentation by the U.S. Air Force of their operational requirement for a variable geometry, all-weather strike airplane, fully equipped with targeting radar, an automatic terrain following auto-pilot flight control system and the ability to deliver nuclear weapons. The competition for development of the system was won by the General Dynamics Corporation and in the spring of 1963 the F-111 system emerged upon the scene. It was a unique airplane. With the ability to sweep its wings forward for long range and endurance, and fully back for supersonic dash it captured the imagination of the Secretary of Defense, Robert McNamara and his covey of "whiz kids." One of them thought up the idea of a "navalized" version of the airplane to be a successor to the F-4 Phantom II. What a grand idea! "Cost Effectiveness" and "Commonality" were two buzz phrases which were making the rounds of the Pentagon and Capitol Hill. The concept of an F-111 satisfying the needs of both an Air Force strike airplane and a Navy fleet air defense fighter was most attractive to the young PHDs who were advising Mr. McNamara from the recesses of offices bearing the name, "Systems Analysis." These bright young men were particularly devoid of anything remotely resembling operational experience. That was a serious problem. But, even more ominous was the fact that the importance of including operational experience in the acquisition process was denigrated. Operators, by definition, were too stupid to be allowed into the process.

As a consequence, incredibly inane ideas emerged. Anyone with an ounce of operational experience knew instinctively that many of those ideas were just plain silly. But, incredibly, many of them made their way into the system and proceeded along the path of development much too far before common sense finally killed them. Several made it all the way into the operating forces before the truth came to light. Three such ideas come to mind. There were many more, but these three characterize the flawed process as well as many of them.

The first was something called "agent orange." Some smart young man decided that one way to stop the North Vietnamese from bringing supplies down the Ho Chi Minh trail to the Viet Cong insurgents in the south, using the protective veil of the jungle to obscure their movement, was to eliminate the jungle. Incredible! I distinctly recall my reaction when I heard about it. We were standing in the ready room on board the *U.S.S. Bonhomme Richard* on Yankee Station in the Tonkin Gulf at the time and were acutely aware of the circumstances. All of us began laughing out loud. I finally sank down into my ready room chair. My sides were aching. We had all been flying for months over the vast tropical jungle of South Vietnam. It was a voracious, living thing, that jungle. Its roof, extending at some places, one hundred feet above the ground, was impenetrable. The wreckage of downed U.S. airplanes disappeared in days; devoured by that voracious thing, the jungle. I recall dreading the thought of being shot down and parachuting into the roof of that jungle. Several of my compatriots had been killed in the process of trying to release themselves after their parachutes hung up in the roof. They cut themselves loose from their parachutes and were killed in the fall to the ground. The roof was so dense that it was forever dark beneath it. The jungle was host to so many deadly insects, reptiles and carnivores that survival in it was chancy at best.

And its immensity was just as threatening as its virulence. How could any downed aviator expect to walk out of it? Impossible! The standing instructions were to remain near the wreckage of your airplane and await the arrival of the rescue helicopter. After having flown over hundreds of thousands of square miles of that jungle it was very apparent to me that there weren't enough airplanes, or gallons of "defoliant" in the whole world to eliminate that jungle. How then, could some smart young man think the idea would work? Simple. He worked out a fancy equation, ran it through a computer program, and without moving from his chair, proved mathematically, that it could be done. I watched from the air high above the coast of south Vietnam, those C-117s flying back and forth, low over the jungle, a white misty spray trailing off behind them, hour after hour trying to conquer the monster. It looked ridiculous . . . and it was! We all know what the result was. The only thing the defoliant hurt, in the long run, was our own young men! What a damning indictment!

The second smart idea had actually preceded the agent orange idea. This was to air drop thousands of tiny, miniature electronic listening devices into the jungle at "choke points" (another buzz word) which would detect the quiet footfalls of Ho Chi Minh's army of human pack animals and transmit that intelligence by radio waves to airborne receivers. Thus counted, a better strategy of where to strike at those choke points and when, would be developed. Like the defoliant idea this one was equally ridiculous. But, the two ideas were carried all the way through development, production and operational employment at an enormous cost in dollars and, in the case of the defoliant, American lives. But, there seemed to be no accountability for the ultimate effect of these smart ideas. Not, at least. for those who thought them up. In the long run field commanders were left to explain their failure.

The third bright idea was the one which gave Tom Connolly most cause for concern. It was the idea of building a navalized version of the F-111 for the Navy's next fighter. On paper the notion sounded great, and had so many advantages that analysts were falling all over each other trying to take credit for the idea. Everyone knew that the more airplanes of a given model produced, the lower the unit flyaway cost and the average costs became. In addition the higher the percent commonality achieved the higher were the economies of scale which obtained. The term "commonality" meant the percent of the component parts which the Navy variant contained compared to the Air Force airplane. Wags accidentally substituted the word "deviant" when referring to the Navy variant. The higher the commonality achieved, the fewer Navy unique components had to be designed and fabricated. Commonality became one of the shibboleths of the systems analysts.

Eager to please, the General Dynamics Corporation designed a shorter fuselage, capable of fitting on a standard aircraft carrier elevator. The concept espoused by the whiz kids was a large, variable geometry airplane capable of remaining on combat air patrol station for a long time carrying a large arsenal of very high performance air-to-air missiles. "Put the performance into the missile, not the airplane. It is cheaper and more cost-effective", they espoused. This missileer, as it came to be called, was the analyst's answer to the carrier battle group's outer air battle problems. The missileer issue gets more thorough coverage later on in this story. It is necessary only to say here that aerial battles may start at long range; but they generally end up in what is called in the trade, a "merged plot." This means close-in combat where short range weapons and high agility are the secret to survival. The F-111B, as it was to be called, was a big, slow, under-powered "dog." Tom Connolly's problem was that the analysts always showed the air battle as a long range exchange of missiles with the missileer coming out on top and unscathed. The numbers proved it! Therefore they didn't believe what those stupid naval aviators were trying to tell them. Furthermore Secretary McNamara believed them and had convinced the Secretary of the Navy to fall in line, bowing to the almighty idol, commonality.

But the gentlemen on Capitol Hill knew a thing or two. Their staffers kept them reasonably well informed about how the "blue suiters" felt on the issue. So in due course, the Senate Armed Services Committee, chaired by the powerful Senator John Stennis, invited the Navy to testify on the issue, knowing full well that the crusty Deputy Chief of Naval Operations (Air Warfare) and the Secretary of the Navy were on opposite sides of this issue. Just exactly where the Chief of Naval Operations stood on the issue was not certain. However, it was very clear that he had aspirations to a promotion to the highest military position, the Chairmanship of the Joint Chiefs of Staff. There was also the clear understanding that the Secretary (the highest ranked of the three), would do the talking. The atmosphere in the limousine was tense (at least it was for Connolly). He had been lead to believe that, having done well as DCNO(Air) or OP-05 as the job was called, he was rightfully in line imminently for promotion to a full (four star) Admiral. He knew that any muddying of the waters at this crucial point in his career could do irreparable damage to the tenuous advantage he maintained over the other three star admirals competing for the nomination. As they exited the limousine he reflected upon the three hours of testimony which had gone on in the morning and wondered how the afternoon's testimony would go. All morning the Secretary had fielded question after question. All of his answers hewed to McNamara's party line. The Secretary couldn't say enough nice things about the F-111B. Following the Secretary up the steps to the Senate, he decided to dutifully keep his peace and let that gentleman continue to do all the talking.

About twenty minutes into the afternoon session. Connolly knew it wasn't going well at all. The questioners had heard the Secretary talk laudably about all the positive aspects of the airplane. Now they were focussing on the service unique ones which, in the final analysis, were the serious "show stoppers." The airplane was badly under-powered and couldn't generate the specified acceleration at military thrust in the power approach (landing) configuration. That was a major deficiency. The senators asked questions about alternative power plants. The Secretary was in way over his head and, instead of turning to his uniformed experts seated beside him, he began taking the difficult questions for study and a written reply at a later date. It was patently obvious to all present, that the Secretary did not intend to let either of the uniformed experts speak. Furthermore, he did not intend to admit that engines powering the Air Force version of the airplane were not sufficiently powerful for the Navy variant. But, Senator Stennis was too

This page and opposite: General Dynamics/Grumman Navy F-111B.

CHAPTER 2: THE ADMIRAL'S REVOLT

smart to let that deter him. "Mister Secretary", he asked, "I would like to direct my next question to Vice Admiral Connolly and get his opinion. I hope you don't mind, Sir," he added unctuously. The Secretary, trapped, had to say he didn't mind. "Admiral Connolly", he asked, with a sparkle in his eye, "Do you think that the Navy variant needs a more powerful engine?"

This, it turns out, was a very important moment in the history of naval aviation. Admiral Connolly sensed that fact, perhaps more than anyone else in the room except for the crafty chairman. There was a long pause and a deafening silence in the chamber while Tom Connolly thought about his future. Up until a moment ago, it had been rosy. Now, he wasn't so sure. But there were other futures, more important than his. There were futures for the navy airmen who for the next thirty years would have to fly this dog of an airplane. Their futures would not be nearly secure enough flying an under-powered airplane in combat or simply in the deadly serious day-to-day business of peacetime carrier operations at sea. No, this was one of those moments when it behove a man of integrity to speak the truth and let the devil take the hindmost.

"Mister chairman", he answered in a deep, resonant voice, "All the thrust in christendom couldn't make a fighter out of that airplane."

That was the moment the F-111B died. It was also the moment that the Tomcat was born. The design was waiting in the wings for the right moment, the moment of conception. This was it!

But Chairman Stennis was far too wise to let it go at that. He knew that he also had to get the full approbation and the commitment of the other naval officer present or the F-111B wouldn't be really killed. Again with the Secretary's forbearance he directed the same question to Connolly's immediate superior the Chief of Naval Operations, also an aviator. Connolly told me years afterward, that there was a very pregnant pause before his boss spoke up. Doubtless, he was also contemplating his own future. The Chief finally answered Stennis' question by saying he agreed with Connolly. There was absolutely no conversation in the limousine ride back to the Pentagon. Nor was there any communication between Connolly's office and that of the Secretary for several days. To say that the Secretary was furious would be the understatement of the year. Vice Admiral Thomas F. Connolly retired as a Vice Admiral, United States Navy in September 1971. Men of his integrity and intestinal fortitude don't come down the turnpike very often!

3
THE REQUIREMENT

Naval strategists the world over drew a number of significant conclusions from the World War II campaign in the Pacific between 1941 and 1945. The major conclusion was that the main battery of the fleet shifted from the battlewagons and heavy cruisers to the fast carrier. I emphasize the word "fast" because there were many different sizes and shapes of aircraft carrier at the end of the war. The ones that did the bulk of the fight, the fast carriers were ultimately called attack carriers. The smaller carriers filled very important supporting roles without which the war in the Pacific might very well have had a different outcome. The table in Appendix IV lists the total numbers of aircraft carriers, by designation, in operation at the end of each year from 1940 through 1945. The numbers will be doubtless be startling to anyone familiar with the U.S. Navy's carrier force levels during, say, Korea, Vietnam or the Persian Gulf war. There was a total of ninety-eight aircraft carriers, of all types, in inventory at the close of the war. As one can see, from the progressively larger numbers beginning in 1942, the miracle of U.S. Naval expansion unfolds; and central to that miracle is the amazing story of the *Essex* Class aircraft carrier.

The principal weapon of destruction which sent the proud Japanese fleet to the bottom during the war shifted from the huge projectile from the sixteen inch gun, to the bomb dropped from carrier-based airplanes. The fast attack carrier came of age during those years. The aircraft which made up its air groups were a combination of special purpose and multi-mission airplanes. The torpedo and dive bombers were, for the most part, single mission airplanes. The multi-mission fighters first took on the fighter forces of the enemy by seizing control of the air over the enemy fleet, and then, over their own forces when the enemy struck back. When air superiority had been achieved, and enemy fighter forces neutralized, Navy fighters shifted to the attack role and participated in the war of attrition against the Japanese fleet. The multi-mission role of the navy fighter is important in its ability to expand the ship-sinking capabilities of the fleet's main battery.

Subsequent to the war, as the cold war between the United States and the Soviet Union became institutionalized, the United States Navy's attack carriers became the target against which the Soviet long-range naval aviation forces were developed. The main threat to U.S. aircraft carriers was the remarkable Tupolev TU-95 Bear bomber and the assemblage of anti-ship weapons which were designed for it to carry. First were the bombs, then came the family of air-breathing missiles each more destructive and more difficult to counter. As the U.S. Navy undertook the difficult task of transitioning to jet propulsion for its carrier aircraft, fighter design efforts were focussed at the Bear bomber. The first jet-powered fighter designs were single mission airplanes designed to shoot down Russian bombers. The concept of sweeping wings to eliminate the constraints which shock waves imposed on straight winged airplanes ushered in the second generation of fighters, still designed for the sole purpose of countering the Soviet bomber.

The first generation airplanes were relegated to the attack role and the "police action" with North Korea saw F9F-2 Panthers attacking targets with rockets, bombs, napalm and cannons.

As the third generation of fighters entered the fleet, earlier swept wing fighters were converted to attack airplanes (F-9F8Bs) and a whole new generation of attack airplanes was embodied in the competition between the A-4D Skyhawk and the FJ-4B Fury to take on the role of carrier based nuclear strike warfare.

Through all of these birth pangs, the requirement for a carrier-based airplane to counter the threat posed to the fleet by the Soviet bomber pervaded. The remarkable range of the Tupolev TU-95 represented a challenge to U.S. naval carrier forces over the uncontested use of a great part of the world's oceans.

Meanwhile, Soviet airplane designers, staying busy, introduced jet propulsion into their bomber forces with

CHAPTER 3: THE REQUIREMENT

U.S.S. Forrestal (CVA-59). (Official U.S. Navy Photograph)

PART I: DESIGN FOR MARITIME AIR SUPERIORITY

Views of Hellcat (left) and Panther (right) landing on early carrier.

a series of very impressive aircraft, each more powerful and capable of carrying more payload faster, farther and higher than its predecessor. The basic driving force in their design efforts was to sink the U.S. aircraft carrier.

The anti-ship air-to-surface missile was the next logical weapons development as supersonic bombers took center stage. Jet powered missiles capable of sneaking in at wave-top level or in steep, supersonic terminal dives added immensely to the difficulty of carrier defense. With this backdrop, the planners of U.S. naval aircraft requirements were faced with developing a fighter plane with capabilities beyond the wildest dreams of their predecessors of the late 1960s.

Russian Tu-95 bomber.

4
THE CONCEPT

Two instances come to mind which serve to highlight the principle benefits of the basic design concept of the F-14 Tomcat. The features of this marvelous airplane which set it apart from all other fighter planes in the world are a variable geometry wing and turbofan engines. To be sure, there are other tactical airplanes in the world which feature variable geometry wings; but, with the exception of the MiG-23, no air superiority fighter planes. In the U.S. tactical airplane inventory there are the FB-111, the B-1A and the B-1B ... all three bombers. The FB-111 is technically called a fighter bomber. In the U.S. Air Force, it is purely out of convention, (in the Tactical Air Force everything except the A-10 is called a fighter). But, the FB-111 is no more a fighter plane than the man in the moon. There is a variable geometry airplane in the North Atlantic Treaty Organization (NATO) inventory, but, like the FB-111 it is purely a strike airplane. Even the Soviet Union produced variable geometry airplanes like the MiG-23 and the SU-24. But, like the Tornado, and FB-111, they are also strike airplanes and perform poorly in the fighter arena. The principal method of varying the geometry of a wing is to sweep it. There have been experimental airplanes which have varied the geometry of their wing by changing the wing camber. But, that became so difficult an engineering feat for tactical airplanes that those efforts were abandoned years ago. There was even an oblique wing design in the late 1970s by the Rockwell corporation. So, sweeping has been the only practical way to exploit the benefits of variable geometry. The obvious reason for varying the geometry of an airplane's wing is to take advantage of the benefits of a forward swept (straight) wing; high aspect ratio for best efficient lifting at low speeds; and low speed for optimum landing performance. For carrier airplanes low landing speed is an extremely important benefit. But, the tactical benefits of a high aspect ratio wing are enormous. A straight wing airplane can turn better than a swept wing airplane by a substantial margin.

There are some serious design considerations in sweeping an airplane's wing. For one thing, the basic stability of an airplane changes dramatically during the sweeping process. Therefore, design engineers must carefully consider the stability effects, not only after the wing has been swept, but also, during the sweeping cycle. These design challenges were so severe for the Soviet designers of the very successful MiG-23 that they settled on a design which required the pilot to manually sweep the wing. He had only three positions to select; fully forward, for landings only; fully swept for supersonic, non-maneuvering flight; and partially swept for maneuvering flight. Consequently, aerial combat in the MiG-23 is highly restrictive simply because the pilot must be concerned constantly with selecting the correct wing sweep position for the particular maneuvers he is performing. Furthermore, he must plan ahead for anticipated maneuvers because there are additional restrictions he must observe while the wing is in transition from one position to the next. Full blown aerial combat maneuvering in a MiG-23 is so difficult that only the most skilled combat pilot could master the intricacies and be effective against a well trained opponent.

This, of course, raises the most critical consideration of rate of wing sweep (how long it takes for the wing to sweep through its full range of motion). In both the FB-111 and the MiG-23 the sweep rate is so slow that there is practically no tactical advantage to be gained in aerial combat against a fixed wing adversary. Therefore, the engineering challenges of sweeping the wing of a tactical airplane are threefold. First, and probably foremost, are considerations of wing strength in the various sweep positions. How does one design a wing that can withstand six "g"s at several wing sweep angles (or even a very large number of angles)?

Next in importance are the many stability considerations involved in moving an airplane's wing through a range of almost fifty degrees (as in the case of the F-14). There are many engineering challenges wrapped up in

B-1B and Tomcat in flight.

this single issue. Finally, the question of rate of wing sweep is probably the greatest engineering challenge. A very powerful actuator is needed to sweep a wing the size of the Tomcat's wing in straight-and-level, non-maneuvering flight. Finally, the difficulties encountered in designing a wing that can sustain high "g" forces while sweeping at a high rate make the challenge almost insoluble. The wing sweep rates in the B-1, FB-111, Tornado and MiG-23 are all too slow for effectiveness in aerial combat.

The only airplane in the world which features an automatically sweeping wing which can sustain high "g" loads while sweeping fast enough to keep up with the intense demands of aerial combat is the F-14. The F-14 aircrew can put their airplane through the most demanding and complicated maneuvers with total disregard for wing sweep because they know that a computer is rapidly providing the optimum wing position. The only thing the computer cannot do is anticipate what the aircrew will do next. Therefore, it lags the tactical situation by the time it takes to sweep from present position to the next desired one. A fast sweep rate takes care of the bulk of that problem.

The proof of the adequacy of the sweep rate in the F-14 is the fact that fleet aircrews do their aerial gunnery and air combat fleet exercises with the wing sweep control button in the automatic position. The only times a fleet aircrew chooses to select manual sweep is for parade formation (for cosmetic reasons) and for inflight refueling, a most precise evolution.

The first of the two instances which high-lighted to me the tremendous operational flexibility and combat effectiveness of the F-14's wing sweep system occurred in the fall of 1979 shortly after I had checked out in the airplane. It was on a stop-over cross-country flight from Miramar to Andrews Air Force Base near Washington, D.C It was a trivial incident but it made the point to me. We had filed a two-legged flight plan with a refueling stop at Tinker Air Force Base near Oklahoma City, Oklahoma. The total distance for the leg was only twelve

CHAPTER 4: THE CONCEPT

hundred nautical miles. The F-14 could easily fly fifteen hundred miles on internal fuel but this seemed like a logical mid-point for the trip.

Because of its variable sweep wing, the F-14's best cruise speed was really quite slow. We were about half way to our stop-over destination and were cruising at an indicated airspeed of only 275 knots at an altitude of 41,000 feet. This gave us a true airspeed through the air of about 500 knots. However, we were bring boosted along by a fifty knot tailwind and, therefore, were making a speed over the ground of roughly 550 knots. I was astonished to note that the fuel flow per engine was only eighteen hundred pounds per hour. A total of only thirty-six hundred pounds per hour; or sixty pounds per minute. By comparison, an F-4 Phantom would be burning about six thousand pounds per hour, almost twice as much. Certainly, he would be cruising at a speed at least a hundred knots faster. But, the point sank home that best cruise was very close to loiter speed for the Tomcat. That, was the point. The F-14 was designed to loiter on a combat air patrol station several hundred miles from the carrier to provide air superiority for the carrier operations. The F-14 could loiter longer on station, with a larger, more lethal load of air-to-air weaponry than any other fighter plane in the world. The loiter and radius advantages of the Tomcat were brought home to me as we cruised lazily along the airways of the great western desert.

Obviously, if we had wanted to cruise faster, we could have done so. However, it would have shortened our range. The benefits of only making one refueling stop enroute to Washington, D.C. were obvious.

"Navy Jet 4203, this is Oklahoma City Center, how do you read, over?" The radio transmission startled me from my thought process. Frank Brown's response was crisp and clear from the back seat.

"Oklahoma Center, this is Navy Jet 4203, loud and clear, over."

"Roger, 4203, this is Oklahoma Center. We have a flight of Naval Reserve Phantoms behind you. They have an overtake speed of fifty knots and are at your altitude. I'm going to have to move you to a lower or higher altitude to let them through. Which do you prefer, over? You can have flight level 450 or 370." Before Frank could answer, I told him on the intercom that I would answer. "Oklahoma Center, do you have a ground speed read-out on me. over?", I asked.

"Affirmative, 4203, you are making a ground speed of 549 knots, over", came the quick response.

"Oklahoma Center, this 4203, watch this", I announced as I rammed both throttles to the fire wall and into maximum zone five afterburner. I'd be dammed if I would move out of the way for a flight of Phantoms . . . especially Reserve Phantoms. No god damned way! The immediate increase in engine thrust threw me back against the seat as that Tomcat squatted and took off like a rocket. The airplane will accelerate at 50 knots a second in straight and level flight or almost 100 knots per second unloaded. The unloaded acceleration is an important tactical capability in combat. Even straight and level it was eye-watering. Exactly two seconds later I came out of afterburner and returned the throttles to a new fuel flow setting of twenty-two hundred pounds per hour per engine and was now looking at an indicated airspeed of 375 knots. I knew that my new ground speed would be about 675; more than enough to leave the Phantoms in the dust. After all, there is such a thing as dignity!

"4203, this is Oklahoma Center, Wow! Would you please do that again, my fellow controller wasn't watching, over?"

"Sorry, Oklahoma Center, if I did it again I would have to change my destination." I knew that there wouldn't be sufficient fuel left to make it to Tinker. Federal Aviation Regulations require that a change in cruise speed of over ten percent would have to be approved in advance. I knew that, but was counting on the controller not to be a stickler under the circumstances. So, I followed with. "Oklahoma Center, this is Navy Jet 4203, request a change in cruise speed to 675 knots, over."

The answer came quickly, "Roger, 4203, your request is approved." I quickly asked Frank to run the cal-

Tomcat Mach/Airspeed indicator.

PART I: DESIGN FOR MARITIME AIR SUPERIORITY

CHAPTER 4: THE CONCEPT

culation to see if we could still make it to Tinker at the new ground speed and fuel flow. In three seconds the answer came back that we could still make it but that our fuel reserves would be considerably lower at estimated time of arrival at Tinker. The remainder of our trip to Washington was uneventful. The point of the story is important. The F-14 can loiter on combat air patrol station very efficiently. It also has the excess thrust to accelerate very rapidly to a combat speed; and still be able to fight . . . and stay in the fight, better than any other air superiority fighter in the world. The new F-14D, with a thirty percent increase in thrust, as well as a 29 percent increase in loiter time represents an enormous increase in overall combat capability for the fleet. I could imagine that air controller that evening at home describing to his family how some crazy Navy fighter pilot accelerated his airplane nearly one hundred knots in less than three seconds on the airways just to keep another flight of jets from passing him.

There is one other aspect of a variable wing geometry design which is often overlooked by superficial analysis. This is the fact that the wing area (from which combat wing-loading is derived), varies with wing sweep angle. This is obvious to anyone who has walked around an F-14 and examined the enormous flat plate area on the under side of the fuselage between the engine nacelles.

Whenever the wings are fully aft (68 degrees in flight), the flat plate area provides what aerodynamicists call the fuselage contribution to lift. In the case of the F-14, the fuselage contribution to lift is enormous. The normal wing area is 565 square feet. When this number is divided by the combat weight of the airplane it yields a wing-loading of about 90 pounds per square foot (psf). There is a direct relationship between wing loading and agility; the lower the better. A wing-loading of 94 psf is about average for a modern fighter. However, when the wings are swept fully aft, the fuselage lifting area of 443 additional square feet increases affective wing area to 1,008 square feet, resulting in a wing-loading of about 55 pounds per square foot. Of course there is a drag penalty associated with all this lifting area which can only be compensated for by thrust. A fighter plane blessed by large wing area but low thrust will not have the ability to accelerate under "g" loading (Ps) and therefore will not be considered agile. That is why the F-14s with the new engines (F-14A+, F-14B and F-14D) are able to beat up so easily on new generation airplanes like the F-

VF-301 F-14A section over San Clemente runway.

16, F-15 and F/A-18s. It is the unique combination of low wing-loading, high thrust-to-weight ratio and high Ps which yields what I call agility.

As an example, an F-14D with a basic operational weight empty (OWE) of 44,000 pounds, half a load of internal fuel (8,200 pounds), two Sparrow and two Sidewinder missiles (1,400 pounds) in a fighter escort mission configuration has a wing-loading, with wings swept, of only about 55 pounds per square foot. This is comparable to the wing-loading of a MiG-21 . . . and much better than that of the F-15, F-16 or F/A-18 . . . by a long shot.

The second incident, which adds another dimension to the remarkable operational flexibility of the F-14 occurred in April of the following year. I had joined a carrier qualification class at the F-14 fleet replacement squadron (VF-124) at Miramar to see what it was like to land the Tomcat on a carrier. The idea had been, all along, to get with the youngsters of the troubled west coast fighter community and find out why their pilot retention rate was so disastrously low. By doing a little bit of everything they were required to do, I might find out what the problem was and, more importantly, do something to change it! I had checked out in the F-14, done some air combat maneuvering in it with fleet squadrons, some night intercepts, some aerial gunnery, some day and night in-flight refueling. Now, the only thing left to do with that wonderful machine was to take it to the boat!

The carrier qualification class which I joined comprised about a dozen aircrewmen besides me and the radar intercept officer assigned to keep me from killing us both, Lieutenant Commander Joe Motzinger. Aside from me and Joe, all the others were youngsters going to the boat for the first time in the F-14. I sensed a certain amount of anxiety and excitement in all of them about taking this monster aboard an aircraft carrier. I also sensed a certain wonderment as to what the hell this fifty year old fart was trying to prove by going to the boat with them. There was plenty of skepticism in their faces the day we all gathered in a briefing room for our first lecture on carrier qualifications in the F-14.

Since it was the first time for me in the F-14, the squadron had assigned a very experienced radar intercept officer, an instructor, to watch over me. I didn't envy Joe Motzinger. He introduced himself to me and announced the he and I were going to the boat together. All the while he, along with all the others, was sizing me up. He had an expression on his face like what I imagined a World War II Japanese kamikaze pilot might have. But, I could also see that Joe was determined to see this thing through. He was of medium build with brown hair, brown eyes and a large handlebar moustache. He also possessed a naturally exuberant nature and a wonderful sense of humor. I thought we hit it off well from the start . . . maybe!

For three weeks Joe and I flew twice a day; always the same mission, field carrier landing practice (FCLP). We started at Miramar for a couple of periods of day FCLP. A portable optical landing system was positioned on the left runway at Miramar (24 Left). We used it to make simulated carrier touch and go landings until we convinced the landing signal officer instructor that we were competent enough to advance, as a class, to the next phase of training. The next phase was night FCLP at Miramar. Deprived of the usual visual cues which daylight provides to aviators, we all took a few "bounce" periods to get the hang of the night carrier landing pattern. It was a little different from the day pattern. It was flown at the same altitude but was slightly wider and longer in the groove so that we started down on glide slope from a wings level attitude rather than from a turning start. But, it was artificial. There were too many lights on the ground to make it anything more than a transitional step. The gradual encroachment of housing and industrial development around the field made it difficult to simulate the dark environment of a carrier at sea. It only took one bounce period on runway 24 Left at Miramar to discover that the best turn in point was directly over a drive-in movie. As a consequence, as soon as the landing signal officer determined that we were ready to advance to the next phase of training he announced that we were ready for El Centro.

El Centro was a different story. There were no lights on the ground by which to cheat . . . just darkness. Except for the few homes in the area around the Naval Air Station it was very dark. The pilots had to refer to their instruments to fly the correct landing pattern for the two runway approaches used for carrier landing practice . . . the east-west runways, 08 and 26. By the time we got to the El Centro stage of training it was the first week in October 1980. I remember well the flight on the sixth of October. We took off from Miramar at about eight o'clock in the evening with a full internal load of fuel and crossed over the Laguna mountains to El Centro, a flight of about 100 miles. On arrival, we were cleared into the "bounce" pattern and commenced making carrier landing approaches. We completed ten approaches and were considered by the landing signal officer to have completed our mission. To be sure, we could have continued because there was still plenty of fuel on board. However, night FCLP is a very intense kind of flying. After about ten approaches, aircrew performance begins to degrade and further landing practice becomes counterproductive. So, we were "bingoed" back to Miramar. On arrival at Miramar the back seater suggested that I make a few ground-controlled landing approaches using the standard radio talkdown method. My training syllabus called for so many of them before going to the "boat." Since there was still plenty of fuel we flew two "GCAs" and then made our final landing. Each GCA took about ten minutes grinding around in a much longer pattern with wheels and flaps down. When I shut down the engines and punched the elapsed time clock I saw that we had logged exactly one and one half hours of flight time, nearly all of it at sea level with the wheels and flaps down and had landed with enough fuel for another half hour if we had so desired. I know of no other Navy airplane that could get that much carrier training out of a single load of internal fuel. This wonderful capability comes from several features unique to the F-14. First of all, the large amount of internal fuel that the airplane is structurally allowed to carry on its first carrier landing approach makes for plenty of training fuel available. By contrast most other fighters I have flown must burn down or dump fuel to low fuel states before beginning landing practice. The other two unique features, already discussed are the variable geometry (sweepable wing) and the turbo-fan engine which is so fuel efficient at low altitudes. The combination makes the airplane a clear winner in terms of operational flexibility over any other Navy tactical airplane. Our training period at El Centro was completed in about a week and again the landing signal officer determined that we were ready for San Clemente. This was the final, and most difficult stage of training before heading for the boat. San Clemente is a large uninhabited island about sixty miles off the coast of Southern California. It is owned by the U.S. Navy and has at its northern tip a single runway. Oriented roughly east and west, this 9,300 foot landing strip comes as close, at night, to the actual carrier environment as can be found anywhere in the world. As the landing signal officer put it, the night he

San Clemente Island.

briefed us for our flight to San Clemente, "this is where we separate the men from the boys." And, he was right.

Joe Motzinger and I climbed into our Tomcat on the evening of seventeen October for our final, and most intense, portion of the carrier qualification training. Nothing I had experienced thus far was as black as that patch of water at San Clemente. To add to our difficulty was the fact that there is usually a crosswind which is something which rarely occurs in real carrier operations. After an hour of groping around in that black hole, I felt physically brutalized by that god damned cross wind in that god damned black hole out there. Even though my landing attempts hadn't been very good at all, I was relieved when the LSO bingoed us to Miramar. The next two nights at San Clemente saw sufficient improvement in my landing performance for the LSO to certify us as ready for the boat on the night of the twentieth. On 21 October we went to *Kittyhawk* and the rest is history.

I recognize that there is more to optimizing the combat effectiveness of a navy fighter than illustrated be these few rather mundane examples. However, I distinctly recall sitting in the Tomcat one of those evenings after an FCLP period at El Centro. I was shutting off switches preparatory to getting out of the plane when the realization came to me that the Tomcat was really quite a unique airplane. The total effect of all the features I have described make for what I still consider to be the best all around carrier airplane and the most lethal fighter in the world!

PART II
DEVELOPMENT OF A NAVY FIGHTER

The specifications which, out of necessity, are placed on a Navy tactical aircraft are unique when compared to their land-based counterparts. The most obvious "penalty" paid by the developer of a carrier airplane is the penalty of weight. To operate from a flight deck one thousand feet long conventional airplanes must be catapulted to get them airborne and arrested to get them back. It is commonly thought that, of the two, the arrestment imposes the greatest demand for structural penalty. Not so. The F-14A, for example, routinely lands with only a small fraction of the ten tons of fuel which it carries internally and which it carries for the catapult launch. Since the energy needed to launch an airplane is directly proportional to the product of its mass multiplied by the square of its velocity. The velocity difference between an F-14A landing at an approach speed of 130 knots and one being catapulted at 155 knots is substantial when squared. Combine that with the difference in mass and the answer is clear.

The weight penalty is derived from several factors; beefed up landing gear, the carry-through structure for the arresting hook and the carry-through structure for the launch bar. During a catapult stroke all of the energy imparted to the airplane to accelerate it to flying speed is imparted at one point, the launch bar attached to the nose wheel assembly.

Similarly, all of the kinetic energy an airplane has at touch down must be absorbed at one point, where the tail hook assembly attaches to the airplane's keel. But, these three elements are not the only ones imposing unique penalties on the carrier airplane. There is also the weight penalty imposed by the necessity to fold or oversweep the wings, and sometimes even fold the vertical stabilizer. There are many other restrictions which are more subtle but equally important. The ingestion of steam from the catapult by an airplane's engines imposes engine design constraints. The constant presence of salt water imposes constraints on aircraft materials and coatings as well as corrosion control needs. Weight and size limitations are also imposed by aircraft elevators, jet blast deflectors and hangar bay overhead structure. The list goes on and on but, the point is made. It is a far greater engineering challenge to design and develop a Navy tactical aircraft than it is to design one for the more benign environment of an air base equipped with commodious support facilities and a twelve thousand foot runway.

As the number of specifications increases, so also do the number of tests needed to ensure their compliance. The testing of the F-14A's weapons system has been one of the costliest and time-consuming in the history of tactical aircraft. With such a wide range of weaponry, the testing process took an enormous amount of time and resources to complete. Finally, the multi-mission requirements of Navy tactical aircraft add to the testing as well as training time. First flight of the Tomcat occurred on 21

F-14 and SR-71 in flight.

December 1970. The Bureau number 157980 was stencilled on the either side of the rear fuselage just beneath the horizontal stabilizer. The pilot, Bob Smyth and the radar intercept officer, Bill Miller were the aircrew marking this significant event. Only six weeks had passed since the airplane was rolled out of the Grumman factory. And, only twenty months had transpired since the contract had been awarded to the Grumman Corporation for the research, development, test and evaluation of the winning design in the VFX competition. The Grumman proposal, called Design 303, was the distillation of the lessons derived from the Navy's aerial combat experience in the skies over Hanoi in the nine year war in southeast Asia. There is an interesting contrast in the development efforts of Grumman in introducing relatively high tech variable wing geometry onto the flight decks of U.S. Navy aircraft carriers in the early 1970s as compared to Lockheed's SR-71 program. In roughly the same time-frame the Navy marched the F-14 design through all the wickets in the acquisition process to field a revolutionary new design concept to the operating forces.

The U.S. Air Force, under the cloak of secrecy of the Lockheed "Skunk Works", fielded an equally high technology aircraft, virtually avoiding those same developmental constraints. Each airplane in its own right represents a whole panoply of monumental engineering achievements. The SR-71, the relatively unconstrained design, has since left the operational scene.

Meanwhile the F-14, which struggled so hard during the development process, continues to serve the Navy as an aging warrior but still unmatched in overall capability, by any existing fighter in the world. For those iconoclasts who would ruthlessly overhaul and streamline the defense department's acquisition process, there is a not-so-subtle lesson!

5
THE ACID TEST

Commander John R. "Smoke" Wilson, Jr. and his radar intercept officer Lieutenant Commander Jack Hawver walked the hundred yards or so from the line shack to the F-14A bearing the side number two zero nine the same way they had done several dozen times since they had begun the series of tests on the AIM-54 Phoenix air-to-air missile test program. "Smoke" was the Operations Officer of the Navy's Joint Evaluation Team or JET Team, as it was called.

The team was made up of aircrews and test engineers from the Weapons Test Division at the Naval Air Test Center, the Naval Missile Center at Pont Mugu, and one aircrew from Air Test and Evaluation Squadron FOUR (VX-4) also stationed at Point Mugu. The team's mission was to conduct, jointly, the Weapons System and Guided Missile Trials of the F-14/AIM-54 while avoiding duplication of effort and maximizing the utilization of test data.

Today, 21 November, 1973, however, was going to be a very special day! Because, today would be the acid test of the F-14's weapon system. In a sense, the future of the Tomcat hung on this one, single flight. All other test flights, as singular, successful and important as they were would have very little meaning if today were a failure. Needless to say, "Smoke" and Jack felt the pressure. They understood, as well as the bureaucrats in the Pentagon, how important this flight was. By the time they reached their airplane and began the exhaustive preflight inspection the sun was well up and the day had begun to warm. The airplane sat there on the ramp looking particularly sinister, mainly because there were six AIM-54 Phoenix missiles hanging on her. Four were on pallets in the semi-submerged missile stations under the fuselage and between the engine nacelles. The other two were suspended on the shoulder stations where the wing sweep pivot point was located. It was a six thousand pound weapon load, and it was lethal!

"Smoke" Wilson and his radar intercept officer (RIO). Jack Hawver were the Navy aircrew who conducted the most extensive and most expensive series of air-to-air missile test firings in history. And, the grand finale test was the most costly test in the history of air launched weapons testing. But, beyond being expensive the tests represented the vindication of a concept and the proof of effectiveness of a design that does not have, in my view, an equal in today's, world of sophisticated weaponry.

Of the many weapons which the F-14 carries, the AIM-54 Phoenix is the biggest, most lethal and has the longest range of any air-to-air missile in the world. To be sure, all of the Tomcat's weapons were tested. But, the series I refer to in this chapter covers only the Phoenix.

The tests under discussion used the early version of the Phoenix missile designated the AIM-54A built by the Hughes Aircraft Company. It is a big missile, thirteen feet long, fifteen inches in diameter with a three foot wingspan and weighing nine hundred seventy-five pounds. Its warhead, of the annular blast fragmentation type (continuous rod), weighs one hundred thirty-two pounds. The missile can operate in several modes. It is an active homing missile using a small radar for terminal guidance and an impact or proximity fuse to detonate the warhead. The missile has a launch-and-leave capability, but in its long range mode uses an autopilot and semi-active mid-course guidance with active radar for terminal guidance. In it's long range mode the missile comes off the launcher, ignites the rocket motor, climbs to over eighty thousand feet, accelerates to a speed in excess of Mach four and, after burn-out, conducts its terminal guidance in a descending trajectory converting potential energy (altitude) into kinetic energy for high performance end-game maneuvering. The F-14's principal Phoenix stations are four semi-submerged wells in the underside of the fuselage. Pallets containing Phoenix-unique hardware and electronics are fitted into these wells and the Phoenix missiles are suspended from the pallets. If the smaller AIM-7 Sparrow is to be carried on

CHAPTER 5: THE ACID TEST

Above and below: VF-111 F-14As landing on U.S.S. Kitty Hawk (CV-63).

Airborne F-14 loaded out with six AIM-54 Phoenix missiles.

the Phoenix station the pallets are removed to save weight. The pallets weigh over two hundred pounds each. Two more Phoenix missiles can be carried, one on each wing station pylon. In this, the heaviest missile loading configuration, the F-14 can still carry two AIM-9 Sidewinder missiles, one on the outboard side of each wing station pylon. In this configuration even without external fuel tanks the gross take-off weight would be several thousand pounds in excess of the limitations of the new catapults on the *Nimitz* class aircraft carriers.

There are various combinations of the three air-to-air missiles which can be carried ranging from six Phoenix, on the heavy side to four medium range radar-guided Sparrow and four Sidewinders on the lightest side with all stations loaded.

The purpose of this chapter is to describe six tests of the Phoenix missile. It is certainly not the intention to diminish the importance of either the AIM-7 Sparrow, the AIM-9 Sidewinder or, for that matter the lethal M61A1 Vulcan gun. Indeed, the weapon of choice in

Ground view of F-14 loaded out with six AIM-54 Phoenix missiles.

Pilot "Smoke" Wilson (left) and RIO Jack Hawver (right).

CHAPTER 5: THE ACID TEST

the two combat engagements in which the Tomcat has shot down four Libyan fighters has been the Sidewinder. The tremendous capability against the Soviet bomber and air-to-surface missile threat was the reason for the F-14 design, simply put, Maritime Air Superiority. I have tried for years to get people; military officers, Department of Defense civilians, congressmen and even journalists to stop using the worn-out expression, fleet air defense. If the purpose for designing the F-14 were purely for fleet air defense, it never should have been built. Modern carrier aircraft must be multi-mission aircraft. The F-14 has always had the long range strike escort and fighter sweep missions and was originally designed to have a conventional air-to-ground weapons capability. I have heard senior Navy civilians say that the F-14 will never go over the beach. That, of course, is sheer nonsense. In fact the astonishing capability of the F-14A plus (with the big engines) and carrying four two thousand pound Mark 84 bombs was demonstrated to me at Fallon, Nevada in October 1990. In September 1990 the F-14D demonstrated in a fleet airplane the remarkable air-to-ground capability of the new Tomcat. But, on the other hand, it is also true that had the F-14A failed the comprehensive Phoenix tests carried out by VX-4 at Point Mugu and two fleet squadrons from 1973 to 1975 the F-14 program should have, and would have been canceled. The six tests I will describe cover the gamut of the Phoenix weapons system capability and represent as thorough and complete a set of tests as has been devised for an air-to-air weapons system. It should be noted that, because of the price tag of a Phoenix missile, (its unit weapon cost) a very unique fleet operational testing program was initiated which allowed highly qualified fleet aircrews to gain valuable training experience while conducting follow-on test and evaluation test firings.

The tests to be described evaluated the long range capability against a simulated Backfire bomber target; a multiple (two weapon) firing to demonstrate the Phoenix capability in an electronic countermeasures environment; a high altitude, high MACH number firing against a simulated Foxbat target; a simulated sea skimming missile target; and a maneuvering target test. The final test, the acid test was a simultaneous firing of six Phoenix missiles against six targets at various altitudes and airspeeds. It was on that final test that the fate of the F-14 rested. Truly, it was the acid test!

The Phoenix missile's predecessor, the Sparrow missile, was probably the world's most successful radar guided air-to-air missile. It had proven itself to have modest combat effectiveness in the skies over North Vietnam in the early 1970s but the weapon had several distinct limitations which the Phoenix design was supposed to fix. The first limitation was range. Under the best of circumstances the existing AIM-7 Sparrow air-to-air missiles could be fired successfully at an approaching target fifteen miles away. This was not good enough to handle the threat posed by Soviet bombers carrying air-to-surface, anti-ship missiles.

The second limitation was the fact that the radar system of the F-4 Phantom (the airplane which the F-14 Tomcat was intended to replace) could only track one target at a time. Again, this was not good enough against an attack on a carrier battle group by many Soviet bombers carrying many air-to-surface, anti-ship missiles. The F-14's radar can track 24 targets simultaneously. This capability was demonstrated by intercepting and individually tracking the post deployment fly-off of an entire carrier air wing.

The third limitation, inherent in the Sparrow, was the fact that it was a semi-active, radar guided missile. This meant that the guidance and control system of the missile relied upon radar energy return from the target which was generated by the radar of the shooting airplane. In other words, the firing airplane had to keep its radar locked on the target throughout the entire flight of the missile. This was clearly not good enough in defending against a multi-aircraft attack. The combat effectiveness of the Sparrow was limited by not having a "launch and leave" capability. The Phoenix possesses this important feature and it was also an important program "driver" in the later Advanced Medium Range Air to Air Missile (AMRAAM) and Advanced Air to Air Missile (AAAM) programs. The fourth limitation, and one which was becoming more and more serious as the state of the art of electronic warfare advanced, was the fact that the Sparrow missile was not adequately equipped with an electronic countermeasures capability. This was not good enough considering the fact that Soviet bombers could be equipped with a radar jamming capability against the U.S. Navy's fighters.

The fifth, and perhaps most important limitation was what is called "end game" performance. Once the rocket motor of the Sparrow missile burned out, it began to decelerate rapidly. As it lost airspeed, its ability to maneuver diminished. Therefore, any kind of target maneuvering after rocket motor burn-out became increasingly effective in lowering the probability of kill (Pk) of the missile.

The Phoenix missile was specifically designed to correct all of these deficiencies. The missile's flyout range of approximately sixty miles represented a threefold increase. Furthermore, launch range to target could exceed one hundred miles. In addition, the F-14's radar would be able to track twenty-four targets at the same time and control the flight of six missiles simultaneously to their targets. The Phoenix missile would not have only a semi-active homing capability. In fact, the missile would carry its own small radar which would turn on in the final stages of its flight to acquire and guide on the target. As far as electronic warfare was concerned, the Phoenix missile would be equipped with an advanced, state of the art electronic countermeasures capability which would thwart some jamming, and even enable it to home on the jamming aircraft. Finally, and perhaps the most significant feature of the Phoenix missile, it was designed for much greater "end game" performance. The way this "end game" performance was achieved was quite unique. For a long range shot, the missile was programmed to climb to an altitude in excess of eighty thousand feet. Rocket powered vehicles perform better at higher altitudes for range purposes. After rocket motor burn-out the missile is programmed to begin a descent to the target. In the descent, the missile converts potential energy (altitude) to kinetic energy (velocity) thereby maintaining its ability to turn and chase a maneuvering target.

By the time "Smoke" and Jack had completed their thorough pre-flight inspection, the airplane had a crowd of anxious observers watching the small crew of sailors checking all of the Phoenix missiles on all of the weapons stations. There were electrical continuity tests and checks of other aspects of the sophisticated AWG-9 Hughes system. Although the crowd of Grumman and Hughes engineers wanted to jump in and help, the test called for sailors to load and check-out the system just as though they were at sea and in a real shooting war. So, the crowd watched and mentally wrung their hands as the sailors stepped slowly and methodically through the elaborate series of system checks. "Smoke" and Jack participated in the checks and finally, on signal, indicated that they were ready to start engines. Once started they shifted to aircraft power and the electrical power cables running from the electrical power carts were disconnected from the airplane. Now another series of checks was begun to determine that the airplane's engine powered generators were providing adequate power to run the weapons system. The checks were exhaustive and finally a signal from one of the sailors told "Smoke" that they were indeed ready to taxi.

The airplane turned out of the parking ramp and started down the taxiway towards the engine warm-up and arming area at the take-off end of the duty runway. "Smoke" could pick out the vehicles of the arming crew waiting for them in the arming area. As he turned into the area and swung the airplane to the west for arming, he braked the airplane to a halt, set the parking brake and, on signal from the senior ordnanceman raised his hands above his head. The radar intercept officer did the same. This was the signal for the crew of ordnancemen to swarm over the airplane and conduct their final checks of the missiles and the hardware suspending them from the airplane. At last the senior ordnanceman gave "Smoke" a thumbs up signal and they all climbed into their truck and sat waiting for the take-off. Jack called Point Mugu tower for take-off clearance. They were cleared into position with instructions to hold for take-off clearance. Moments later, they were cleared for take-off. The heavily loaded Tomcat accelerated down the runway and lifted off cleanly, tucking in its wheels and flaps and turning seaward towards the firing range.

They checked in with the range controller on the radio and were assigned to a position on the range where they were to hold until the elaborate stage could be set and all targets launched. They reached the assigned altitude and position and "Smoke" leveled off at twenty-eight thousand feet, throttling back to a loitering speed of Mach 0.78 to conserve fuel for what he knew might be a long wait. Now was a time for reflection on some of the more landmark test firings leading up to this acid test. First there was the firing to test the long range capability of the Phoenix missile in April 1973.

Long Range Test: The target was a BQM-34E, a drone containing an augmentation device which made it appear to have the same radar cross-section as a Soviet Backfire bomber. The target was simulating the speed and altitude for a Backfire; Mach 1.5 (one and one half times the speed of sound) at an altitude of fifty thousand feet. "Smoke's" radar intercept officer had acquired the target at an amazing range of 132 nautical miles with his own airplane sprinting along at Mach 1.5 at an altitude of forty-four thousand feet. The target had been acquired in the track-while-scan mode (one of the requirements of the test) and, at a range of 110 nautical miles, "Smoke" fired. With a "whoosh" the huge missile roared off, climbing to a peak altitude of over one

CHAPTER 5: THE ACID TEST

hundred thousand feet and then started its long descent scoring a range (passed within lethal range of the warhead) hit at a distance of 72 nautical miles from the launch point. That was truly an impressive test and established a benchmark for the range capability of the missile. All the more impressive, however, was the fact that, during the test, the target employed a "blinking" noise jamming technique similar to that expected from a Backfire bomber! Then, "Smoke" remembered, there was the test against a high altitude, high speed target.

High Altitude, High Speed Test: This firing occurred on 22 July 1972. The target, a BQM-10B Bomarc drone missile was howling along at an incredible speed of Mach 2.1 at an altitude of over seventy thousand feet. The target was equipped with an augmenting device which simulated the radar cross-section of a Soviet MiG-25 Foxbat interceptor. This had been one of the "fleet" firings. A very well qualified aircrew from fighter squadron THIRTY-TWO (VF-32) launched from the aircraft carrier *John F. Kennedy* climbed to an altitude of forty-one thousand feet, accelerated to a speed of Mach 1.2, acquired the target and fired at a range of fifty-one miles, scoring a direct hit. This shot, in "Smoke's" mind, established the benchmark for the very high altitude, very high speed capability of the Phoenix missile. But, one of the most demanding, he remembered, had been the test firing in an electronic countermeasures (ECM) environment.

Electronic Countermeasures Test: This firing had been completed earlier, in March of 1973. It was difficult for two reasons; there were two targets fired at simultaneously with the trailing target protecting the lead target by jamming the F-14's radar. The lead target was a QF-9 (an old jet fighter modified as a drone target) cruising at an altitude of thirty thousand feet and a speed of Mach 0.8. Twenty-five miles behind the QF-9 was a BQM-34A target drone cruising at an altitude of thirty-five thousand feet and a speed of Mach 0.8. The BQM was noise jamming down the main beam of the Tomcat's radar. This time "Smoke's" airplane had been cruising at an altitude of thirty thousand feet and a speed of Mach 0.8. His RIO had acquired the target through the jamming and "Smoke" fired two missiles nine seconds apart. The first missile, fired at a range of twenty-five miles, scored a direct hit on the QF-9. The second missile, launched at a range of forty-seven miles from the jammer scored a range hit (lethal radius). This was truly one of the most difficult challenges laid upon the weapons system up to that moment. "Smoke" and Jack were exultant about the results. Another difficult test, "Smoke" remembered was the test of the Phoenix against a hard maneuvering target.

Maneuvering Target Test: This firing occurred on 2 February 1973. The target was a QF-86 (drone version of an old Air Force fighter) cruising at an altitude of seventeen thousand feet and a speed of Mach 0.7. "Smoke's" airplane was cruising at an altitude of seventeen thousand feet and a speed of Mach 0.80. The target was acquired and a Phoenix was launched at a range of ten nautical miles. Shortly after the launch the drone's controller rolled the QF-86 into a five "g" descending turn and made a six "g" pull-out at nine thousand feet. The missile arrived just at the pull-out scoring a range hit. The F-14's radar was directed away from the target after initial positioning because this was to be an Air Combat Maneuvering Active launch. In this mode, when the trigger is pulled, the Phoenix's radar comes on immediately and locks on the first target in its field of view. The missile is completely independent of the F-14's weapons system. "Smoke" recalled pulling up after the launch and rolling the Tomcat inverted in order to observe the target's evasion maneuver. Because of the geometry and the maneuvers of both the target and the missile he initially thought that they had missed. Then, suddenly there was a ball of fire where the target had been.

This was also considered a benchmark achievement since, up to this juncture, a hard maneuvering turn had always been a successful defense against air-to-air missiles. But, the test from which "Smoke" derived perhaps the greatest satisfaction so far was the test against the simulated sea-skimming missile.

Sea-skimming Missile Test: One of the greatest concerns the Navy had was its inability to counter the Soviet cruise missile skimming over the tops of the waves. Even if it could be acquired and distinguished from the radar return of the water's surface it was almost impossible for the weapon's fuze to function properly for the warhead to damage the target. Usually, the fuzing action was caused by the proximity of the water's surface resulting in a premature detonation. In this test, which occurred on 8 June 1973, "Smoke's" airplane was cruising at an altitude of twenty-four thousand feet and a speed of Mach 0.92. The target was a QT-33 drone cruising at

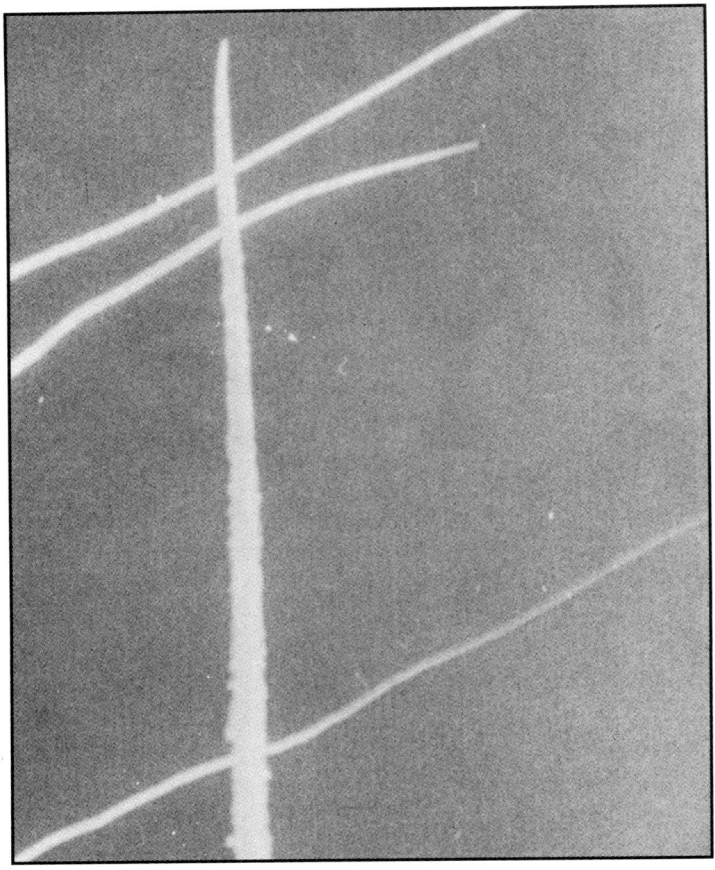
Missile contrails from six-on-six missile shoot.

a speed of Mach 0.72 and a height of just fifty feet over the water. "Smoke's" RIO acquired the target and a Phoenix missile was launched at a range of twenty-two nautical miles scoring a lethal hit. This was a real landmark in the technology struggle between U.S. and Soviet weaponry.

"Smoke" forced his attention back to the business at hand. Of course, a test as important and as costly as the "six on six" should not be attempted without a dress rehearsal. On the day of the rehearsal seven airplanes took off from Naval Air Station, Point Mugu; three QT-33's (with pilots), two A-4 Skyhawks, one F-8 Crusader and the F-14 shooter. "Smoke" and Jack positioned themselves at their assigned orbit position and the other six went to their assigned stations to await the start. The difficulty of achieving such exquisite timing was clear to every one in the air and at the ground control and monitoring stations. The three QT-33s would depart their stations first because they represented the slowest of the six targets. They were to simulate the three targets which would cruise toward the waiting shooter at mach 0.77 in a sort of line abreast. Shortly afterward the two A-4s simulating BQM-34As would depart their stations headed toward the shooter. They were to cruise at a higher mach number, 0.84 and would catch up to the first three at just about exactly a range of forty-five miles. The last airplane to leave its orbit was the Crusader. Its pilot would turn inbound and, emulating the launch of the high speed simulated Soviet Backfire bomber, light his afterburner and accelerate to mach 1.2. If timed correctly, the Crusader would arrive abeam the T-33s just as the two A-4s did. They did it just right and "Smoke" and Jack went through the motions of firing the six missiles in the sequence discussed earlier. Although the dress rehearsal had been a resounding success, there were people with nagging doubts. One of those had been Ken Richardson, Phoenix/AWG-9 program manager of the Hughes Corporation. He had spent a good deal of time going over the many computer simulations of the firing scenario and come to the nasty conclusion that there was too much risk, yet, in the firing scenario as it was agreed upon. He expressed those doubts to Rear Admiral "Swoose" Snead, the F-14 program manager at the Naval Air Systems Command in Washington, D.C. and to Captain John Weaver, the Navy's Phoenix program manager. "We are going to miss one of those targets, I'm afraid", he told Snead. A conference was called to weigh the concerns expressed by Mr. Richardson. All of those present knew what the stakes were. Failure of this crucial test would mean certain cancellation of the entire F-14 program. It was a tough call. But, Snead was tough-minded. He listened to all the arguments, for and against proceeding with the test as scheduled. Then, he made the decision. "We go as scheduled." It was simple and final . . . and terrible in all of its implications. Snead had crossed his Rubicon, for better or worse. Now it was all up to the team he had set up and trained . . . especially the pilot and RIO, "Smoke" and Jack. "Smoke" remembered that meeting as he adjusted the altitude hold mode of the autopilot. In fairness to all those concerned in this decision it should be pointed out that "Smoke" and Jack had also run numerous variations of the "six on six" scenario on the simulators at the Naval Air Development Center at Warminster; the Hughes "roof top" in Canoga Park, and on the Systems Integration Test Station at the Naval Missile Center. The "blue suiters" believed that the scenario was; (1) a fair test of the system, (2) had a reasonable chance of success and (3) a demonstration of the control of six missiles against six targets simultaneously. The Hughes people were naturally nervous and would have preferred a more conservative scenario. The Navy

CHAPTER 5: THE ACID TEST

view was that the test had to be realistic or it wouldn't be worth doing at all.

The sharp voice of the radar ground controller snapped "Smoke" from his reflections with the announcement that the show was about to begin giving them a vector which brought them head-on with a line of six targets. "Smoke" left the throttles where they were to optimize the launching of six missiles in rapid succession against that impossible array of targets. It had been a major achievement getting them all into the air and into a position to present a simultaneous attack by six targets at different locations, aspect angles, speeds and altitudes. As Jack excitedly announced the appearance of each of the targets in succession the weapons system automatically prioritized them for firing sequence. "Smoke" and Jack determined the priority of the first two and left the remaining four up to the computer to prioritize. There was a good reason for this. If left to its own devices, the computer would always select as the first priority, the target which would arrive first. That, of course would be the BQM-34E which was traveling at mach 1.2 at fifty thousand feet. If the first missile launched, was aimed at that target, it would reach it before all the missiles had been launched. In that case the testers could not really claim that the AWG-9 weapons system had truly tracked six missiles in flight simultaneously. For this reason "Smoke" and Jack decided to select two of the slower targets, one of the BQM-34As and one of the QT-33s as threats one and two. Tracking had begun at over fifty nautical miles and as the Tomcat turned toward the threat vector aircrew's pulses were racing like trip hammers. They had good track files on all six targets and Jack was excitedly calling out the rapidly decreasing range to optimum launch time. The other targets included three QT-33s (drone versions of the old Lockheed jet trainer, two BQM-34As and one BQM-34E.

At a range of thirty-one miles to the closest target the first Phoenix missile was launched. Thereafter, in rapid succession the two men worked in concert to launch the other five missiles at the other five targets. "Smoke" fired the first missile. Jack fired missiles two through five, and "Smoke" fired the final missile. In only thirty-eight seconds all six had been launched. There were four direct hits on the simulated bombers (two of the three QT-33s, one of the BQM-34As and the BQM-34E). The flight control module failed in one of the two BQM-34As causing it to veer to the right of the intended course. The ground controller used full left control stick displacement but the drone continued to the right and outside the control volume of the missile's radar causing it to break lock. One of the Phoenix missiles experienced a failure in an antenna causing it to miss the QT-33 against which it was targeted. In all, the test was scored a success with five of the six missiles functioning correctly, four direct hits and one lethal miss. It certainly represented the basis for selling the F-14 program to the congress, the Department of Defense and, most importantly, to the United States Navy. In a light moment years later "Smoke" tried to give me a feel for the magnitude of the dollar cost of all those missiles, and the drones, and the range and fuel costs. It was a staggering number. The firing sequence lasted thirty-eight seconds, amounting to $154,000 per second. He summed it up by saying, "It was like setting fire to a ten story parking lot filled with new Cadillacs!

6

THE GREAT REBATE

I will never forget marching down the E-Ring of the Pentagon in a flying wedge toward the door with the inscription, "Office of the Deputy Secretary of Defense, The Honorable William Clements." The three of us were in what I call a flying wedge with Dave Potter, Undersecretary of the Navy, in the lead. I was flying the left wing position as his Executive Assistant, and John Bierworth, Chief Executive Officer of the Grumman Corporation on the right wing. It was late in the evening in November of 1974. There had been a great deal of difficulty in the F-14 development program. There had been an in flight fire, several crashes, cost overruns and substantial schedule slippage . . . all the ingredients for a program cancellation. Added to the distress were Grumman's bleats of financial problems. The additional development costs had eaten up all profit margin and all indications were that more costs would surely put the corporation into receivership. The Navy's refusal to share any more of the pain had been adamant.

The press had a hey day with all of this. The questions came thick and fast. Could the Navy afford a development program that seemed to be nothing more than a bottomless pit? How much would the F-14 program really cost the taxpayer before it was all over? Do we really need such an expensive airplane to do nothing but defend the aircraft carrier? In the midst of all the bad press came the announcement of a General Accounting Office (GAO) investigation into advanced payments made to the prime contractor, the Grumman Corporation by the United States Navy. The GAO report asserted that the payments were illegal. The contract called for periodic payments on the basis of performance. Since the development program had failed to make the progress stipulated in the contract, recent payments should have been withheld. When the press got its hands on excerpts of the report leaked by opponents to the program on Capitol Hill there was hell to pay. Great pressure was exerted by the Congress on the Deputy Secretary of Defense, Bill Clements. Being the politician that he was,

Mr. Clements yielded and sent a memorandum to the Secretary of the Navy insisting that restitution be made to the federal government of dollars paid illegally to the Grumman Corporation. The Secretary of the Navy, the Honorable William Middendorf, directed that the Under Secretary of the Navy, the Honorable David S. Potter look into the matter. A short inquiry by Mr. Potter resulted in a memorandum to the Secretary of the Navy, from him recommending that the Grumman Corporation be ordered to return the total of the advanced payments. The Grumman Corporation was hard pressed to come up with an easy way out of their dilemma. They were on the verge of embarking on the most profitable program in the history of the corporation; and here they were faced with a serious cash flow problem. Fortunately, the Shah of Iran came to the rescue. The Bank that represented the Shah in the United States made a favorable loan to the Grumman Corporation to permit the Grumman Corporation to respond to the United States Government.

In due time, the Grumman Corporation announced that they were ready to comply with directions from the office of the Under Secretary of the Navy. Mr. Beirworth, Chief Executive Officer of the Grumman Corporation, showed up in the Office of the Under Secretary of the Navy. As Mr. Potter's Executive Assistant, I received Mr. Beirworth and announced his arrival to Mr. Potter. There was a call from Potter to Clements and we started down the E-ring with Mr. Potter in high spirits. He was going to slap the check, in the amount of fifty-two million dollars, on Clement's desk and get the Navy off the hook. We swept into Clement's outer office and were waved into the inner sanctum without a moment's delay. Dave Potter walked briskly over to Bill Clement's desk and ceremoniously slapped the check on the desk along with a few earthy remarks about getting off the Navy's back. Mr. Clements, grinning like the proverbial Cheshire cat, accepted the check with great ceremony and thanked Mr. Beirworth. The Shah of Iran had un-

CHAPTER 6: THE GREAT REBATE

F-14A section from VF-301.

wittingly saved the F-14 program from disaster, and didn't even know it. The delivery of the check was certainly a fortuitous event because, I believe it saved the entire F-14 program. The program was in trouble. Technically, programmatically and politically the F-14 was experiencing severe pressure. The advocates in the Navy, lead by the Deputy Chief of Naval Operations, Air Warfare, Vice Admiral Thomas F. Connolly, were hard pressed to answer the tough questions. As mentioned earlier in "The Admiral's Revolt", they were fighting a daily battle to keep the program alive and the developmental difficulties the airplane was experiencing were making it a hard-fought battle. The civil servants in the office of the Secretary of Defense (OSD) who had advocated the F-111B for the Navy were having a hey day with all of the F-14's misfortunes. I am convinced that the biases weighed heavily in Mr. Clement decision to send the deadly memorandum to the Secretary of the Navy. I have always felt that the OSD Mafia fully intended that the leaked memorandum would be the death knell for the F-14. It is one of life's ironies that an Iranian bank official saved the life of what turned out to be the best fighter plane in the world.

7
SELLING THE SHAH

There are those knowledgeable gentlemen who will insist that the sale of the Tomcat to the Shah of Iran didn't have any real effect on the F-14 program. I disagree. To be sure the Shah only bought eighty of the airplanes (79 were delivered), but their purchase, in my view, represented a very significant milestone in the airplane's history. The reason for this is simple. The sale of the Iranian F-14s came at a time in the airplane's history when it was still getting a great deal of bad press over program cost overruns and schedule slippage. The airplane badly needed some good press and good news. Winning the sale over the aggressive opposition of the U.S. Air Force was both good news and good press.

The fact that the Shah considered the F-14 to be a notch better than the F-15 was a huge morale booster for the proponents of the Tomcat and a serious blow to the U.S. Air Force. The incident warrants a chapter in the history of the F-14.

One of the several key players in the sale of the Tomcat to Iran was the OPNAV Program Coordinator, Captain John R.C. Mitchell. In the summer of 1972 John reported to the office of the Chief of Naval Operations (OPNAV) as Program Coordinator for the F-14 and the AWG-9 weapons system program. He was a Phantom pilot who had not yet flown the F-14. But, his reputation as a very competent Navy fighter pilot gave credence to his selection for this important post. John relieved Captain "Scotty" Lamoreaux as F-14 Program Coordinator, and Scotty, headed for "the promised land" as the next Commander, Fleet Air Miramar. It was only days after Scotty's departure that the letter from the Shah made its way through the bureaucratic maze of the Pentagon to John's desk. Officially, John's title was code OP-506C3. He was assisted in his responsibilities by Commander Denny Strole, a battle tested Radar Intercept Officer (RIO) also from the Phantom community.

The letter from the Shah announced his intention to investigate the possibility of buying the F-14 as a replacement for the aging F-4 Phantoms in the Imperial Iranian Air Force. John was quick to recognize the importance of this opportunity at a time in the life of the Tomcat when its safety record and its program costs were giving the airplane a very bad name in the Navy, the Office of the Secretary of Defense and on Capitol Hill. Of course, the Shah was well aware of the Tomcat's growing pains. Nevertheless, he was evidently determined to give equal opportunity to both the U.S. Air Force's new F-15 and the Navy's F-14 to compete for the role of preeminent fighter airplane in the Imperial Iranian Air Force. The buy, estimated to be about eighty airplanes and two billion dollars, was not a foreign military sale to be sneezed at.

Until this time, the Imperial Iranian Air Force had been considered by the U.S. Air Force as its private turf. But, the Shah wasn't naive. He was quick to recognize that the Phantom which his air force had grown to love was, in fact, a U.S. Navy developed fighter plane. Was it not good business, then, to look at both the follow-on Air Force and Navy fighter programs for a replacement to their venerable Iranian Phantoms? In fact, the Navy's F-14A was substantially ahead of the Air Force's F-15 in the development process, from a calendar standpoint. The first flight of the Tomcat occurred in December 1971, whereas the F-15 first flew in May 1972 some six months later. This time advantage had a pronounced impact on the competition for the Iranian buy.

John Mitchell and Denny Strole went to a full court press to get a briefing ready for the Shah and the Iranian Air Force. When the briefing was ready to show, Scotty Lamoreaux was brought back from Miramar to view it and comment. His total involvement in the program for several years made it logical for him to give the brief to the Shah rather than John, who was new to the Pentagon, to the F-14 and to Washington politics. The Tomcat had many enemies in Washington; not only in the Navy, the Air Force and the Defense Department, but also in the Congress.

CHAPTER 7: SELLING THE SHAH

In his letter, the Shah had expressed the desire to come to the United States to be briefed on both airplanes, to observe a flight demonstration and, perhaps, even to fly the airplanes. Naturally, since the F-15 had not yet made its first flight, the idea of the Shah coming to America was ruled out and the U.S. Navy team, made up of Rear Admiral Harry Gerhardt, Captain Scotty Lamoreaux and John Mitchell went to Iran. They went directly to Tehran, briefed the Shah and returned to the United States. The briefing had been well received by the Shah. They were tolerated by the Iranian Air Force pilots and the Shah congratulated them very graciously. He also reiterated his wish that they come back when the U.S. Air Force was ready, and give back-to-back briefings on both airplanes. After that he reminded them of his earlier request to come to the United States to observe flight demonstrations of both airplanes. It was some months later when the Air Force announced that they were ready to brief the Shah on the F-15 Eagle. The Air Force also argued that, since the F-14 had already been briefed to the Shah the Navy should not come along. But, wiser heads prevailed and the Department of Defense decided that the two airplanes should be briefed to the Shah.

It was determined that John Mitchell should give this second briefing to the Shah and he set diligently to work incorporating the additional information being developed from flight testing of the Tomcat. During their many briefings, they came to the realization that the Imperial Iranian Air Force had been brain-washed by the U.S. Air Force into believing that the F-15 was the end-all fighter of the century, and that the F-14 was a dog and should be ruled out as a replacement for their Phantoms.

It was also decided that, for the second trip to Tehran with the U.S. Air Force, John Mitchell would have more credibility if he flew the Tomcat. Then it was decided by the State Department that an evaluation of the airplane ought to be done by someone external to Grumman and the U.S. Navy, to give it a stamp of approval by the U.S. Government. An Air Force officer, a test pilot stationed at Edwards Air Force Base in the Mojave Desert, Lieutenant Colonel Fred Cuthill was selected to do the "unbiased" evaluation. It was laughable! Imagine, if you can, a U.S. Air Force pilot expected to give an unbiased evaluation of a Navy developed fighter plane that was in direct competition with the premier Air Force fighter plane! Ridiculous! (In recent months I tried several times to get Fred to give me a copy of his report. He has, thus far, been unable to find it).

In good time the flight was scheduled and, with John Mitchell acting as his escort and chase pilot in an ancient F-4B, Fred Cuthill got his flight. The blessings of such a lash-up were mixed to say the least. But, in John's view, there was a hidden benefit for him. After Fred got through his flight, the Chief Test Pilot for Grumman, Bob Smythe, asked John if he would like a second flight in the F-14. In a heartbeat John accepted and within minutes Don Evans, a Grumman test pilot bustled John back to the flight line to fly the F-14. The flight was a hurried up event and the timetable so short that John spent most of the forty minutes of it at high speeds and low altitudes to burn up the eight tons of internal fuel. The high point of the flight came when the pair surprised a twin engined, propeller-driven S-2 Tracker out over the water, dawdling along at a sedate one hundred twenty knots. Later, the shocked pilot of the S-2 reported them to the Federal Aviation Agency for nearly causing a mid-air collision. John said they never got nearer than two hundred feet. However, the fact that their Tomcat was doing over eight hundred knots when it went by probably aggravated the situation! The supersonic shock wave must have really rattled the pilot's cage! Meanwhile, Fred Cuthill wrote his report and plans moved ahead for the briefing to the Shah.

When the briefing was finally ready after many "murder board" reviews, John made plans for the trip which would find them giving the brief many times as they made their way east toward Iran. There were briefs in Washington, London and Stuttgart before the team ever crossed the Iranian border. When the team finally arrived in Tehran they were scheduled to brief a large retinue of senior Imperial Iranian Air Force officers. They had been brought in from air bases all over the country. As before, John and his Air Force counterpart flipped a coin to see who would brief first. As before, the other briefer won the toss and went first. During the pre-briefing introductions, John found that the Iranian Air Force officers were openly contemptuous of the F-14 and somewhat surprised at the trepidity of the two naval officers who had the sheer effrontery to try to sell a Navy fighter to them.

The Air Force briefer was a good speaker and was thoroughly prepared for his work. His pitch went well. However, the advantages John brought to the table were several. First, and foremost, he had a better designed airplane and he knew it. Secondly, his Tomcat had already flown and his data were real. The F-15 was still a paper airplane and the data presented were all estimates.

PART II: DEVELOPMENT OF A NAVY FIGHTER

Finally, and most important, John had flown the Tomcat. It was very important, because when a pilot appreciates the good qualities of an airplane, he can speak about it with an eloquence that only other pilots can appreciate. It shows.

John made full use of his advantages and the real value of the F-14 design began to penetrate the brainwashed Iranian Air Force officers a little. John gave it his all. Both briefings went well. Afterward, several members of the audience came forward and congratulated them both.

The day of the big briefing to the Shah came. The entourage made its way to the Shah's beautiful summer palace in Tehran. It was a sunny day in April 1973. They were led into a beautiful, ornately appointed reception hall. Again, they flipped a coin. Again, the Air Force officer won the toss and elected to go first. John knew that he had some disadvantages as well. First, there had been that terribly unfortunate crash of the first F-14 on its second flight. Then, there was all of that bad press over schedule slippages and cost overruns. But, when his turn came to brief the Shah, John set all of those negative thoughts aside and gave the best briefing of his life. The Shah asked many questions. He was knowledgeable about tactical airplanes and was an accomplished pilot himself. He was also very aware that these very United States Air Force officers who were trying so hard to denigrate their Navy competition, had been weaned on an Air Force version of a Navy designed fighter, the F-4 Phantom II.

At long last the briefing ended and John felt totally exhausted from the intensity of the briefing and the questions and answers. The Shah stood up and a hush fell upon the group. First, he thanked both briefers for doing such a splendid job of presenting the unique capabilities of their airplanes so eloquently. The Shah had a perfect grasp of the English language, as did most of the Iranians in the room. He singled out the F-15 first and spoke in glowing terms of its spectacular performance, weapons system and flying qualities. Certainly it would make a wonderful airplane to satisfy the requirements of the Iranian Air Force (John's heart began to sink). It was truly, the Shah continued, the premier air superiority system of the western world! (John's heart began the long descent to the pit of his stomach).

However, the Shah added, the F-14 was also a very impressive airplane. With its long range air-to-air missile capability, its variable geometry wing, turbo-fan engines and its broader range of weaponry, it was truly the premier air supremacy (the Shah put meaningful emphasis on the word) airplane in the world! With that, the Shah strolled regally from the room leaving the gathered eagles in a state of shocked stupor.

In utter amazement, John looked over at the broad grin on the face of Rear Admiral Harry Gerhardt, Director, Foreign Military Sales. They had won this round and the next, and last, round would be the flight demonstration at Andrews Air Force Base, near Washington, D.C. That was scheduled in July, 1973.

As the time grew short for the big shoot-out several meetings were held with Air Force and Navy representation. A member of the Department of Defense refereed these meetings. It was decided that each airplane would do the identical flight demonstration, flying identical profiles, each lasting about twelve minutes. John Mitchell quickly put together a proposed demonstration profile and submitted it up the line for approval by the Air Force. They bought it completely, confident that the higher thrust-to-weight ratio that the F-15 possessed would be capitalized upon with the Navy profile. Indeed, the Air Force openly wondered at the naivete of the Navy planners for suggesting a profile that would clearly favor their airplane. None of them suspected anything devious . . . no hidden agenda.

The flight would begin with a high performance take-off to an Immelman turn and climb-out. The next maneuver would be a descent to a high speed fly-by, followed by a couple of high "g" low altitude maneuvering turns, a slow speed fly-by in the landing configuration and a final landing. The flight profile was carefully planned out so the total time from first take-off to final landing of the second airplane not exceed 30 minutes. Again, a coin was flipped; and again the U.S. Air Force won the toss, electing to go first.

The big day arrived. The assemblage of ground support equipment and trailers was substantial, indicating that the two contractors fully understood the importance of the flight demonstrations to be executed that day in July 1973. All of the Air Force and Navy big wigs were assembled at Andrews Air Force Base at Camp Springs, Maryland. The Shah's motorcade arrived at the flight line. The base was essentially closed for the next thirty minutes. The reviewing stands had been assembled the night before and the Shah's entourage was escorted to the stands. The company F-15 pilot and the Grumman aircrew walked across the parking ramp to the two sleek fighters parked there. Don Evans and Dennis Romano began a detailed pre-flight inspection of their F-14 as

CHAPTER 7: SELLING THE SHAH

USAF F-15 Eagle on takeoff.

Irv Burrows, in the F-15, started engines and taxied out to the take-off end of the longest north-south runway. Both aircrews had earlier been given a special meteorological briefing before the flight. Don and Dennis caught a nuance in the weather briefing which perhaps the F-15 pilot missed. It was a subtle point, but one which would prove to be decisively important in the outcome of the flight demonstration.

There was a shear wind at about 1,000 feet over the field. There was a slight surface wind blowing essentially down the long runway from the north. But, the wind shear, which began at 1,000 feet caused the wind to change direction almost 180 degrees and increase to twenty knots. Don decided to reverse the direction of his slow speed fly-by so that, by flying a little bit higher, he could appear to be flying much slower over the ground than the F-15, which would be flying at a lower altitude and into a head-wind of just a few knots.

The difference in speed over the ground (and past the reviewing stand) would amount to over seventy knots. That was the net effect of the wind shear, the 126 knot approach speed of the F-14 (Don actually flew the pass at 95 knots), as compared to the 155 knot approach speed of the F-15. This may not seem important, but, in fact, the ability of an airplane to operate from runways that had a high probability of bomb damage from enemy air strikes was a very important factor in the Shah's criteria for an Iranian fighter. Slow landing speed equates to short landing distance. The braking system in a tactical airplane has to absorb the energy of a landing airplane. Energy equals the mass of the airplane multiplied by the square of its approach velocity. Lower landing speed, therefore means less roll-out distance. Don and Dennis, in their last minute change of plans, decided to raise the altitude of his low speed pass to get fully into the wind shear and take full advantage of the apparent lower landing speed of the F-14. He further intended to take advantage of a lower internal fuel load than agreed upon. He started engines ahead of schedule and sat out in the warm-up area burning down fuel during the F-15 flight demonstration. This would reduce the difference in thrust-to-weight ratio between the two fighters. Of course, this would reduce the reserve fuel agreed upon by the two services. But, Don and Dennis were born risk takers and reveled in the notion that they were going to make the Air Force look bad.

On schedule the F-15 taxied onto the runway, stopped briefly, lit both afterburners and simultaneously released the brakes. What followed was a truly spectacular twelve minute flight demonstration! The sleek machine accelerated rapidly down the runway for about twelve hundred feet then lifted off gracefully and almost gently. The pilot was good. He kept the airplane no more than twenty feet off the runway while accelerating as the wheels folded into the fuselage and the flaps programmed up. About three thousand feet down the runway the plane rose smoothly in a steep climb out, accelerating all the way until it was almost out of sight. When it was noth-

PART II: DEVELOPMENT OF A NAVY FIGHTER

F-14 during flight demonstration.

ing but a blue speck the pilot came out of afterburner, rolled the airplane inverted and came racing back earthward. There was no sound as the small blue speck grew rapidly toward the reviewing stand at just under the speed of sound. He was probably doing six hundred and fifty knots when he went by the reviewing stand about one hundred feet over the same spot on the runway where he had released his brakes only thirty seconds earlier. It was a spectacular maneuver.

It was impossible for the pilots watching not to salivate at the demonstration of raw, brute power! At the far end of the runway the airplane went back into full afterburner and, rolling almost into a vertical bank, did a 90/270 degree reversal that brought him back down the runway at the same speed even though he had pulled an incredible seven "g"s throughout the 360 degrees of turn. The brute airplane had also accomplished the reversal entirely within the field boundaries, pulling soft vapor trails from the wing tips. There was another identical reversal at the take-off end of the field and the roar of the engine abruptly quieted as the pilot chopped both throttles to idle rpm, put out the speed brakes and lowered the wheels and flaps. The airplane rolled out of the reversal decelerating all the way to about 160 knots and an altitude of about two hundred feet . . . nice and slow. Then at mid-field he "broke" to the downwind while at the same time banging both engines to full power. The climbing turn to the downwind leg was almost an oblique Immelman turn, rolling out on the downwind leg,

very close abeam with the wheels and flaps down. The pilot made a nice approach, touched down gently at the approach end of the runway and rolled to a complete stop in about 2500 feet, and directly in front of the reviewing stand. It was an impressive show, indeed! Everyone was impressed. The pilot continued to the first taxiway and cleared the runway.

Don and Dennis had observed all of this and were ready to go. Their work, they knew, had been cut out for them. There were smug looks on the faces of all the Air Force officers in the reviewing stands. They were all evidently waiting for the underpowered Tomcat to fall on its face. What they didn't know was that Don Evans and Dennis Romano had remained at a high power setting during the F-15's performance and had only about 2,500 pounds of fuel remaining. They knew that at the end of their short performance they would be "running on fumes." But, they also knew that with only one eighth of their internal fuel capacity they had the same thrust-to-weight ratio as the F-15. They had one more thing going for them, variable geometry, and it would make all the difference in the world.

The Navy entourage were all holding their collective breaths as Don taxied onto the runway, came to a halt, held his brakes, ran the engines to a setting where the brakes would barely hold and then simultaneously rammed both throttles to full zone five afterburner and released the brakes. The Tomcat leapt forward, rolled about six hundred feet when the nose lifted off the run-

CHAPTER 7: SELLING THE SHAH

way, the wheels came up and the plane continued accelerating up into the burning blue sky, its afterburners trailing two twenty foot long sheets of flame as it executed a perfect Immelman turn. At about three thousand feet the Tomcat rolled out of its Immelman turn and, remaining in afterburner did a quick 90/270 degree reversal back to the original runway heading and then its graceful wings swept back all the way, as it fell earthward like a stone. It came by the reviewing stand at about 325 knots in a knife-edge pass (90 degree bank and one "g" lateral) while sweeping the wings from fully swept (68 degrees) to fully forward (22 degrees). When it had reached a point a little past mid-field it snapped into another maximum performance turn reversal in the same manner as the F-15 except that as the Tomcat started the turn the wings swiftly programmed full forward in a matter of seconds (thereby greatly enhancing the airplane's turning ability) and there was a large puff of vapor off the wings causes by the shock wave. As the F-14 approached mid-field at about 1,000 feet and 350 knots with the wings swept to 40 degrees, it went into a full after-burner 360 degree turn staying within the field boundary and during its 8 1/2 "g" turn, accelerated to 400 knots. This final turn was truly eye-watering! Being much lower than the F-15, the Tomcat's reversals seemed more spectacular. He then added one more turn so that his slow speed fly-by was in the opposite direction from that of the F-15's pass and at an altitude of five hundred feet, right in the wind shear. Although the "dirty" pass was made at 95 knots, by comparison, it seemed to be flying at a much slower airspeed . . . unbelievably slow! The difference was noticeable.

When the airplane came in for what was thought to be its final approach, Don added the finishing touch, a touch-and-go landing. Just as the mainmounts touched the runway, he ran both throttles to full zone five afterburner. The fuel tanks were almost empty, and the Tomcat completed a climbing vertical turn in the landing configuration placing it directly over the reviewing stand at less than five hundred feet inverted. Then he rolled upright flew out to a very close abeam position and made a flawless carrier landing approach coming to a full stop in less than one thousand feet of roll-out! The Shah was visibly impressed and the U.S. Air Force entourage were stunned. The Tomcat had clearly stolen the show from the Eagle – and by a large margin. Several times during the F-15 performance, flown by Irv Burrows, the F-15 had gotten completely out of sight of the reviewers.

Immediately following the show the Shah walked directly to the F-14, ignoring the Eagle parked nearby. He talked to the Navy aircrew, sat in both cockpits for a few minutes before departing the scene.

It was almost as if the Eagle didn't exist. As soon as the show was over the Air Force attempted to file a flight violation against the Grumman aircrew for "conducting low-level acrobatics over a crowd." Fortunately, Don and Dennis had gone to the FAA officials before the show and briefed them fully on their demonstration flight. The FAA officials in the tower threw out the Air Force flight violation report.

That evening, in a statement to the press, the Air Force's F-15 program manager, Major General Ben Bellis called the F-14 performance a "hot-dogging stunt" which placed the Shah in great jeopardy. The sour grapes display was vintage U.S. Air Force! The Shah was sold!

F-14 during flight demonstration. (Official U.S. Navy Photograph)

8
KHATAMI

The Shah of Iran is probably one of the most misunderstood of the "enlightened despots" of the twentieth century. He was well-educated in the western world and understood, better than his peers in the middle East, the transitory nature of "petro dollars." Iranians, by the way, are quick to point out to ignorant westerners that they are not Arabs. They, along with their Syrian neighbors, consider themselves a different race from what westerners think of as Arabs . . . an important distinction to them . . . an even more important distinction for the west to keep in mind when dealing with Iran.

The Shah was determined that Iran should achieve status as an economic industrial power before the country ran its oil resources dry. As a consequence, he ran his oil producing machinery at a faster pace than his neighbors in order to fully fund the transition from a fourteenth century monarchy to twentieth century world power. In the attempt to bridge the gap between a medieval monarchy to a modern industrial giant he squandered billions of dollars on what seemed to most observers as gold plated weapons of war. F-14s and "Ayatollah Class" *Spruance* destroyers are two examples of this "gold plating."

In the process of equipping Iran to defend herself against neighboring Iraq and the Soviet Union, the Shah overshot his mark by a considerable amount. He built the third largest war machine in the world armed with the most sophisticated weapons systems money could buy. The F-15, F-14 and the "Ayatollah Class" DD-963 destroyers are but examples of such sophistication. Not only were his weapons the finest money could buy. So also was the complicated infrastructure that accompanied them.

The air base at Khatami is a perfect example. Covering almost fifty-five square miles of high Iranian desert, it became one of the finest major jet bases in the world. The runways were eleven thousand feet long. The aircraft revetments were enormously strong (massive walls

Above and top opposite: Imperial Iranian Air Force F-14 in flight.

CHAPTER 8: KHATAMI

forty feet thick protected the openings to these revetments. The maintenance and repair facilities on the base were equally impressive, as were the training facilities, classrooms, simulators and programs. The field's control tower looks larger and more modern than the one at Dulles International airport in Chantilly, Virginia.

The major weakness of the whole system built to support a modern air force were the people who were funnelled into the training pipeline. The aircrews came, for the most part, from the well-educated elite class. The real maintainers of the weapons systems were a highly trained cadre of what would be the equivalent of warrant officers in the United States Armed Forces. The lower enlisted ranks came from the mainstream of Iranian society and were, for the most part, uneducated, semi-literate and unskilled.

The Imperial Iranian Air Force (IIAF) patterned itself after the air forces of the western world . . . notably the U.S. Air Force. As a consequence, there was a dearth of qualified radar intercept officers (RIOs). The U.S. Air Force didn't employ RIOs in their F-4 Phantom IIs. Neither, then, did the IIAF. The "GIBS" (guys in the back seat) were all pilots who knew something about radar and intercept geometry. The word "something"

IIAF F-14 on the ground with support equipment.

PART II: DEVELOPMENT OF A NAVY FIGHTER

IIAF F-14s in flight aerial refueling from a USAF KC-135 tanker en route to Iran.

covered a wide range of expertise from "brilliant" to "abysmal."

The Iranian F-14 pilots, on the other hand, were all veterans of other aircraft, mainly Iranian F-4 pilots. The range of Iranian pilot expertise, as described by one of the United States instructors, ran the full spectrum from "dangerous" to "brilliant." They were definitely the strongest element of the Iranian F-14 fighter force. The radar intercept officer trainees, on the other hand, were not very good. In general, their educational background was not as high as the pilots' and their overall performance in the training program was not as high. The overall combat effectiveness of the F-14 fighter force would probably reflect the fact that there was never a strong effort to generate the team aircrew concept which was generated in the U.S. Navy's fighter force. Whereas, in the U.S. Navy, the F-14 aircrew shares equal responsibility for their performance, this has never been the case in the Iranian F-14 fighter force. If a U.S. Navy F-14 aircrew shoots down an enemy airplane in combat, the aircrew each gets the same award. If they have an accident, each shares equal blame. In the Imperial Iranian Air Force the RIO was definitely a second class citizen.

The first F-14 was delivered on 24 January 1977 under the terms of a foreign military sales (FMS) contract. In accordance with FMS policy, U.S. Navy aircrews picked up the airplanes at the assembly site at Calverton on Long Island and delivered them to the Imperial Iranian Air Force at Khatami. Delivery flights were flown either through an enroute stop at Naval Station, Rota, Spain, or direct from Calverton to Khatami. In either case, U.S. Air Force KC-135 tankers were used during the transit flights.

Subsequently, a total of seventy-nine airplanes were delivered. The eightieth airplane was never delivered. It had been identified as the prototype airplane for conversion to the Air Force boom and receiver type aerial refueling system. The "revolution" in Iran occurred during this conversion process. It was never completed and the airplane ultimately ended up in the U.S. Navy F-14 force. At present, it sits in deep storage at the preservation facility at Davis-Monthan Air Force Base at Tucson, Arizona.

Prior to the decision to buy F-14s, the IIAF had purchased a number of U.S. Air Force KC-135 aerial refueling tankers which were intended to provide the fighter force with an aerial refueling capability similar to that of the U.S. Air Force. The boom and receiver systems were used with the F-4 Phantom II fighters and were intended to continue in that role with the F-15s. The F-14, on the other hand, was configured with the standard U.S. Navy probe and drogue system. The long-range plan of the IIAF was to reconfigure all the F-14s to the Air Force system.

IIAF F-14s taxiing at Khatami.

CHAPTER 8: KHATAMI

These three photos are of the IIAF base Khatami, showing the elaborate ground support infastructure; (above right) the control tower, and (below right) aircraft revetments.

In the interim, a few of the Imperial Iranian Air Force's fleet of KC-135 tankers were modified to a drogue configuration to accommodate the F-14s until the conversion could be accomplished.

The initial cadre of the F-14 training team, a group of six pilots and RIOs, went to Iran in November 1975 where they spent two months writing the training plan. Upon approval of the completed training plan, the team returned to the United States where they underwent refresher training in the F-14. Upon completion of that training they began deliveries of the F-14s to Iran and went into full training operations.

Khatami was the principal training site. It was built especially for the F-14 fighter force and was located about fifteen miles north of the ancient capital city of Isfahan in the high desert. The other major F-14 base, Shiraz, was located further south. With the exception of some operational flights made out of the air base near Tehran, all other F-14 operations were flown from Khatami and Shiraz. When training began in earnest the training team grew to eleven instructors and ultimately grew further to about twenty-seven people by June of 1976.

The tempo of operations at Khatami was never as high as it gets at a typical F-14 base in the United States, like Naval Air Stations, Oceana and Miramar. As one of the U.S. instructors put it, no one began work in the morning until they had enjoyed their morning tea. During the holy season of Ramadan, no flying was done at all except for operational necessity. A typical flying day at Khatami might comprise 15-20 sorties. During the transfer period about two to four F-14s were delivered per month. By U.S. standards the "fleet introduction" of F-14s to the Imperial Iranian Air Force was a fairly leisurely process.

In the four years that the Grumman/Navy training team was in Iran, they trained about eighty pilots and forty to fifty radar intercept officers. The civilian U.S. head of the Iranian training team was retired Rear Admiral "Swoose" Snead who, during his active duty Navy career had been the F-14 program manager and later the Pacific Fleet fighter wing commander. After retirement, he went to work for Grumman and headed the team from an office in Tehran where Grumman International conducted liaison between the U.S. Government and the Imperial Iranian Air Force.

A Grumman employee, Chuck Zangas, was the aircrew training manager at Khatami. The FMS contract

between the U.S. Government and the Iranian government included the construction of a substantial infrastructure at Khatami of brand new personnel housing facilities. Built to western standards, this small village housed all of the U.S. Navy and Grumman/Hughes training personnel. The facilities were to revert to Iran at the completion of the training program. This normal reversion was cut short by the "revolution" and the last of the U.S. Navy/Grumman/Hughes training team left the country in late 1979. The aircraft transfers had been completed, through aircraft number seventy-nine by late 1977. On the Iranian side, Major General Abdi Minuspeher was the principal "go-between" in the Iranian F-14 team. He was "two-hatted." On the Iranian side he was the base and wing commander at Khatami. He was also a member of the Military Industrial Organization and occupied the position of F-14 Project Manager.

A good example of the scrutiny which the team underwent occurred when the it experienced its two operational losses. Both losses were spin related. The airplanes were operating in simulated aerial combat, each experienced a one engine after-burner blowout. This induced a high yaw rate in the direction of the problem engine, which the pilot attempted to correct with aileron. The aileron input aggravated the yaw rate and a flat spin resulted. As mentioned previously in this story, this sequence of "compounding felonies" resulted in ejection attempts by both aircrews. One of the four received fatal injuries because he waited too long to eject. He was an Iranian student pilot. The back-seater, an American instructor survived. As might be expected, the Shah expressed great interest in these two losses and an extensive investigation was conducted. Ultimately, the chief Grumman test pilot, Chuck Sewell, was called in. After examining all the evidence, Chuck concluded that both Iranian pilots followed the proper procedures and the fault lay with the engine whose basic weaknesses were, by now, legendary.

In a scenario where "supervisory error" would be expected as a partial causative factor, the ultimate supervisor, General Minuspeher was totally exonerated and the training of Iranian Tomcat aircrews proceeded apace.

The F-14 training program was well underway and beginning to function smoothly when unrest took over the country, the Shah was ultimately deposed, and in the bloody purge which followed his departure drove many talented and essential Iranian military officers into exile. Along with the political emigres went a flood of Americans . . . civilian and military; including virtually all of the cadre of instructors who made up the F-14 transition team.

In all, over eighty pilots were trained and something slightly less than that in the radar intercept officer ranks. What has followed in the ensuing years is cloaked in secrecy. The combat record of the F-14 is not well documented. But, the F-14 has shot down somewhere around ten Iraqi fighters, a few with the Phoenix missile.

Where the F-14 has been the most useful, however, has not been in actual aerial combat. The airplane has been employed as an early warning and airborne combat director aircraft. By staying at medium altitude with its powerful radar turned on, the F-14 has been used to vector other Iranian fighters against the low-flying Iraqi fighters attempting to sneak into Iranian airspace using low-altitude ingress and the cover of the rugged mountains to mask their approach.

Before the embargo was imposed, the Imperial Iranian Air Force had set in motion an elaborate logistics pipeline with a central office in the United States for acquiring crucial airplane parts and supply support and shipping them to Iran, direct to Khatami. After the ousting of the Shah and the seizure of the U.S. embassy in Teheran, the flow of parts was reduced to a trickle. Extra-legal and illegal means were employed to keep the essential flow of repair and replacement parts flowing. For the most part, the logistic problems are almost insurmountable with aircraft "cannibalization" becoming an increasingly standard procedure to keep but a few of the airplanes still flying on a minimal basis.

This was the down side of the Shah's military modernization program. The sophisticated weapons of war which he purchased from the United States have become virtually useless to the Iranian armed forces today. It is much easier to keep F-4 Phantom IIs flying because of the wide support base for the airplane available in other countries. The same can be said for the other weapons systems which abound in third world countries. But, the Tomcat is a uniquely American airplane. It is operated by no other countries in the world. The very features which have made it, in the Shah's own words, "the finest air supremacy airplane in the world" have also made it an airplane which the Iranian Air Force cannot operate effectively.

9
THE LITTLE ENGINE THAT COULDN'T

I do not believe that anyone who has ever flown the F-14A Tomcat would argue with the statement that the airplane's greatest single weakness is the engine. The design of the F-14's original engine dates back to the spring of 1958 when it was designated the JTF-10A to be built by the Pratt & Whitney engine manufacturing giant. It was to be a turbofan engine and its military designation was TF-30. Its first military use was in the U.S. Air Force's long range tactical bomber the F-111 built by General Dynamics. The engine designation in the bomber was the TF-30-P-12. (The navalized version of the airplane, the F-111B, is the subject of Chapter 2 entitled, *The Admiral's Revolt*.) In this engine, the manufacturer had produced the first turbofan engine equipped

The Pratt & Whitney TF-30 engine.

with an afterburner. When the U.S. Navy won the battle of the F-111B, and it was cancelled, the follow-on airplane had to accept it as the only available powerplant in its class. The engine designation was the TF-30-P-412.

The latest F-14A engine is the TF30-P-414A. It produces a little over 10,875 pounds of thrust at military (non-afterburning) power and 17,077 pounds in full afterburner. The engine weighed a little under 4,000 pounds. The airplane's designers were not entirely satisfied with the engine but accepted it as the only alternative presently available with the idea in mind of replacing it with a common core variant of the more powerful Pratt & Whitney TF-100 engine under development for the U.S. Air Force's new F-15 Eagle. The U.S. Navy was participating, jointly with the Air Force, in the development of this fine engine on a 60%-40% cost share basis in a "cost plus" contract which was experiencing serious cost overruns. The bill was beginning to get out of hand for the Navy. The amount of funds set aside by the Navy for the development of the TF-100 engine had been a great deal smaller than the counterpart Air Force development budget. Furthermore, the "buy" of Navy engines was much smaller. As a consequence, the unit cost of the engine for the F-14 was increasing at an alarming rate. The TF-100 variant engine was supposed to cut into the F-14A production line at ship number seven. Number seven would be called the F-14B.

As a longer term engine development program, both the Navy and Air Force were participating in an engine program called the Advance Technology Engine (ATE). This would be a more powerful engine taking advantage of new, high technology such as new turbine blade materials, designs and production methods. The best estimates at that time were that the new engine could be cut into the F-14B Tomcat production line in ship number 37.

By way of comparison, the TF-100 would produce over 13,000 pounds of thrust in military power, 23,000 pounds in full afterburner. It was a rather dramatic 35% increase. The Advanced Technology Engine, on the other hand, was intended to produce an additional increase of 5% over the TF-100 engine for a whopping 13,800 pounds in military and 23,600 pounds in afterburner. Today's F-14D is powered by the F110-GE-400.

By the time that engine came into production there would be an improved avionics suite to put into what would be called the F-14C. According to plan, the F-14C would arrive in the fleet roughly in 1990.

What a grim irony that turned out to be! What the designers did not realize was that the engine's two weaknesses, which were known from the start, were far more serious than originally thought. The two weaknesses were: poor compressor stall margin and not enough thrust. The first, and principal weakness would contribute ultimately to the loss of over forty airplanes valued at over a billion dollars. The factors leading to this monumental miscalculation, will be developed further in this chapter.

In a nutshell, a jet engine uses its compressor to pump air to the turbine where fuel is added and ignited. The combustion products flowing out the tailpipe produce the thrust that powers the aircraft. In high speed and low altitude non-maneuvering flight there is plenty of available air to pump and burn. But when a jet powered airplane begins to maneuver, the engine intake assumes the increased angle of attack of the airplane's wing, and air entering the engine intake must turn the corner created by the increased angle of attack. This has the net effect of decreasing the amount of air available to the pump (compressor) to supply to the turbine.

As maneuvering is increased the angle of attack increases, further aggravating the problem. As angle of attack is further increased (more "g"s), a point is reached where the smooth flow of air through the engine breaks down, and the compressor stalls. Compressor stalls lead ultimately to flame-out. To add to the problem, when altitude is increased and ambient air becomes less dense all of the above problems are aggravated. Stall margin is a measure of the distance between smooth air flow and compressor stall expressed as a function of pressure. Stall margin need not be as great in commercial airplanes as in tactical airplanes because they don't maneuver as violently. Early generation tactical jet aircraft could never achieve angles of attack which modern airplanes now reach, and still maintain controlled flight. The F-14, on the other hand, is capable of achieving extreme angles of attack and still retaining reasonably good flying qualities. Adequate stall margin, becomes very meaningful for modern tactical airplanes which have the ability to reach extreme angles of attack. The match between the airframe and the engine was, and still is, a bad one for the F-14A. For the most part, efforts to improve the engine in the F-14A have been of the bandaid variety. That is to say they tended to fix the symptoms rather than the problem. During my tenure as Director, Aviation Plans and Programs (OP-50) I went to the effort to add up all the money paid by the Navy to the

CHAPTER 9: THE LITTLE ENGINE THAT COULDN'T

 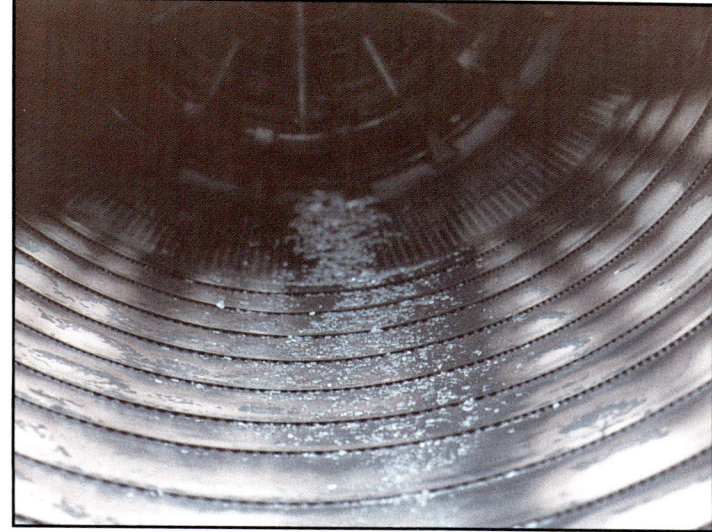

Two views of a TF-30 engine with catastrophic turbine failure (view from afterburner section). Note the metal shards, all that is left of the failed turbine section.

engine manufacturer to design and incorporate those bandaids. That was in 1983. The total came to roughly a quarter of a billion dollars . . . for bandaids!

There were those of us who thought the manufacturer should have shared that bill. One of the fixes involved designing a protective shroud to surround the fan section of the engine. The idea was to contain the turbine blades during a catastrophic failure to prevent them from doing damage to the other engine, the airplane and the crew. Incidentally, that bandaid proved successful. But the worst fixes of all, and the ones which drew great resentment from the fleet, were what I call the non-fixes. These were little disclaimers written into the airplane flight handbook restricting throttle movements at certain airspeed, altitude and angle-of-attack combinations. It was almost insulting to tell a fighter pilot that in the extreme corners of the flight envelope, the very places where he flew to win in aerial combat, he had to limit his movement of the throttles to avoid disaster.

In aerial combat a fighter engine should be able to stand all the throttle chops and jams to full afterburner that are necessary to execute the winning maneuvers.

Every airplane I have ever flown has had its "gotchas." They are those peculiarities which, if ignored, get a pilot in trouble. The F-14A had its share of gotchas. One of them was serious trouble. The engines are mounted in nacelles which are nine feet apart. The nine foot dimension represents a large yawing moment whenever there is unbalanced thrust. The most extreme out-of-balance thrust circumstance would be with one engine in maximum afterburner and the other one flamed out. This is the situation which could develop in a slow speed, high angle-of-attack maneuver in which (unfortunately) the engine has a tendency to stall and flameout. A pilot in the heat of aerial combat maneuvering normally is devoting most of his attention to his opponent's maneuvers and relative position and relies on the seat of his pants to tell how close to the edge of the envelope he is flying.

This "gotcha" is complicated by the fact that even with the engine alarm signalling a stalled condition, the large yawing motion is not always recognized as such since it generates a rolling motion, and it all happens fast. If the pilot recognizes the rolling motion and tries to correct for it with opposite aileron (a natural tendency) it aggravates the yaw and puts the airplane into a flat spin (the worst kind). But, the worst is yet to come.

Since the yaw rate increases very quickly, the "eyeballs out" "g" forces generated in a well-developed flat spin tend to throw the aircrew forward against the shoulder and lap restraint harnesses. The F-14 flight handbook calls for locking both harnesses as the first step in the emergency procedures. If that is not done early, the rapidly building "g" forces make it impossible for the aircrew to lean back and position themselves for an ejection.

There are a few more complications in this "gotcha." One of them is the fact that it is difficult to recover the F-14 from a flat spin. Another, is that the canopy, does not separate from the fuselage (the first action in an ejection sequence) as rapidly as it would at higher speeds. This slow separation has caused the aircrew to strike the canopy as their ejection seats separate from the airplane. It is a long and complicated "gotcha", but also a very fatal one . . . all caused by the poor stall margin of the engine.

The death blow to the F-14A engine program was dealt to it by Deputy Secretary of Defense Packard on 27 May 1971. Cost overruns had become so serious and so highly publicized that the scrutiny of the Department of Defense was brought to bear in a Defense Systems Acquisition Council (DSARC) review on that day. The briefing was conducted by the Phoenix program manager, Captain John Weaver with the Secretary of the Navy, the Chief of Naval Operations and his Deputy Chief for Air Warfare sitting in the hot seats. When the bottom line was delivered by John Weaver, that the F-14A program was over four hundred million dollars in the hole a deathly silence fell over the room. (Incidentally, that same number was roughly the amount that the Grumman Corporation reduced in total program cost in between the final Request For Proposals [RFP] competition between Grumman and McDonnell and the subsequent Best and Final Offers competition on 5 January 1969).

After about ten seconds of this uncomfortable and deafening silence, Mr. Packard spoke in a soft voice. He had a pencil in his right hand. He pointed it at the Secretary of the Navy and said, quietly, "I should fire you." Then the pencil point sought out the tense figure of the Chief of Naval Operations. Mr. Packard added, "and you." Again the deadly pencil shifted to the Deputy Chief of Naval Operations (Air Warfare) adding, again, "and you, too." Then he waited a few seconds for what he had said to sink in an added, "Now, here's what we are going to do."

In the next five minutes Mr. Packard performed merciless major surgery on the F-14 program. In Pentagon parlance he "down scoped" the program. The total number of F-14s to be produced was drastically reduced. Little program features calculated to fall into the category of "bells and whistles" fell victim to Packard's scalpel. It was swiftly and brutally done with a bureaucrat's technical precision. Nobody even thought of objecting to the final, and most disastrous of cuts. Mr. Packard told the gathering that the TF-100 engine for the F-14 was cancelled. The Air Force was to stay with the engine development program for their F-15 program.

It is too bad that no one present spoke up in defense of this last cut. It turned out to be a terrible mistake. Hindsight is always twenty-twenty. The naval officers, in their defense, could not have known what the terrible consequences would be. And, they must have been intimidated by a very angry Deputy Secretary of Defense. It is also possible that they perceived that the entire F-

VF-51 F-14A.

CHAPTER 9: THE LITTLE ENGINE THAT COULDN'T

General Electric F-110 engine.

14 program was at the ragged edge of extinction. Whatever the reason, no one spoke up and the F-14B program died stillborn. Nonetheless, the engine decision, destined U.S. Navy fighter aircrews to fly on the pointed end of the spear in F-14s powered by what they referred to as "two pieces of junk" for an unprecedented eighteen years. It was not until November 1987 that the first F-14A Plus configured with the new General Electric GE-F-110 engine reached VF-101 at Naval Air Station, Oceana, Virginia.

10
NASA

F-14A, Bureau number 153991, also called 1X, had been a fixture at NASA's Dryden Space Flight Facility at Edwards Air Force Base for a long time. It was first used to conduct spin trials, having been equipped with a spin recovery chute. Thereafter it was used to conduct a speed run to Mach 2.40 using untrimmed engines.

During the early days of fleet introduction, the F-14 experienced some controllability mishaps which were attributed to aileron rudder interconnect (ARI) problems. In response, the Navy bailed 1X to NASA to do an investigation into possible ARI solutions. Dick Gray, a former Navy ACEVAL/AIMVAL pilot who got out and was hired by NASA, began investigative test flights in 1979.

The ARI fix recommended by NASA was accepted by the Navy and combined NASA/Grumman tests were flown by NASA test pilot Einar Enevoldsen and Grumman test pilot Chuck Sewell.

There were a total of four different ARI fixes conjured up by the engineers:

1) The "cadillac fix" came from the NASA engineers at their facility at Langley Air Force Base.

2) Fixes #2 and #3 were developed by Dryden engineers.

3) The fourth, and final, fix, called the cross-control fix was developed for the new production F-14Ds. What finally went into all Fleet F-14s was a combination of the cadillac fix and the cross-control fix. During the major portion of this testing the ARI was disconnected in all fleet airplanes (this entailed disabling some of the hydraulic system monitors).

It was during the investigations that NASA determined that the recommended spin recovery procedures used in

NASA F-14A with full combat load: 2 Phoenix missiles, 2 Sparrow missiles, 2 Sidewinder missiles, and 600 rounds of 20mm ammunition. Note the absence of the RIO as the rear cockpit contains test instruments.

CHAPTER 10: NASA

NASA F-14A with spin chute attached – used during high AOA/Spin Testing.

the fleet were wrong. NASA was right! The centrifuge at the Navy testing facility at Warminster, Pennsylvania was put into use. The concern, early on, about F-14 spin recovery problems was certainly warranted. Because of the spin characteristics which were being evidenced in the fleet, a set of very rigorous spin investigations was developed.

At Warminster, for example, tests included "eyeballs out" "g" loads of up to 6 (harness locked) and 5 (harness unlocked) to determine the pilot's ability to initiate and hold spin recovery controls and, as well, to initiate ejection. It took yaw rates as high as 90 degrees per second to develop those "g" loads.

NASA test pilot Ed Smith began to fly the spin tests in 1983. The airplane was returned to Patuxent River, Maryland in 1985. The positive fall-out from all of the NASA spin testing was an updating of fleet simulators to more realistic flying qualities in the rigorous NASA "2 x 4" (2 external fuel tanks, 2 AIM-9 Sidewinder air-to-air missiles, 2 AIM-7 Sparrow air-to-air missiles and 2 AIM-54 Phoenix air-to-air missiles) configuration. Another F-14A was used by NASA for basic aerodynamic research into "natural laminar flow." What was particularly interesting about these tests was the new liquid crystal display technology employed in the tests. As a step beyond the traditional tufting of the upper wing surfaces, this liquid crystal material was painted on the surface to be examined. The color of the material changed when the air flow over it went from laminar to turbulent. During my tour of duty as OP-50, I had the opportunity to visit the Dryden facility to watch Chuck Sewell do some of the high angle of attack ARI tests. The post stall gyrations and spins resulting from some of those tests were some of the most spectacular maneuvers I had ever seen. However, somewhat more spectacular were the wing sweep asymmetry tests conducted by Chuck Sewell and Grumman engineer Paul Canigliaro.

Speculation had been going on in the fleet and the testing community for years about wing sweep asymmetry. The tests came about because of several fleet wing sweep actuator failures. The system design incorporates a mechanical cross-shaft that synchronizes the left and right wing position, preventing a single failure from causing an asymmetric wing condition.

In a couple of cases a double failure of the actuator and cross-shaft occurred, producing a relatively small wing position asymmetry. None of these failures resulted in a mishap, however they highlighted the fact that Navy standard operating procedures (NATOPS) contained no recommended procedures for asymmetric wing sweep.

The flight tests produced some amazing results. At normal cruise airspeeds, the airplane was controllable at all possible asymmetries. Just as important, safe field landings were demonstrated up to and including 20 degree/60 degree asymmetries and were considered feasible to the maximum 20 degree/68 degree position. Planned demonstration of a landing at the maximum asymmetry was precluded when the final flight was canceled.

The tests were accomplished by locking one of the wings at the full forward sweep position of 20 degrees. The other wing was gradually moved aft (greater sweep) in flight to do the evaluation. As long as the sweep angle was not greater than 50 degrees, flaps could be employed. Therefore, approach speeds for 20/35 and 20/50 were reasonable at 135 knots and 145 knots respectively.

The greater asymmetry and the loss of flaps past 50 degrees produces approach speeds around 155 knots at 20/55 and 170 knots at 20/68 degrees. These approach speeds are acceptable around the field but would be unacceptable around the ship.

It is worth noting that Chuck Sewell was sanguine that a carrier landing approach could be safely made in the 20/68 degree configuration of asymmetry. I have

CHAPTER 10: NASA

Laminar airflow test aircraft top and side views.

known the man since we were at Patuxent River together in 1959. He was a superb aviator, an incisive test pilot, a wonderful human being and a good friend. But, he tended to get overly enthusiastic about his projects.

There is absolutely no doubt in my mind that Chuck Sewell would have taken the F-14 to the boat and attempted to land it aboard in the 20/68 degree asymmetry, with a high degree of confidence in his ability to do it safely. But, I also know, having far more carrier experience than Chuck, how serious the problems of coupling between axes can be in a carrier approach. In my view, the Navy was right in terminating the asymmetry testing when and where they did. In all, NASA made a major contribution in the resolution of ARI problems in the fleet, conducted important high alpha and spin tests and made an important contribution to the understanding of the effects of wing sweep asymmetry on controllability.

OPPOSITE: *Cockpit view of NASA F-14A test aircraft #47.*   **Above:** *Asymetrical wing testing.*

PART III
IN THE FLEET

The first F-14As were delivered to fleet replacement squadron ONE HUNDRED TWENTY-FOUR (VF-124) in June 1972. Fighter Squadrons ONE and TWO (VF-1 and VF-2) were commissioned on October 14, 1972 at Naval Air Station, Miramar, CA. Known as the Wolfpack and the Bounty Hunters respectively, the two squadrons were elements of Air Wing Fourteen and were subsequently reassigned to U.S.S. RANGER. They deployed first on the U.S.S. ENTERPRISE in September 1974. The first east coast fleet squadrons to transition from the F-4 Phantom to the F-14 were the Tophatters of VF-14 and the Swordsmen of VF-32. Both squadrons, based at Oceana deployed on the U.S.S. JOHN F. KENNEDY in the summer of 1975 as elements of Air Wing ONE.

The schedule for transitioning all but four fleet squadrons from the F-4 Phantom to the F-14A Tomcat continued. The two squadrons in Air Wing FIVE based overseas on the U.S.S. MIDWAY were never intended to make the transition because there were no plans to modify her to take the larger jet blast deflectors required by the F-14. MIDWAY retained her Phantoms until they were replaced by two squadrons of F/A-18s in 1988 The same was true for U.S.S. CORAL SEA which was decommissioned in 1990. MIDWAY is presently being decommissioned. Because there were plans for Phantoms on these carriers for the immediate future, an F-4 fleet replacement squadron, VF-171, was created at Oceana and all VF-101 F-4s were transferred to that squadron. Fighter Squadron ONE HUNDRED ONE thus became exclusively the Atlantic Fleet F-14 fleet replacement squadron.

In 1976 the two squadrons in U.S.S. AMERICA's Air Wing SIX, the Ghost Riders of VF-142 and the Pukin' Dogs of VF-143 completed the transition to the Tomcat. In 1977 the transition schedule was accelerated and the U.S.S. CONSTELLATION's Air Wing NINE completed the transition for the Renegades of VF-24 and the Checkmates of VF-211. That same year both U.S.S. KITTYHAWK and U.S.S. NIMITZ's transitioned their fighter squadrons to the Tomcat. The Aardvarks of VF-114 and the Black Lions of VF-213, elements of Air Wing ELEVEN were the KITTYHAWK west coast squadrons. The Black Aces of VF-41 and the Jolly Rogers of VF-84, elements of Air Wing EIGHT were the NIMITZ east coast squadrons. No fighter squadrons transitioned in 1978. But, in 1979 KITTYHAWK received two newly transitioned squadrons in her new Air Wing FIFTEEN, the Screaming Eagles of VF-51 and the VF-111 Sundowners. Air wings were shifted from carrier to carrier as the transition continued. The Red Rippers of VF-11 and the Tomcatters of VF-31, both elements of Air Wing THREE completed their transition to F-14As on U.S.S. KENNEDY in 1982. Later that same year the Diamondbacks of VF-102 and the Starfighters of VF-33, both elements of Air Wing ONE on U.S.S. AMERICA completed their transition to the F-14A. The next squadrons to transition from the Phantom to the Tomcat were the Bedevilers of VF-74 and the Sluggers of VF-103. As elements of Air Wing SEVENTEEN, they joined U.S.S. SARATOGA's team in the summer of 1983. The last two squadrons to transfer from the F-4 to the F-14 were VF-21 and VF-154. They made their first deployment in F-14s on U.S.S. CONSTELLATION along with the first west coast deployment of the F-18 Hornet.

The only remaining squadrons to transition were the four reserve fighter squadrons who received old F-14s. The Devil's Disciples of VF-301 completed the transition in 1984 and the following year the Stallions of VF-302 finished transition as Miramar-based elements of Reserve Air Wing THIRTY. Reserve Air Wing TWENTY's fighter squadrons, VF-201 and VF-202 completed their transition in 1989 and 1990 at their home base at Naval Air Station, Dallas, Texas. It is noteworthy that the transition to an all F-14 fleet fighter force took ten years to complete. There is a subtle axiom hidden in the statistics here. As airplanes get more costly their transition takes longer.

VF-124 F-14A section over the Pacific Ocean.

PART III: IN THE FLEET

VF-1 F-14A off the California coast returning from W-291 warning area, 1974.

VF-2 Bounty Hunters F-14A.

PART III: IN THE FLEET

VF-32 Swordsmen F-14A carrying six Phoenix missiles.

VF-14 Tophatters F-14A holding over carrier.

VF-142 F-14A is launched down No. 3 waist catapult on the USS Dwight D. Eisenhower (CVN-69). (Official U.S. Navy Photograph)

PART III: IN THE FLEET

VF-143 F-14A section over Fallon, Nevada.

VF-24 F-14B over W-291.

PART III: IN THE FLEET

VF-211 F-14B carrying six Phoenix missiles.

VF-114 F-14A section.

VF-213 F-14A landing at NAS Miramar.

PART III: IN THE FLEET

VF-51 F-14 launching from catapult #3 on USS Kitty Hawk.

VF-111 F-14A holding over USS Kitty Hawk.

PART III: IN THE FLEET

VF-41 F-14A preparing for landing at Oceana.

VF-84 F-14A over the Atlantic Ocean. (Offical U.S. Navy Photograph)

VF-11/VF-31 F-14D section. This unit was the first to transition from the F-14A to the F-14D.

PART III: IN THE FLEET

VF-102 F-14.

VF-33 F-14 returning to Oceana.

Division of VF-74 F-14Bs in a diamond formation.

VF-103 F-14B over the Italian Alps. (Official U.S. Navy Photograph)

VF-21 F-14A over southern Iran, 1987 USS Constellation.

VF-154 F-14A over Mt. Fuji.

VF-191 F-14A at the ramp. (Offical U.S. Navy Photograph)

VF-194 F-14A over southern California.

Topgun F-14 painted up to resemble an Su-27 Flanker.

Topgun F-14 painted up to resemble a Russian Su-27 Flanker for combat training.

11
THE FIRST TOMCAT DEPLOYMENT

As mentioned earlier, the F-14 was introduced into the Pacific Fleet first then the Atlantic Fleet next. The Fleet Replacement Squadron (FRS) at Naval Air Station, Miramar, Fighter Squadron ONE HUNDRED TWENTY-FOUR (VF-124) received the first airplanes and the first two fleet squadrons, Fighter Squadrons ONE and TWO (VF-1 and VF-2) were commissioned. The reasons for beginning in the Pacific Fleet are a bit obscure, but that isn't important. What was important was establishing the first fleet replacement squadron co-located with the first two fleet squadrons. The whole issue of logistics support for the introduction of a very sophisticated weapons system was wrapped up in the politics of an airplane which many of its critics thought was to complex for the fleet to operate.

The army of Grumman (airframe), Hughes (radar) and Pratt & Whitney (engine) field service representatives descended on Miramar with firm directions from their home offices to render whatever help was necessary to make the system work. Although this support

VF-124 F-14A during first fleet carrier qualifications.

VF-1 F-14A carrying one Phoenix, one Sparrow and one Sidewinder missile. (Official U.S. Navy Photograph)

VF-2 F-14A over USS Ranger.

was initially helpful, it was in the long run counterproductive. The sailors in the squadrons who were charged with maintaining the systems grew to rely too heavily on the representatives and, as the time to deploy them to the fleet grew nearer, realized that they hadn't developed their own skills sufficiently to operate without their assistance. As with all new systems there were problems, mostly associated with the engines and the radar. The fleet and the reps dealt with them, clumsily at first, but they dealt with them, nonetheless. Finally, Fighter Squadron ONE and TWO deployed to the western Pacific.

Those who planned the fleet introduction decided to transfer the two initial Atlantic Fleet squadrons to the west coast, train them at VF-124 and then transfer them back to their east coast base at Naval Air Station, Oceana, Virginia to get ready for their first deployment to the Mediterranean. This began shortly after the squadrons returned from a Mediterranean deployment. Those personnel who would remain with the squadron (officers and enlisted) were given permanent change of station orders to Miramar for the duration of the transition.

The two squadrons were assigned the same hangar where the Navy Fighter Weapons School aircraft were located. Captain Scotty Lamoreaux, Commander, Fleet Air, Miramar personally got involved in making the transition go smoothly. Despite those efforts, the two east coast squadrons never felt entirely welcomed by the fleet squadrons home-based there. VF-1 and VF-2 were just completing their transition when the east coast fighter squadrons began their's. The transition involved training not only of aircrews but enlisted personnel as well, learning the secrets of maintaining the complicated Tomcat. There was not a great deal of flying involved. Each pilot got a transition phase and enough advanced training flights to take and pass the standard naval aviation training and operating system (NATOPS) check flight. As soon as they had completed their NATOPS checks they flew back to Oceana. It was late summer of 1974. All of their enlisted personnel were back and in place by fall of that year.

They began their training in preparation for a Mediterranean deployment in *Nimitz* scheduled for May of 1975. It was decided to take an air combat maneuvering (ACM) detachment to Naval Air Station, Jacksonville, Florida that fall. They chose Jacksonville for several reasons. The weather was better that time of year and the air station was not particularly busy at the time.

ACM training, to be accomplished most efficiently, ought to have good weather, ready access to an over water operating area and be able to get into and out of the field with minimum delay. ACM missions are short and intense and often returning flights are low on fuel. The Skipper of "Topgun" sent one of their new F-5 airplanes all the way from Miramar to serve as an adversary air-

Topgun F-5s over the southern California desert.

CHAPTER 11: THE FIRST TOMCAT DEPLOYMENT

VF-41 F-14A.

VF-32 F-14A.

plane. The east coast adversary squadron, VF-43 sent a few of its airplanes down from Oceana. Much experience was gained during the short detachment while the aircrews were building up flight time and expertise in their new airplanes.

There were the usual growing pains. The newly installed logistics system lagged the transition and caused the squadrons to do a great deal of cannibalizing of parts from their own airplanes to fix others. There were also engine problems. The compressor section had a bad habit of stalling as has been mentioned in an earlier chapter. The compressor also had a bad habit of disintegrating once in a while. The result was often the catastrophic fire, explosion and loss of the airplane.

In time those problems were solved. When it came time to prepare to go aboard *Nimitz* for work-up training, the west coast fleet replacement squadron sent some landing signal officers to Oceana and the deadly serious business of carrier qualifications began. In due course, Fighter squadrons FOURTEEN and THIRTY-TWO became fully qualified on *Nimitz*, each aircrew getting his ten day and six night carrier arrested landings. The air wing headed for the Sixth Fleet and a Mediterranean deployment with the first two F-14 squadrons in the Atlantic Fleet.

The east coast fleet replacement squadron was the next step in the transition of all east coast fighter squadrons from F-4 Phantoms to F-14 Tomcats. The east coast F-4 fleet replacement squadron, VF-101, was picked to become the F-14 FRS and a new squadron was commissioned as Fighter Squadron ONE HUNDRED SEVENTY-ONE to fulfill the mission of over seeing the stand down of the Phantom community. Eventually, VF-171 was decommissioned when it had fulfilled its function.

VF-101 F-14A section.

12

"FIGHTERTOWN, U.S.A"

It was a cold winter day in 1979 at CINCLANTFLEET headquarters in Norfolk, Virginia when I received notification that I had been selected for flag rank, Rear Admiral, U.S. Navy. It was momentous, to say the least. But, just as momentous was the telephone call I received the next day telling me that my first flag assignment was as Commander, Fighter Airborne Early Warning Wings, U.S. Pacific Fleet. That meant I was going to "Fightertown, U.S.A." The same telephone call informed me that I should start immediately to renew all of the training and aviation physiology requirements to resume flying fleet fighters. It was literally like being thrown into the briar patch. I had long since given up any hope of military flying. Now, being told that I would have to resume an active flying career, in fighters to boot, was almost too much for my 50 year old psyche to handle.

There was a flurry of activity in which I took time from a busy schedule to go to Naval Air Station, Oceana, Virginia to requalify in the low pressure chamber, water survival training, ejection seat training, night vision training and complete several hour in the F-4 Phantom flight simulation trainer. It was a brutal schedule involving fifteen hour days but it didn't phase me. Nothing could phase me. I was in seventh heaven, and it was obvious.

Finally, the orders arrived. There was a brief "frocking" ceremony and I was off to my resurrection. ("frocking" means assuming the next higher rank, but without pay). My arrival at Miramar was singularly inauspicious. Certainly, there was the usual change of command ceremony but the atmosphere at "Fightertown" was reserved. There was a sense of wondering what would happen next as the leadership changed. The Bureau of Naval Personnel had warned me prior to my departure for Miramar that morale was low in the Pacific Fleet fighter community and that pilot retention was a horrible twenty-eight percent and dropping. That, they told me was to be my biggest problem. But, I instinctively knew that morale was not a problem, it was a symptom. My concern would be to find the real problem causing the symptom. In retrospect, I believe the real problem was not whether aircrews could wear their leather flight jackets away from the hangar area. Nor was it whether they could wear their flight suits at the Officer's` club on Friday nights at "happy hour." The real problem was that they were not flying enough. Give fighter aircrews plenty of flight time . . . good flight time and all other difficulties fade into insignificance. The reason why they were not getting enough flight hours was the terrible reliability and maintainability of the F-14 coupled with an unresponsive supply system. I didn't know enough about the maintenance of the F-14, but I sure as hell knew how to jack up an unresponsive supply system. We invited a Lieutenant Commander "Skip" Holden, who was my Maintenance Officer's counterpart on the east coast, to visit us and share the secrets of his recent success in maintaining his F-14s extremely well. Of course, Skip's proximity to the wellhead of supply at Norfolk helped a great deal. Nevertheless, the East coast fighter wing had just announced by message to the world that they had reached an unprecedented "Zero NORS" status. It blew my mind! Not Operationally Ready, Supply (NORS) simply means that an aircraft is not available for flight because it lacks a repair part. For the east coast fighter wing to have no airplanes down for parts was unprecedented, and certainly a cause for celebrating and telling the world just as they had done. But, it made me feel all the worse for being so bad in the same arena. Skip Holden offered some good advice and we, my staff and the commanding officers of all twenty-eight squadrons in the wing, set about to fix things in the west coast fighter community.

The first order of business was the supply problem. We instituted daily supply status briefings. It turned out I had the best aviation supply officer in the Navy and didn't know it! I visited the supply department and noticed something which would come back to haunt me. My Supply Officer, Commander Dick Scharff, was standing in the supply office introducing me to his staff.

CHAPTER 12: "FIGHTERTOWN, U.S.A."

VF-194 F-14A over "Fightertown, U.S.A.", Miramar, California. (Official U.S. Navy Photograph)

While introductions were going around I heard a truck drive up to the loading dock just outside the window. I saw the driver open the rear door of the truck and throw a very large carton onto the dock with a loud thump. He then walked in, got his invoice signed and left. Nobody in the office even looked at the carton. Thirty minutes later I left and noted the carton still sitting on the loading dock untouched and, for all practical purposes, unnoticed. (Readers please remember this scene. I am going to recall it to you later in this chapter).

At one of my morning briefs I recall looking at a slide projected on the screen listing all of the NORS items for the wing. I remember distinctly the number. It was 132. The list was almost too long for the supply officer to do anything more than mention each of them, what airplane they were ordered for, which squadron, how many days the part had been on order and so forth. It was a tedious ten minutes while he reviewed the NORS status of the wing.

Next, my wing Maintenance Officer stood up turned on the slide projector and showed the days status of Not Operationally Ready, Maintenance (NORM). NORM meant, simply, that an airplane was not ready to fly because of a maintenance action necessary to be done on it. The long list was equally tedious. The Maintenance Officer next showed a slide listing the "bare firewalls" in the wing. A bare firewall is an empty hole in an airplane where an engine should be but isn't. I distinctly recall the number. It was twenty and the total had been climbing steadily.

Finally, the Maintenance Officer showed a slide listing all of the SPINTAC airplanes. SPINTAC stands for Special Interest Aircraft and means, simply, that an airplane has been in a non-flying status for more than 30 days. The existing maintenance regulations prohibit the cannibalization ("borrowing") of parts from a SPINTAC airplane to fix another airplane. Cannibalization is an everyday occurrence and a necessary evil. In 1979 the average F-14 landed from each flying sortie with 1.5 discrepancies. It took an average of seven days for a part to arrive once it was ordered. For the seven days that an airplane was downed awaiting that part someone would borrow several more parts from it to fix other airplanes. The SPINTAC rule was to prevent certain airplanes from becoming "hangar queens." The problem was serious. Even when the rules were followed there were difficulties. A mechanic would remove a part from an airplane downed for some reason. He would turn the bad part in to supply for repair and attach a tag to the place from which the part had been removed explaining the action and often containing the nuts, bolts, sheet metal screws or fasteners that had been removed to borrow the part in the first place. After a while the bag would get lost and now one NORS became five or ten more NORS. It was a nightmare to figure out what was missing. Thus, the SPINTAC rule issued by the type commander. As in the NORS numbers, the bare firewalls and SPINTAC numbers were so great that none of us could remember them all . . . just the totality of the problem; and it seemed insurmountable. The bottom line at this particular daily status brief was 132 NORS, twenty bare firewalls and eleven SPINTAC airplanes. What a mess! No wonder the morale was low!

The first problem to attack was the supply system. We knew from checking the records that once a part requisition reached the supply depot at Norfolk the turn around time for east coast requisitions was several days less than the west coast requisitions. There was only one explanation for this. Somehow the east coast requisitions were getting some kind of higher priority even though the system was not supposed to do this. At a meeting with my staff and squadron COs I asked them all if they would sign up to a program to reduce the NORS to zero, no matter what the price in time, energy or personal sacrifice. There was a moment's pause then they all raised their hands. Commander Scharff sent a red hot

F-14s on the ramp at "Fightertown, U.S.A."

CHAPTER 12: "FIGHTERTOWN, U.S.A."

junior supply officer to the supply center at Norfolk. I agreed to pay his per diem expenses as long as it took. His orders were simple. Go to the desk where incoming requisitions enter the supply system. Every time a Miramar requisition arrives in the "in" basket keep putting it on top of the pile until it gets logged in. Then hand carry each requisition from basket to basket as it moves through the supply process. Finally, the young man was told to stay in Norfolk until the NORS was zero, however long it took. What an unusual set of orders that young man was given! In two days after the young supply officer was in place the number of daily NORS began to go down. The downward swing was inexorable. When it went below 100 we all cheered. When it passed seventy-five the supply officer was now able to fill us in on fine details of all of them from memory. We were all learning a lesson. When the number dropped to fifty I began to remember squadrons connected to some of the items. When the number dropped to twenty-five the supply officer no longer need to expound on each of them because we all had them memorized and associated each item with not just particular squadrons but also with airplane side numbers. It was synergy in action and I went to each daily brief with anticipation rather than dread.

One morning the number of NORS items on the Supply Officer's slide said only nine parts keeping airplanes out of commission were on order. I found myself suggesting that our man in Norfolk find them, drive to the airport and put them on a plane himself, thereby saving twelve hours of lost time. I knew it was silly but I found myself wanting to reach that Zero NORS goal more than anything else in the world. I suspect that nobody in that room a month ago really believed that the wing would ever get the number below twenty much less to zero. But, now all of us, having agreed to sacrifice anything to get to zero, wanted it so bad we could taste it. We also knew that a Zero NORS status would only last long enough for an F-14 to land with a discrepancy requiring a part . . . perhaps only hours. But, we would have done what no one thought we could do. The transformation of the atmosphere in that briefing room was magical. It was charged with excitement. Finally, I asked Dick Scharff to prepare a message to our Boss at COMNAVAIRPAC with information copies to the world, including our counterpart on the east coast that we had achieved Zero NORS. As a dig we used verbiage identical to the east coast's announcement. I knew we were close. It was late one afternoon several days later when I found myself standing in that same supply office. There was only one item to go. It was quiet. The same faces were there doing the same things they had been doing at the same desks when the sound of a truck engine could be heard approaching. Typewriters stopped. Paper shuffling stopped. Heads turned inquiringly. The familiar slam of a parcel on the loading dock was followed by a scraping of chairs as several people scrambled for the door. Someone bent over the parcel, looked up grinning and headed for a truck to take it in person to the recipient squadron. Someone else yelled, "That's the part. We did it!" Several other people cheered. Dick Scharff turned to me and we silently shook hands. "Send the message," I directed.

"Aye, aye, Sir", he answered in mock seriousness, adding the question, "May I bring my lad home from Norfolk?"

"Bring him home." I answered, adding, "And tell him he done good!"

As a postscript, some people chided me for pulling a stunt. But, they missed the whole point. Sure, we were only Zero NORS for a few hours. Sure, it cost me several thousand dollars in travel and per diem expenses for a Zero NORS condition that only lasted a few hours. However, the wing never went back to 132 NORS. They never even got close. The numbers got into the twenties over my remaining time at Miramar. Never did the number get so high that I didn't know them by memory. And the team at Miramar learned a few lessons from the drill. One lesson was that if you want something badly enough you can probably get it. The other lesson, the more important of the two, was that challenging a group of talented people to do the very difficult, then stepping out of their way is a sure recipe for success. That was the proudest message I had ever sent in my naval career.

The next shibboleth was those goddamned bare firewalls. Jet engines are changed when they reach a prescribed number of flight hours. They also have to be changed when they develop oil leaks, experience Foreign Object Damage (FOD) and for a host of other reasons. They are removed and taken to the jet engine repair shop at Miramar's Aviation Intermediate Maintenance Department (AIMD). There they are disassembled and repaired. There is a repair line, much like a factory assembly line, for each different type of turbine engine on the base. The F-14, F-4, F-5, A-4, T-2 and E-2 all have different engines. AIMD has a separate disassembly and repair line for each. The supply department keeps spare engines on hand in large hermetically sealed cans.

VF-111 F-14 landing at "Fightertown, U.S.A."

It can generally keep up with the scheduled removal and repair rate of engine changes. It is the unscheduled engine removals which so often outstrip the number of spare engines the supply officer is allowed to keep. A good, aggressive Foreign Object Damage control program is essential to keep bare firewall numbers to a minimum. To me there is something obscene about the sight of an F-14 parked in a hangar with a gaping hole where an engine should be. One is bad enough, but twenty of them is a disgrace! That is what I told them assembled staff at the morning status briefing. I asked for a show of hands of who would be willing to pull the plug in going for a zero bare firewall status. This was a little more complex a problem than the Zero NORS program we had just achieved. It involved AIMD for decreasing engine turnaround time in repair, increasing efficiency and increasing throughput. It involved the squadrons for increasing their FOD control program, improving their organizational level engine maintenance efforts. It involved the supply department to ensure a higher rate of engine parts availability. It was a big team effort, and everyone in the room knew it as they all raised their hands. With the Zero NORS success behind them they were showing a lot more of what I called, "piss and vinegar." To add a little motivation to the folks who would bear the major brunt of the effort I stood before the gathered engine repair crews at the huge hangar bay of Miramar's engine repair facility and announced the prize for achieving zero bare firewalls at Miramar. "The moment we achieve zero bare firewalls here at Miramar, your Boss is going to give me a call, regardless of the hour or the day. I am going to stop whatever it is that I am doing and come over here. We are then going to lock up this place and go to the enlisted club and I am going to stand for a keg of beer and we are going to finish it off." There was the exchange of skeptical looks, then some grins and a gnarly looking mechanic, his hands darkened with the continual soaking in engine oil spoke up.

"Admiral," he said, "You got yourself a deal!" This was followed by some whoops and hollers as I walked out of the building wondering whether I would ever have to buy a keg. I suspected I would.

CHAPTER 12: "FIGHTERTOWN, U.S.A."

Again, as in our NORS experience we watched the numbers of bare firewalls at the morning status briefing. A similar thing occurred. We became more familiar with which squadron had the bare firewalls, where the engines were and when they were expected to get put back in. Nothing happened for a few days then the number dropped from twenty to eighteen. The supply officer had gotten permission from his supply boss to keep a few extra spares on hand just for a few weeks. Then, all of a sudden the number of bare firewalls began to decrease steadily. I was elated. One bright Monday morning I was thrilled to see the number at nine. We had broken the ten barrier. It hadn't been below that number since the F-14s first arrived at Miramar I was told. As I recall it took another three weeks of steady decreasing numbers. I was called out of town for a week and, when I returned for a Monday morning recap of the previous week's performance I noted one bare firewall. That evening I put a fifty dollar bill in my money clip since I don't normally carry that much cash on me. I had a presentiment. The following morning's brief still carried the one bare firewall and the AIMD officer informed me that the troops were hard at work on the engine. At about two o'clock he called me and said, "Admiral, I think you'd better get over here. There's something I want you to see." I went over. He met me outside the building and led me in through the side door indicating he didn't want the troops to catch sight of me. We peeked around a corner and I was aghast at what I saw. All of the work stations were vacant except for the F-14 engine station. Although there were normally four or five people in a work crew, this jet engine was literally crawling with workers. It looked like a bee hive. Many of them were getting in each other's way but, nonetheless, they were lightheartedly hammering away like a bunch of excited kids. They were wrapping up the job and excitedly getting ready to surprise the Admiral. We returned quietly to his office and had a cup of coffee while we waited. After half an hour his phone rang, he listened for a minute, said, "thanks", and hung up. "Let's go, Admiral", he said, adding, "This is it!"

When we reached the work station the whole crew were standing there grinning like Cheshire cats. They told me we were zero bare firewalls. I turned to their boss and said, "Lock her up." There were a series of war hoops and rebel yells as we left the building and headed for the club. I slapped the fifty down on the bar and spent one of the most satisfying afternoons of my two years at Miramar. As in the NORS experience, the bare firewalls number went back up a little but never exceeded three or four, at the most, for the rest of my stay at Miramar.

The final, and by far, the toughest hurdle remained, the SPINTAC problem. At that time, there were eleven special interest aircraft around the base. They were easy to recognize. They sat in corners in hangars looking a little neglected, dirty, forlorn, without many parts and covered with tags where parts had been removed and little bags of fittings and fasteners attached. This was a problem much more complex than the NORS or bare firewall problems. There was genuine skepticism in the eyes of my staff and in the expressions of the squadron COs gathered around the conference table. We talked a long time and then all concluded that they were all ready to sign up to a Zero SPINTAC effort but it had to be a team effort. The CO of the fleet replacement squadron offered to provide some expert technicians and form a team of talented maintenance technicians, assisted by the full support of the civilian representatives who were stationed at Miramar by the several aerospace companies like Grumman, General Electric, Hughes, Pratt & Whitney and others. This team would attack one SPINTAC airplane at a time and work through all eleven of them until the job was done. In particular, the Grumman senior Field Service Representative offered to appeal to the F-14 production line back at the plant for unique replacement parts if that were ever necessary. The team went to work and I was astonished how quickly the effect of their effort began to show up in the morning statistics. I don't recall how long it took. We all agreed to give the fleet squadrons top priority holding the several SPINTACs in the fleet replacement squadron until last. There was a good deal of assistance from the type commander, called COMNAVAIRPAC, over at North Island as wind of what we were doing caught on in that staff. It was several weeks later that the last SPINTAC was worked off in the fleet squadrons an we started on the last two at Fighter Squadron ONE HUNDRED TWENTY-FOUR. The first one went well but there was nothing but trouble with the last.

The way the rules were written an airplane couldn't be removed from special interest status until it got airborne on its post-maintenance test flight. Twice it had taxied out to the warm-up area at the end of the runway and twice it had failed its critical engine run-up checks prior to taking off. It was a Friday afternoon and I decided to go on over to the VF-124 hangar to see how they were doing. As I got out cf my car and started up the outside staircase to the administrative spaces on the gallery floor of the hangar I could hear a full power run-up occurring at the take-off end of the duty runway. I stopped on the stairs listening, wondering whether this was our final SPINTAC airplane getting ready a third time for its flight. If it were I knew that many people were, like me, paused in mid-stride and listening. Then I heard a slightly different sound of an F-14 in full afterburner now in motion. From my position the sound source was moving from my left to my right just as it would if it were on take-off roll on runway 24. So, I stayed on that step and listened intently. From my position I knew I couldn't see the plane lift off but I knew hundreds of other eyes in this hangar could do so. So, I waited for an interminable several seconds then it came. It was a roar of hundreds of cheering voices and I couldn't move. What a sound! What human emotion! Sailors and officers, men and women, secretaries and civilian workers all cheering at the top of there lungs to celebrate one of the finest team efforts I had ever been involved in. I changed my mind, turned around, retraced my steps. I was sure the squadron CO wanted to relish this moment with his own troops.

There were other famous firsts. But throughout the NORS, bare firewall and SPINTAC efforts tremendous energy and team spirit was building in this wing. I could see evidences of it all around me. Morale was definitely picking up. The aircrews were beginning to fly a lot more. The troops were rebuilding their own morale through hard work and meeting challenges. Now, I thought was the time to add a little of fun to all the work.

Someone on my staff thought up the idea of a major electronic warfare exercise involving other squadrons from other bases all exercising their unique systems in a series of scenarios designed to train the various units involved in their own equipment in a realistic over water exercise off the southern California coast. My Boss approved the idea and we were designated the host air wing for what was to become a semi-annual exercise named "Hey Rube." The name (my idea) came from the old traveling circus days. When local town toughs came to the camp site to roust the circus workers the call "Hey Rube" summoned help from the troupe. The periodic exercise was a resounding success.

Another fun event we dreamed up was an annual aerial gunnery meet. Any squadron in the air wing equipped with guns could enter a four plane team in the contest. The shooting was done over the Chocolate Mountain Gunnery Range north of Yuma, Arizona and was an occasion for great fun and games, an award ceremony and an award party. F-5s from the Fighter Weapons School (Topgun) and F-14s from the fleet squadrons were the principal participants. There were, in 1980, two reserve and two active fleet Phantom squadrons based at Miramar who didn't carry any guns and, therefore could not participate in this great event. Because of this we started up the greatest contest of all, the annual fighter derby. This was the best of all because the rules we drew up required that every aircrew in every squadron participate. All of the simulated aerial combat was done on the instrumented Tactical Air Combat Training System (TACTS) range just east of Yuma, Arizona. The Data Display System (DDS) saw all and told all so there could be no lying or cheating. All the facts about all the participants could be read out in real time by the judges. The derby was an instant success and a great morale booster. The derby lasted a week and the awards ceremony was conducted in flight suits at the officer's club amidst loud and spirited rivalry.

But, the most important of all the famous firsts was the "no-notice" missile shoot. This was the toughest contest to win and also the toughest to initiate. Each day each squadron was required to report on the readiness status of each missile station on each of its airplanes. My weapons systems officer reported to me. Every once in a while I would select a station on an airplane and the squadron CO would receive a telephone call informing him that he had to fire an air-to-air missile from that station on that airplane that day. He would be given a shoot time and the missile would be delivered to him. The safety experts on my staff would watch and grade as his sailors loaded the missile. Then an airborne observer would chase the flight out over the Pacific Missile Test Range and watch them shoot at an aerial drone target. There simply couldn't be a tougher test and the squadrons proved that fact by failing dismally in the first few tests. But, by the time I left Miramar, squadrons were routinely passing this most difficult of all tests. It was, in my view, the real determinant of combat readiness. It was just this kind of readiness and professionalism which determined the outcome of the shoot downs in the Gulf of Sidra in 1981 and 1989. U.S. Navy fighter aircrews have a reputation for being the best trained and most professional in the world, and the reason is simple; they have proven it again and again. "Fightertown, U.S.A." was the best job I ever had!

13

AIM/ACEVAL

One of the most important assemblages of tactical aircraft in the history of air warfare occurred over the barren Nevada desert in 1976-77 a period of eighteen months. It was called Air Combat Evaluation/Air Intercept Missile Evaluation, or ACEVAL/AIMVAL. One of the most extensive weapons tests in history, it was also one of the most comprehensive and therefore one of the most important.

It was a joint U.S. Air Force/U.S. Navy test and it employed large numbers of aircraft in an environment meant to be as real as simulation could make it. The test was comprehensive because it tested not just weapons, but entire weapons systems. It also tested procedures and tactics, in an environment as close as possible to real life war.

But, by far the most important element tested was the human element. Plane captains, aircraft maintenance personnel, radar air controllers and, above all, aircrews were tested. The "fog of war", that unmeasurable element of combat; real anxiety when real bullets are flying past the canopy, came as close to being given a dimension as it ever has. The results of ACEVAL/AIMVAL were a true assessment of the combat effectiveness of the F-14 Tomcat and the F-15 Eagle. It was also a true assessment of the AIM-9 Sidewinder, the AIM-7 Sparrow and the twenty millimeter Gatling gun. In addition, it was a test of Navy and Air Force combat tactics as well as the relatively new air combat maneuvering range (ACMR) and the newer air combat maneuvering installation (ACMI). Communications procedures and equipment came to be examined in the light of things which were learned from captured hardware from communist country arms inventories.

Lessons learned from this important test were legion. Some of them the participants instinctively knew, but couldn't quantify or, up until then, prove. Other lessons were surprises and very instructive. Some equipment items were exonerated. The Weaver rifle telescopes which F-15 pilots had bolted to the top of the instrument panels exonerated a development program (TVSU) which took over twenty years to get turned into real hardware, the F-14 Television Camera System (TCS). Another important high tech tactical tool was the visual tactical aircraft system (VTAS) with which all Navy and Air Force "blue force" airplanes were equipped. (the U.S. Air Force used VTAS only during AIMVAL when carrying the AGILE concept missile.)

The bottom line is that AIM/ACEVAL finally put the lie to the popular media contention that the military establishment procures gold-plated equipment that costs too much and doesn't work. If acquired, maintained and trained with properly, weapons will work. AIM/ACEVAL proved that fact. Of course, key to all of this is proper testing. Testing, like ACEVAL/AIMVAL should be a recurring element in the business of defense. The air combat evaluation (ACEVAL) was the first of the two tests. The air intercept missile evaluation (AIMVAL) came as an added feature of the test program. The author of the test plan was Irving Kaufman, Phd.

The question which ACEVAL sought to answer was; "Can a few high technology airplanes (F-15/F-14) defeat a large number of low technology airplanes (MiG-21)?"

The question which AIMVAL sought to answer was; "What should be the follow-on missile to the AIM-9 Sidewinder? Should it be a small, cheap, low performance air-to-air missile like the US Air Force proposed Ford-Philco 'Ladyfinger'? Or, should it be an advanced, high technology weapon like the U.S. Navy proposed 'Agile' missile?"

ACEVAL was the first of the two tests to be conducted. The players were six U.S. Air Force pilots and six F-15A airplanes. The U.S. Navy players were six air crews flying six brand new Block 90 F-14A airplanes. The adversary services were provided by a joint team of U.S. Air Force adversary pilots and U.S. Navy "Topgun" instructors.

PART III: IN THE FLEET

F-15A from the 49th TFW (Holloman, AFB) over Red Flag Range, Nevada, carrying dummy AIM-9 and ACMI pod.

AIMVAL/ACEVAL F-14A with Keith Ferris' camouflage paint scheme.

The Navy aircrews were headed up at first by Commander J.W. Taylor, former Commanding Officer of one of the first two fighter squadrons to deploy the F-14. The Navy line-up follows:

First Section; Pilot Cdr. J.W. Taylor/ RIO Lcdr. Dudley Bouck, pilot Lt. Dick Grey/RIO Lt. Phil Hubbs

Second Section; Pilot Lcdr. Joe Satrapa/RIO Lt. Bill Hill, pilot Lcdr. Dan Pentacost/RIO Lcdr. Frank Schuemacher

Third Section; Pilot Lcdr. Boomer Wilson/RIO Lt. Bill Riger, pilot Lcdr. Dave Berke/RIO Lcdr. Mike Marnane

The joint adversary force, a group of very talented pilots, was led by Major Murray Sloane. They flew twelve U.S. Air Force F-5Es equipped with an operable, but modest air-intercept radar and an air-to-air missile which had the capabilities of the very latest infra-red homing missile in the U.S. inventory; the AIM-9L Sidewinder.

The joint test force was headed up by an Air Force Colonel and a Navy Captain named Russ Davis. Overseeing the entire evolution for the Navy was rear Admiral Julian Lake who was followed by Rear Admiral Eugene Tissot who was followed by Rear Admiral Robert McKenzie.

Most of the Navy aircrewmen came from the two first F-14 squadrons (VF-1 and 2) as they were just completing their first deployment to the western Pacific. The selected aircrews were transferred to a new parent squadron, Air Test and Evaluation Squadron FOUR (VX-4) located at Naval Air Station, Point Mugu, California. VX-4 has the responsibility for the testing and evaluation of all airplanes and weapons associated with the maritime air superiority (fighter) mission. The air crews trained at Point Mugu until it was time to move to the desert. They remained as VX-4 Detachment, Nellis Air Force Base, Nevada and were headed up by Cdr. J.W. Taylor until he was reassigned and the mantle of authority was passed on to Boomer Wilson.

Both the F-15 and F-14 were new airplanes. The F-14 was slightly ahead of the F-15 in timing of fleet introduction. Other than that, the airplanes were roughly equal in terms of their position in the acquisition and development process.

It is worth saying a few words about the maintenance approach employed by the two services. The air force airplanes were maintained using their standard wing concept which vested full support responsibility in the 57th Tactical Fighter Wing home based at Nellis. The logistics support package provided by the Air Force to the wing commander was substantial.

The Navy, on the other hand, chose to maintain their airplanes using the organizational level maintenance concept extant on all deployed aircraft carriers at the time. There was a group of roughly 150 officers and enlisted men (the size that would have been necessary to maintain six airplanes) assigned to keep the airplanes in operating condition. The logistic support package (AVCAL) normally assigned to a deploying aircraft carrier was "borrowed" from an East Coast carrier for the duration of the tests. In addition to the AVCAL and personnel, there were a number of contractor representa-

CHAPTER 13: AIM/ACEVAL

AIMVAL/ACEVAL F-5.

tives assigned to "help out" in much the same way that fleet squadrons are "helped out" on their first few deployments.

It was about this time that the F-14 ran into some fairly serious developmental difficulties with the TF-30 engine. These difficulties, characterized by basic unreliability, compressor stalls, afterburner blow outs and catastrophic engine failures had a pronounced effect on the performance of the airplane and the aircrews to the extent of imposing rather stringent throttle movement restrictions for the high angle of attack maneuvering essential for successful air combat maneuvering. It is a distinct tribute to the airmanship of the Navy aircrews that there weren't more problems than actually developed. Some amount of luck was also involved.

It was not until the summer of 1976, well into the trials, that most of the engine restrictions were lifted and the Navy aircrews were able to operate their airplanes with a bit more reckless abandon and tactical freedom. Daily logistic flights were flown from Nellis to Miramar to assist in providing a ready supply of spare parts for the Tomcats. As in all new airplane fleet introductions, however, the newness of the Block 90 F-14s was probably the single most important factor in the remarkable maintenance record which the F-14s established during both tests. The internal fuel capacity of the F-14 (16,000 lb.) was substantially larger than the F-15's fuel capacity. As a consequence, the staying power of the F-14 was a little greater on the range during test engagements. The F-14s, averaging about 2.5 successful engagements per sortie, began to outdistance the F-15s which averaged about 1.5 engagements per sortie, in terms of test progress. At some point in the testing, the U.S. Air Force decided to configure their F-15s with a centerline external fuel tank. After that, the test completion rate evened up somewhat.

Both the F-14 and the F-15 were able to out maneuver the F-5s when the engagements closed to close-in maneuvering. The F-15 had a higher thrust-to-weight ratio than the F-14 but higher wing loading. The F-14, with its variable geometry wing had superior turning performance due to much lower wing loading. The exchange ratios achieved by the two airplanes over the entire course of the tests were, roughly, two to one over the F-5s.

In the early part of the tests it became obvious that ascribing the air-to-air missile capability of the AIM-9L Sidewinder to the F-5s gave them a substantial advantage over that missile performance which existed in even

VX-4 "Black Bunny" Tomcat.

the most well equipped Warsaw Pact countries. That, combined with the small size of the F-5, gave it a distinct advantage in the visual engagement arena. The "rules of engagement" (ROE) also required that visual identification was required before simulating the release of weapons. The TVSU in the F-14s and the rifle scopes in the F-15s became important in this aspect of the engagements. Navy airplanes were also equipped with VTAS and over 90 % of all radar locks occurred with VTAS.

Nevertheless, in the early portion of the tests, because of its small size the F-5 was doing much better than anticipated. Beyond about three miles, head-on, the F-5 was extremely difficult to acquire visually. The test monitors occasionally sent an unidentified airplane through the test range to ensure that the aircrews adhered rigidly to the visual identification requirement. The participants were warned that three mis-identifications by any crew would be cause for disqualification.

However, despite all of the ROE and the fidelity of the combat simulation, participants still found that they could "game" the system to some degree. Adversary pilots, eager to succeed, often fired their IR weapons when they did not actually have a good lock-on. The ACMR, at that time a second generation system, was not always good enough to properly assess these events.

On the blue force side, pilots found that they could "game" the system and, therefore, achieve a higher personal exchange ratio by adopting practices which never would have been permitted in real life. "Gaming" can best be described as taking unfair advantage of certain artificialities in the simulation to enhance performance. At times these "gaming" techniques enhanced some pilot's exchange ratios at the expense of test objectives. Leadership on both the Air Force and Navy side of the "blue force" was necessary to ensure that these effects were minimized.

The range of the tests was extensive. The 30 nautical mile ACMI range circle was divided into six entry points. Each test involved the blue force and red force each starting out at one of those points. To enhance survivability, and the ability to "bug out" (disengage suc-

VF-111 F-14A firing AIM-7M.

cessfully), the blue force aircrews found that entry onto the range at very high airspeed was desirable. "Bug outs" were not considered acceptable unless the disengager departed the range at the point of entry. All twelve blue force pilots/aircrews had to complete tests using all of the entry points and in engagements involving one-versus-one, one-versus-two, two-versus-two, two-versus-four and four-versus-four engagements.

Neither blue or red force air controllers were allowed to turn on their ground-controlled-intercept radars until start of each engagement. Participants never knew the set-up in advance and each engagement had to faithfully fulfill all criteria to be counted as a completion.

Each service was allowed to pick their airplane paint configuration. The U.S Navy airplanes sported a dark gray on light gray camouflage configuration designed by the noted military artist, Keith Ferris.

Most of the current dogfight modes in the F-14 weapons system were developed during ACEVAL/AIMVAL. The F-15 radar was better suited for the scope of the tests than the F-14 radar. The small initial range set-ups (less than 30 miles) gave the edge to the simpler F-15 radar.

A typical set-up would involve a head-on visual identification which would permit an AIM-7 launch by blue force airplanes (employing a shoot-shoot philosophy), followed by both blue and red forces firing forward hemisphere IR missiles just before the plots merged. Close-in engagements or bug outs ensued. If close-in engagements occurred, the kill weapon often became the gun.

There was one mid-air collision between an F-15 and an F-5 in which the F-15 was lost.

The blue force weapons configuration for ACEVAL was AIM-7 and AIM-9 missiles. For AIMVAL the weapons configuration was Sidewinders and Agile missiles for the Air Force and AIM-7 and "Ladyfinger" for the Navy. Halfway through AIMVAL the close-in air-to-air missile suite was switched and the Air Force ended up with their "Ladyfinger" concept; and the Navy aircrews with their Agile missile.

In September 1977 the Navy aircrews completed their tests. One month later the Air Force pilots finished. Since that time much has been said and claimed about AIM/ACEVAL by many pundits, analysts, would-be experts, armchair strategists and tacticians. The following are some of the more important findings:

• F-14 and F-15 equipped forces can achieve exchange ratios of 2:1 against a well-trained, larger force operating low tech (MiG-21) airplanes.

• A close-in weapon with seeker head sensitivity, tracking rate capability and off-boresight acquisition capability at least as good as the AIM-9L is essential for modern aerial combat.

• First visual acquisition usually determines the successful outcome of the engagement.

• Visual enhancers like TCS and slewing devices like VTAS are critical in influencing the outcome of an aerial engagement.

• Two of anything can beat one of anything assuming the two apply basic air combat tactical principles and work as a team.

• Four eyes are usually better than two in the visual arena.

• Small airplanes have a distinct tactical advantage over big airplanes.

• Speed is life!

• Fuel is life!

• In a multi-plane engagement, following a predictable trajectory for more than a few seconds will be fatal!

• Regardless of equipment, the better trained force wins!

If it did nothing else, AIM/ACEVAL served to validate aerial combat principles which had been developed and applied by U.S. Navy fighter aircrews in earlier generation fighters in Vietnam and Korea . . . and, as a matter of fact, in World War II!

14

TELEVISION CAMERA SYSTEM

The tests conducted over the Nevada desert under the name AIM/ACEVAL concluded that aircrews equipped with systems which enhanced their ability to identify the enemy early in an engagement, nearly always won the engagement.

That is what TCS does for F-14 aircrews. The two principal advantages which it brings to an aerial engagement are: 1.) the ability fire foreward quarter missiles in a visual environment by extending identification ranges; and 2.) the ability to distinguish friend from foe during a multi-plane engagement.

The conclusion, drawn over the years by tactical aviators, that he who makes the first identification in an aerial engagement usually wins is as true now as it was in World War I.

Lessons from AIM/ACEVAL dealing with regard to visual target acquisition can be summarized as follows:

1) The adversary who makes the first contact of the opponent, by any means, usually wins the engagement.

2) In a multi-plane engagement there is always a need to identify a target before firing.

3) Visual augmentation, by any means, substantially increases an aircrew's chances of winning an aerial engagement.

4) In an aerial engagement two pairs of eyes are always better than one.

There were, of course, many more lessons derived from AIM/ACEVAL. But, the ones listed above are particularly pertinent to aerial engagements were the plots eventually merge. Indeed, as far back as 1954 I can recall being designated as the person in the CO's four plane division of fighters to wear binoculars. I wore them around my neck on a strap and even had an elastic tie-down tab to hold them close to my chest during carrier catapults, arrestments and even, perish the thought, during an ejection.

We were flying Grumman Cougars from a straight deck carrier off the North Korean coast at 45,000 feet. I soon learned how to scan the horizon very efficiently with eight power binoculars while on combat air patrol. I remember very distinctly calling out a contact on a particular bearing. The CO duly relayed my sighting to the ship's air search radar. Even through my binoculars they were only four dark specks on the horizon. The ship duly corroborated my sighting as a division of fighters from another carrier at forty miles. A rudimentary system of visual enhancement was effective forty years ago for jet fighters.

It was thirty-six years later, while flying F-14s out of Miramar, with the Black Lions of VF-213, that I used a Weaver rifle scope in a similar fashion. The Skipper of the squadron, Commander Monroe Smith had designed another rudimentary visual enhancement system using a home made set of metal mounting brackets and a rifle telescope purchased at a local sporting goods store. He gave it the bureaucratic acronym "TITS" which, of course, stood for Tactical Integrated Telescope System.

The pilot simply adjusted the forward mounting bracket, after the engine was started, to align the scope with the armament datum line on the HUD. Then, all the pilot had to do to gain a visual sighting was find a target with the radar, point the airplane at the target, look through the scope and identify the target at remarkable distances. This enabled the aircrew to make a target iden-

CHAPTER 14: TELEVISION CAMERA SYSTEM

TCS chin pod on F-14A.

tification far enough away to use the full capabilities of both the Phoenix and Sparrow radar-guided air-to-air missiles . . . under rules of engagement which might require target identification before firing.

During AIM/ACEVAL the Air Force F-15s used a similar telescope rig and found it very advantageous. But, by then, the Navy F-14s had a far better arrangement called the TVSU (Television Sight Unit). It represented a development which had been ongoing in the U.S. Air Force for over ten years. The predecessor to TVSU was a television camera in the leading edge of the wing on an F-4 Phantom II. The TVSU was a further advancement in the technology and was built by the Electro-mechanical Division of the Northrop Corporation. The final version of the system, that which we now have in the F-14, called Television Cockpit System, gave the F-14s an enormous advantage in the AIM/ACEVAL tests at Nellis.

The system, first appearing in later block number F-14s was manifested by a single pod mounted under the nose of the airplane. A video display of what the television camera saw was projected in both front and rear cockpits of the F-14. With the advent of an infra-red search and track sensor system in the F-14D a dual chin-mounted pod has evolved. The best example of the value of the TCS occurred during my tenure as wing commander at Miramar in 1980.

As wing commander, I was assigned administrative control over Air Test and Evaluation Squadron FOUR at Naval Air Station, Point Mugu, California. Operational control of the squadron was exercised by Commander, Operational Test and Evaluation Force at Norfolk, Virginia. As a consequence, I kept in close touch with the activities of VX-4 and with all ongoing projects which might eventually have an effect on the Pacific Fleet fighter force. I knew in February 1981 that VX-4 had installed in one of their F-14s a TVSU from Northrop and were evaluating it. A call came in from one of my spies in the Pentagon that some funding had been cut from the TVSU project to cover over-runs in another program considered to be of higher priority. The CO of

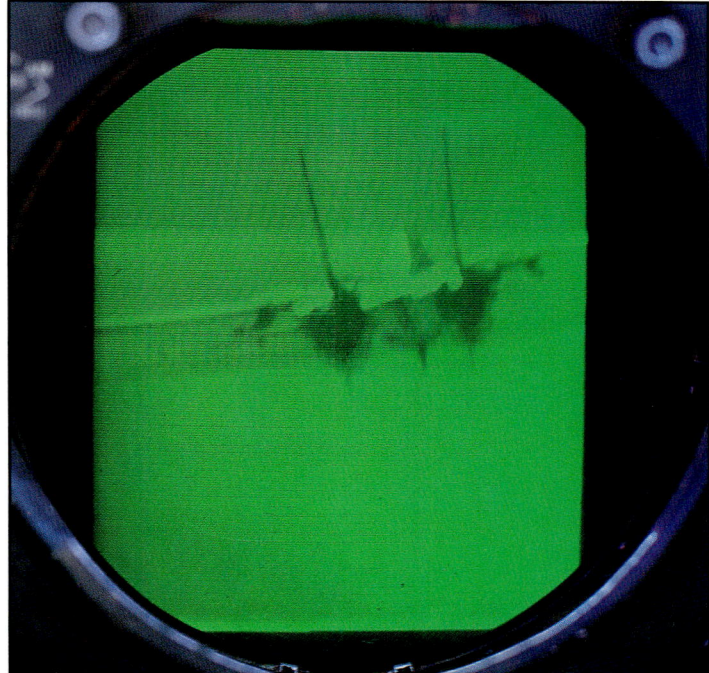

Two views of the TCS display on TID in the rear cockpit of an F-14A.

F-14D TCS/IRST pod.

VX-4 offered to bring his TVSU airplane to Miramar for me to fly. Delighted, I accepted and on 11 February the airplane arrived from Point Mugu.

I climbed into the machine with "Rocky" Deal in the back seat as VX-4 project officer and, in this case, instructor. The flight plan called for a series of head-on runs against a pair of Topgun adversary airplanes over the water west of San Diego. Target aspect angle was varied as well as look-up and look-down angles, so that I could get a proper appreciation for how far away I could distinguish between the two airplanes, an A-4 Skyhawk and an F-5 Tiger. It is worth noting that both airplanes are very small, and out at the limits of normal visual acquisition, in a head-on situation, the distinction between the two is extremely difficult.

The TVSU system included a zoom television camera with two different magnifications and two fields of view. The standard tactic was to use the wider field of view to acquire the target and lock on. Then the radar intercept officer (RIO) would shift to the zoom mode (with its smaller field of view) and observe at what range I was able to distinguish which airplane was which. Inside the front cockpit on the right console was a four by four inch video display showing the pilot what the TVSU was seeing. "Rocky" kept a running tutorial on his tape recorder not only for my benefit but, more importantly, for potential viewers of the tape.

The video, with "Rocky's" audio commentary, was quickly duplicated and I got on the schedule to see the Deputy Chief of Naval Operations (Air Warfare). On 17 February Frank Brown and I "borrowed" an F-14 from one of the fleet squadrons and headed for Washington, D.C. Bright and early on the 18th I rolled a portable television set into Vice Admiral Wes McDonald's outer office and took a seat. His staff viewed me with a jaundiced eye. They knew from experience that whenever a flag officer came in from the fleet he wanted something. More often than not, the visitor got what he wanted if he presented his case reasonably well.

This always meant reversing a funding decision that the staff had gotten their boss to make. What always ensued was a stirring around looking for a source for the requested funds; and somebody else's pet project would take the hit. On schedule I wheeled the television set into the inner office, explained what the man was about to hear and see, and turned the machine on.

Of course, his staff had already briefed him on what the issues were, but they hadn't seen the video. I settled down and let the Admiral watch and listen to "Rocky's" tutorial. It was magnificent. I cannot reveal the actual ranges because they are still classified. But, I can say that they were as startling to the Admiral as they were to me a few days earlier when I experienced them personally from the vantage point of an F-14's front cockpit.

The point made by the video was that it made it possible for an F-14 aircrew to identify an enemy far enough away to fire an air-to-air missile with a forward quarter capability (radar-guided missile or otherwise). The Admiral was as impressed as I had been and, when I explained the adverse funding decision he reversed it. Then he told his money expert to find the necessary funds from another source. The following morning Frank and I climbed into our F-14 and headed it for Miramar with a solid feeling of satisfaction.

15
FLEET AERIAL RECONNAISSANCE

The primary mission of the F-14 is maritime air superiority; the achieving and maintaining of air superiority in a maritime environment. This is more than, simply fleet air defense. It includes going to an enemy battle group and defeating its airborne defenses over the battle group. It means escorting strike groups to targets over water or over land. It means combat air patrols, fighter sweeps and deck launched air intercepts. In the late 1970s and early eighties, when the RA-5C Vigilante and the RF-8G reconnaissance had begun to phase out of the fleet the idea of adding a reconnaissance mission to the F-14's widening range of mission

TARPS equipped VF-102 F-14, over Oceana.

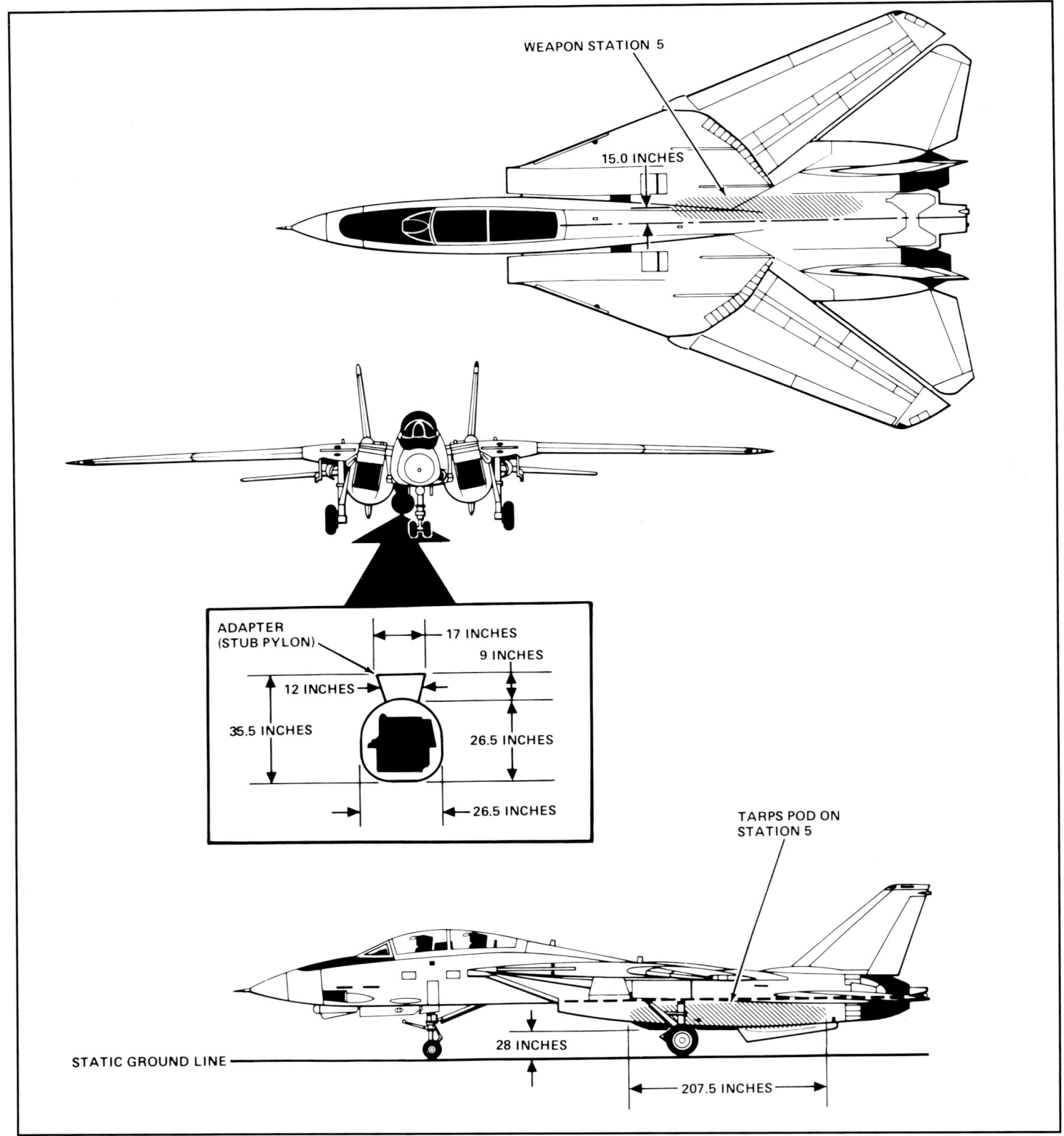

TARPS COMPONENT LOCATIONS

CHAPTER 15: FLEET AERIAL RECONNAISSANCE

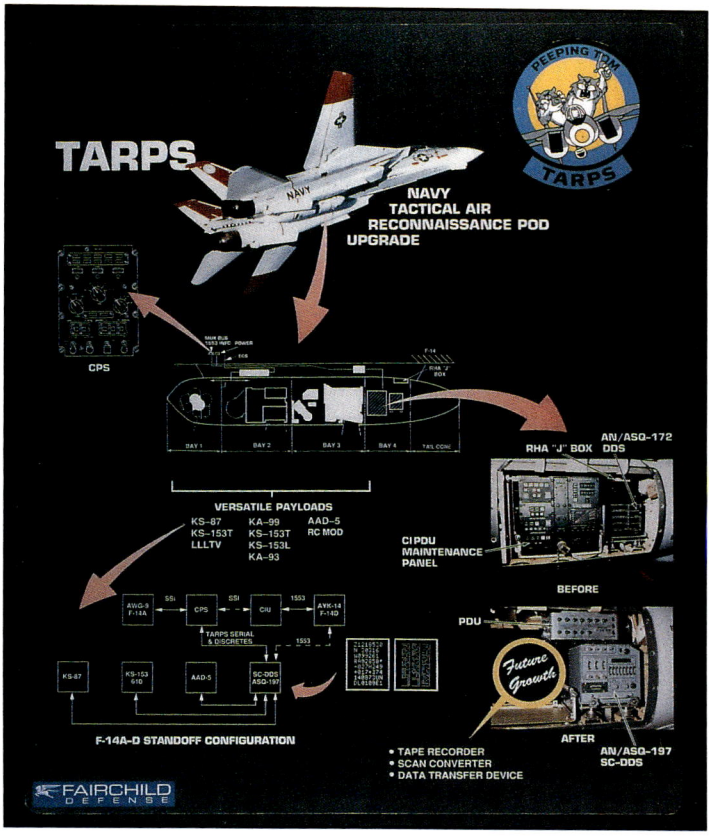

capabilities was conceived. The tactical airborne reconnaissance pod system (TARPS) was born. A large pod suspended from a wing or fuselage missile station, the system is 207.5 inches long, weighs a hefty 1,750 pounds and contained a two position framing camera mounted in the front of the pod where it can look forward and obliquely down through the forward window, or straight down through a vertical window in the bottom of the pod.

Immediately behind the framing camera is a low altitude panoramic KA-99 camera. In the rear of the pod is an AAD-5/RS-720 infra-red reconnaissance set. These sensors give the TARPS equipped F-14 a fairly effective system for medium and low altitude clear air mass reconnaissance. The two carriers (*Coral Sea* and *Midway*) which were not configured for F-14s, were supported by a detachment of US Marine Corps reconnaissance RF-4 Phantoms.

The TARPS system was originally intended to be an interim measure until a reconnaissance version of the F/A-18 could enter the fleet. In about 1985 the decision was made to develop a less expensive kit to change out an F/A-18's gun system and temporarily replace it with a reconnaissance modification. That system is still in

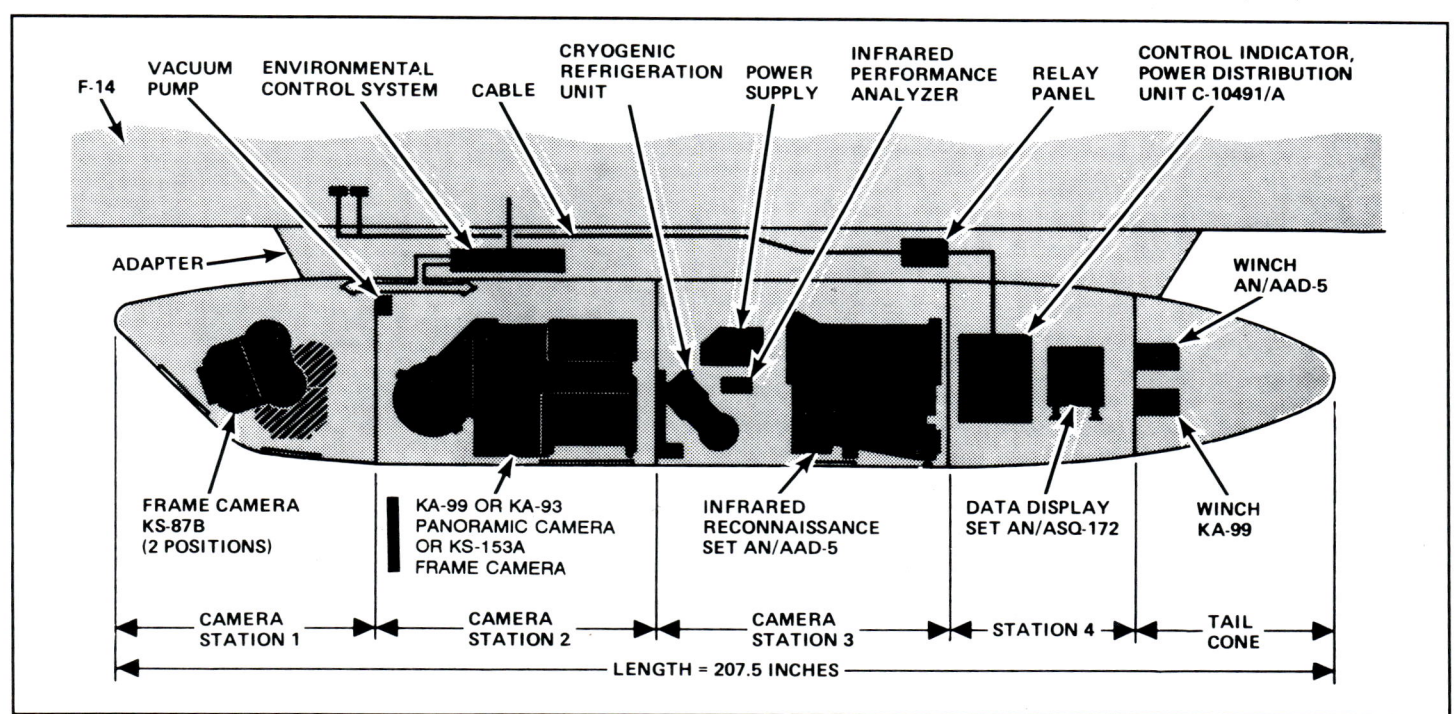

TARPS SYSTEM

TARPS photograph of road/bridge intersection.

the development stage as of this writing. The basic elements of a good sea based aerial reconnaissance system are still long range, high speed and agility. The Hornet cannot be characterized as a long range platform.

In early 1990 serious efforts began to equip all F-14A Pluses and F-14Ds with an air-to-ground strike capability. At any time on U.S. aircraft carriers all over the world one can see F-14s in a large number of configurations ranging from strike to reconnaissance to a pure fighter role. In the latter role there are still a large number of configurations depending on the mission. The versatility is there to be a strike airplane also equipped to carry enough air-to-air weapons to fight its way into and out of a target area. Typical fighter configurations include weapons loads of two AIM-54 Phoenix missiles, two AIM-7 Sparrow missiles, two AIM-9 Sidewinder missiles and six hundred rounds of twenty millimeter ammunition. Variations from that baseline fighter configuration abound, depending upon where the carrier is and what it expects its F-14s to do. But, more and more the two 280 gallon external fuel tanks are becoming a standard part of most of the configurations seen on deployed carriers.

16

THE GUNFIGHTER

It is an absolute certainty that the first Tomcat aircrew to shoot down a MiG with the gun will be cast in bronze and their statues, in heroic scale, will be placed outside the main entrance to the Officer's Club at Naval Air Station, Miramar, California.

There is something almost mystical about a gun in a fighter plane. Despite misguided efforts by theoreticians, statisticians and aerodynamicists to get guns out of fighters, they persist; and for good reasons. A gun cannot be jammed electronically. Decoys don't deceive its bullet stream. It has no minimum range and when it is in the hands of an aggressive and dedicated airman, it can be as deadly as any air-to-air weapon. As an air-to-ground weapon the gun still has no equal for first pass accuracy against lightly armored moving targets. I can still recall a U.S. Air Force combat veteran returning from a Korean combat tour. He was being badgered by an aggressive reporter about what he thought was the most difficult target to hit. His answer stopped the reporter cold. It was, he said, a nun on a bicycle! Then he added, parenthetically, that the only weapon that could hit that difficult target on the first pass was a gun.

The principle reason why the gun is not listed as a high ranking air-to-air killer in modern aerial combat history is that the pilot must pass up several other opportunities with other weapons to close to gun range. There is risk in wasting those chances if he has any of those other weapons in his limited inventory. The weapon which will accomplish the kill quickest, and with least risk to the shooter, is invariably chosen. The gun is rarely in that category. But, when it is used skillfully, it is deadly.

How well I remember being invited to the Douglas Plant in El Segundo, California to render an expert opinion. I was an aerial gunnery instructor at the predecessor to Topgun, the Fleet Air Gunnery Unit, Pacific at El Centro, California. The year was 1956. It was flattering to me, a mere Lieutenant, to be considered an expert on anything. But there we were, three of us, all instructors in aerial gunnery giving advice to aircraft designers.

The fire control design engineers whom we were assisting were trying to get the bugs out of the new Douglas F-5D weapons system. It was a beautiful airplane. We spent quite some time in the mock-up of this follow-on to the famous, record-holding F-4D. It had a longer fuselage, greater internal fuel capacity, a newer model of the Pratt & Whitney J-57 turbojet engine with increased thrust and, best of all, an improved flight control system. The new airplane held great promise and the prospects of fixing all the bad features of its predecessor (and there were many) while retaining all of its advantages.

But, we had been invited to give them our ideas on the way they were solving the problem of displaying the gun sight symbols on a collimating lens in front of the pilot. The whole reason for the problem, explained one of the engineers, rather loftily, was because of the huge kinematic lead angles necessary in the high altitude employment of a gun against a high speed bomber target. He explained that the airplane shouldn't have a gun at all. For the mission it was being built to perform, a gun was stupid. A radar-guided missile or a pod of un-guided rockets would be the only weapons which could do the job. He illustrated the thesis with a diagram showing a typical target, a Russian Bear bomber at 45,000 feet and Mach 0.8. Emanating from the bomber's tail were a series of curved lines called "iso'g's." His diagram proved without a doubt that the fighter was physically unable to pull enough "g"s at those altitudes and speeds to get close enough to generate a firing solution for a gun.

I found his attitude so condescending I wanted to puke. Technically he was correct. Operationally, he was just plain ignorant. A classic high side gunnery run would be suicidal. But, we knew from experiences playing with our own B-36 bombers at high altitude that the job could only be done by several airplanes making simultaneous attacks from several aspect angles not precluding, incidentally, the head-on attack. German fighters employed that tactic in World War II over Europe.

103

F-14 gun port.

But their solution was as ridiculous as their argument. They had proposed automatically lowering the ejection seat from the fully raised position at the start of a run to the fully bottomed position at the firing position. This was proposed simply to permit the pilot to keep the pipper in view during the entire run.

We sent them back to the drawing board. I never did find out how they solved the problem. Perhaps they never did solve it. Shortly after our visit to El Segundo the F-5D program was canceled. The half dozen or so preproduction airplanes were given to the National Aeronautics and Space Administration for its pilots to fly for proficiency.

But, the designers still kept up their efforts to get guns out of fighters. It was not too long after our trip to El Segundo that plans were being solidified for a Navy fighter, a follow-on to the F-8, which would not have a gun at all. It was the F-4H-1 Phantom II. At the time, I was still going through the test pilot school syllabus at NAS Patuxent River, Maryland. Just before graduation each class was given a field trip lasting a week during which we visited all the major aerospace contractors. It was a fortuitous time for such a field trip because the great shoot-out was going on between Ling Temco Vought's F8U-3 and McDonnell's F-4H-1. Again, we heard all the convincing arguments about not needing a gun to do the mission. The shoot-out, in the final analysis, became an argument between the two-man, two-engine adherents and the single crew, single engine Mafia. The leading Navy design engineer later stated that from a design engineering standpoint, the Navy selected the wrong airplane. I recall being fairly vocal about the need for a gun, but nobody was interested in advice from a fledgling test pilot.

Seven years later I sat in a briefing room at the U.S. Air Base in Ubon, Thailand. I was the Commanding Officer of a fighter squadron based onboard the *U.S.S. Hancock*. We had just finished up a line period on Yankee Station in the Tonkin Gulf. The Air Force wing commander, Colonel Robin Olds and his vice commander Colonel "Chappie" James were our cordial hosts for three days of rest and recreation.

CHAPTER 16: THE GUNFIGHTER

We arrived just as Olds was climbing out of the cockpit from a combat mission. He raged at the idiots who handed him a plane without a gun. "I could have been an ace two times over if I had a gun", he shouted during a session of reviewing gun camera combat footage. He described being directly behind a MiG-17 and chopping both throttles to idle while thumbing out the speed brakes to slow down so that he could open to beyond the three thousand foot minimum range for a Sidewinder kill. That one got away. In the next gun camera sequence, the film showed a MiG-17 flashing by just a few hundred feet in front of the camera and much too close for a missile shot. I spoke up in the darkened room and asked the Colonel if he could have the projection booth run that one back again slowly. He did so and when the plane was framed in the middle of the wind screen I asked him to freeze it there. Again he did as requested. At that point I said, "Colonel Olds, right here is where I would have cut him in half with my Crusader's four twenty millimeter guns." The room was silent for a full five seconds before the Colonel bade the show to continue.

Of course, in their defense the designers of the Phantom II could never have guessed that their high altitude interceptor would ever be used against sprightly MiGs at tree top level. But, that is why we have operators involved in the acquisition process these days . . . or do we? And whatever happened to "lessons learned?"

When the time came for the weapons suite for the F-14 to be determined, there were combat veterans on hand to press the case for the gun. But, again the naysayers had to be overruled. They never quit.

About half way through my two year tour of duty as the wing commander at Miramar the Skipper of the Black Lions entered my office with a boyish grin on his face. "Gator", he began in that country boy way he has of speaking, "I think you ought to come on over to El Centro and shoot with us." He did it as though he were inviting me to shoot quail. I demurred, observing that I hadn't gotten to that point in my F-14 training to be using the weapons system. But, I couldn't convince him. He was adamant. "Hell", he expostulated, "There really ain't nothin' to it." Then, as if to convince me, "Tell you what, Gator, I'll put my squadron expert in the back seat with you and Joe won't let you screw up." I got a crash course from my aide, Frank Brown on gunnery aspects of the fire control system that afternoon. The next day I flew over to El Centro experiencing no small pangs of nostalgia. Twenty-five years ago I had been a weapons delivery instructor in this same place. Had anyone told me then that I would be coming over, twenty-five years later, to shoot at a banner from the front seat of a mach two, variable geometry winged, twin engine, thirty million dollar fighter, as a Rear Admiral, I would have laughed in his face.

On the short flight over I became acquainted with Joe, Monroe's expert. From the back seat Lieutenant Commander Joe Zahalka reviewed the switches and controls used in aerial gunnery. It was a great deal more complicated than the simple F-8 fire control system that I had used on my last aerial gunnery flight twelve years earlier. That had been my last aerial gunnery. I began to feel foolish already. What the hell was I trying to prove? How dumb can you get? It takes a week of two flights a day to get the gunnery pattern and run down to the proficiency where you can even hope for hits. All the way to the briefing room, despite Joe's assurances to the contrary, I was mentally kicking my ass. This was just crazy! All I was going to accomplish was to embarrass myself in front of the whole squadron.

There were ten people jammed into the small briefing room containing two more empty chairs and a blackboard on the wall. Introductions were made all around and Joe and I sat down. I remembered about the "century" (one hundred hole) and "double century" (two hundred hole) banners that Monroe Smith, the Skipper had told me about. He was proud of the record setting that his aircrews had done in aerial gunnery on this gunnery detachment. Indeed, I had never heard of such shooting performance in an F-14 squadron. I had to see for myself. The banners were all there, proudly displayed on the outside walls of the hangar. I was impressed.

Now, I wondered if the Skipper had suckered me into flying against the hottest shooters in the squadron. I wouldn't have put it past him. The flight leader stood up, a piece of chalk in his hand, and wrote down the line-up, names of front and rear seaters, airplane side numbers, call signs, places in the line-up, radio channels and so on. I was to be number four in the four plane flight. The tow pilot (the squadron was using its own planes and pilots to tow the banners) was given his instructions, tow speeds and altitudes. I recall being shocked. The only differences between this gunnery flight and the ones I used to brief as an instructor was that the towline was fifty percent longer, the banner was seventy-five percent larger, the banner was towed ten thousand feet lower and fifty knots slower and the airplanes were thirty-eight times more expensive. Other than that, Mrs. Lincoln, nothing else had changed.

We took off and rendezvoused with the tow plane at the same "Chocolate Drop" and proceeded up the range with the same pattern spacer runs and the same calibre bullets dipped in the same paint colors for distinguishing the hits after the flight. It was déja vu! We would make one circuit around the range in a counter clockwise direction firing from the east on the northern leg and from the west on the southern (return) leg. I reflected on something the instructor had said before beginning the forty-five minute brief. He had said, "The same bets apply." I had stopped him right there, asking what that meant. With a trace of a grin he said, "the low hitter buys the beer", with a 'what else' tone to his voice. Everyone in the room grinned at that. Then I said, "Okay, I was on for that."

It was the standard bet from the old days. (Even the bets were the same). Then I asked one more question. How many hits had this flight scored on its previous gunnery flight? The flight leader grinned broadly and answered, "One hundred ten, Sir." A chuckle ran through the room and I knew that I was about to be had.

But being had by this cocky bunch of bright, exuberant, vibrant young men was really, I reflected, why I had come to Miramar, in the first place. I considered it an honor and a pleasure . . . but, by Christ, they were going to have to earn that beer. It was not going to be a god damned gift. No Sir, not from the Gator.. no way!

My first run was terrible! Joe shouted to me range to the banner in hundreds of feet in a rapid decreasing sequence followed by, "Breakaway, breakaway, breakaway!" The gunsight display on the heads up display (HUD) was totally different from any I had ever used in a gunnery pattern before. Instead of the single gunsight pipper I'd become accustomed to in the F-8 Crusader, the F-14's head's up display included another moving symbol which the pilot had to corral during the final part of the gunnery run. It was the armament datum line, the symbol which indicated where the gun was pointed and was employed in the first two thirds of a typical gunnery pass to position the airplane into the small cone which represented the tracking part. It was the part during which the airplane's radar was locked on to the radar reflector mounted on the bottom of the banner bar. The radar fed the range to a computer which calculated the kinematic lead angle necessary for the bullet stream to strike the bull's eye in the center of the banner, twenty feet behind the reflector.

The tracking pipper was a small illuminated circle two mils in diameter which floated around in the HUD. The pilot's task was to move the airplane's flight controls to keep the pipper on the bull's eye in the center of the banner. It was hard work keeping the limp pipper on the bull's eye while racing down towards the banner at a closure rate of over two hundred miles an hour. Since the firing envelope was from an outside range of twelve hundred feet to eight hundred feet from the target there was only a firing opportunity of 1.5 seconds.

The gun fired at an amazing rate of three or six thousand rounds per minute. The system even counted the bullets fired and displayed this important intelligence to the pilot. Compared to the chug-a-chug-a-chug of the old twenty millimeter guns in the Crusader, the high-pitched shriek of the gatling gun was startling. It made a "bzzzst" kind of sound and it was a certainty, with that rate of fire, that if a pilot could get his opponent within the trajectory of that stream of steel the enemy airplane would suffer mortal injury.

The second run was a little bit better but no where near good enough to even consider firing. I was getting the pattern down, but slowly . . . perhaps too slowly for me to get a firing opportunity in the next eight or ten opportunities that remained before we were off the range. I got slow on the third run and Joe advised me to push the throttles into minimum afterburner coming off the "perch" and leaving them there until the reversal. At that point, if I pulled the throttles out of burner and left them at full military power it would leave us with about the proper airspeed for the firing run.

On the fourth run I was tempted to try shooting but my tracking was much to rough . . . just not nearly good enough. By now I was beginning to panic. Jesus, four god damned gunnery runs and not a round expended! I could just imagine the other guys in the flight punching dozens of holes during each run and here we were, Joe and I, flopping around in the gunnery pattern like a drunken turkey buzzard wasting precious opportunities while Joe was obviously wringing his hands wishing he had never climbed into the airplane with this clown in the front seat! The fifth run was a joke and during the sixth, and last, run on the northern leg I got into a "sucked" (low angle off) position and, for safety reasons could not fire. I was in a rage at my ham-fistedness!

The tow pilot called the range "cold" and started the shallow turn which would bring him back onto the southern leg along the western side of the Chocolate Mountain gunnery range. The flight leader called "off, range cold" and we joined up in a loose trail formation while the tow plane reversed course. Just moments before the

CHAPTER 16: THE GUNFIGHTER

Ordnancemen use an Aero-21A weapons skid to load 20mm ammunition onto a VF-142 F-14A on board the USS Dwight D. Eisenhower (CVN-69). (Official U.S. Navy Photograph)

tow pilot called the range "hot", our flight called "in on a spacer run." We all followed him in a two thousand foot trail. He called "off, the range is hot" as he flashed by the left wing of the tow plane and started the steep climbing turn toward the perch for his first firing run of the southern and final leg.

During the turn I took advantage of the opportunity to set up the cockpit for precision flying. It was a technique I had developed in the old Crusader days when I needed to do real precision stuff. I rolled back the rudder pedals as far as my stiff left knee could stand, moderate pain, and then rolled in a substantial amount of forward (nose-down) trim. This left me with my knees drawn up into a semi-fetal position and my right forearm resting on my right thigh. It was not a position which one could stay in for more than a few minutes; but, it was the one I had used when doing three precision maneuvers in the Crusader; aerial tanking, night carrier landings and aerial gunnery.

As I pulled off my spacer run and commenced the steep right climbing turn toward the perch I felt a little less apprehensive and a bit more optimistic of, at least, not bringing back a "virgin" (no Gator holes) banner. The first run on the return leg was a little too acute and the excessive "g"s I pulled prevented me from holding the pipper on the bull's eye in the final part of the run. But, at least, I thought, the pipper is somewhere on the banner. Joe's voice was patient as he called off the range to target and the breakaways, but I could sense the frustration in his voice. He thought he was going to help buy the beers, I knew. I also sensed that Joe Zahalka was not used to buying beers.

We started the seventh run from a good starting position and I began to feel good. Maybe, I thought, this is the run where I'll get a couple of hits. I came out of burner at the reversal and began good, vernier pipper control from my fetal position. It was a tight run and as we roared on in towards firing range the "g" forces began to build rapidly. Programming the stick back, I saw the pipper drift slowly behind them bull's eye and wanted to cry. But I was able to stop the pipper about one bull's eye width behind the bull and it stabilized there as Joe's voice shouted, "Twelve, eleven, ten, nine, eight, breakaway . . ." Just as he started to say breakaway I squeezed the trigger to the first detent, felt the gun camera start grinding. Joe was already into his second breakaway call when I squeezed the trigger into the second detent. The banner filled the wind screen and I knew we were much too close, but by Christ this was going to be a hitting run! Joe's third breakaway call was frantic as the gun went bzzzzzt and I released the trigger slamming the stick to the left. The airplane rolled wings level as we went by the banner just a few feet above it.

"Jesus, Gator" was all he said as we roared by the tow plane and began our arcing climb to the perch. I didn't say anything. The next two runs were not quite good enough to shoot about but, obviously the runs were getting better. I estimated we only had two more runs to go before we exited the southern edge of the range as I rolled in once more. The anxiety was gone and the fervor to really hose the banner on this run seized me. It was a pretty good run and as I fired at eleven hundred feet the banner stopped in mid-air, flashed past my left field of view and out of sight. We had shot it off. Joe's voice came up on the air, exultant and relieved, "This is four, we have just shot off the banner." I couldn't help myself, keying my microphone button and adding, "All bets are off."

It was several days later when "Hawk" (Monroe Smith's call sign) walked into my office beaming broadly. He had a Cheshire cat expression on his face and was holding a wrapped package under his arm. "Gator, this is for you to hang on your wall." He announced. "It is living proof that you hit the banner on your first gunnery flight. In fact," he continued, "you were really hosing it when this picture was taken." He handed me a beautiful framed photograph, one frame, taken from my gun camera and blown up for framing.

The firing symbol in the upper right hand corner of the frame showed that the gun was firing. The pipper was slightly aft of the banner's bull's eye. "Gator", he continued, "You were really punching holes in it on this run. Congratulations!"

It was several years later in the Pentagon that the last battle of the gunfighter was fought and won. I was Assistant Deputy Chief of Naval Operations (Air Warfare) at the time. The F-14 program coordinator called me with bad news. I can still remember the sense of outrage that swept over me at the last serious threat to the gun in the Tomcat. Westinghouse had developed a marvelous set of software which enabled the pilot of the F-14D to dramatically increase the effectiveness of the gun in aerial combat. It was put into the F-14D program. In the process of reducing costs in that program, the head of the Naval Air Systems Command selected that software program to cut. During his review he deleted the Westinghouse software program with the reported remark, "The F-14D really isn't a fighter plane anyway."

The author of that remark was a zealous F/A-18 Hornet advocate and obviously thought he could get away with it. Since the establishment of requirements lay entirely within the purview of the Chief of Naval Operations, I was highly and understandably incensed. I was Acting as the Deputy Chief of Naval Operations (Air Warfare) for a few months pending the arrival of the new Deputy from London. I can only assume that the Commander, Naval Air Systems Command thought that, wearing three stars, and dealing with a two-star lame duck, he could pull off this final indignity to the F-14. He guessed wrong.

I told the program coordinator, Captain "Hank" Kleeman, to inform his counterpart in the Naval Air Systems Command, the F-14 Program Manager, that the capability was specifically spelled out in the operational requirement (OR). He had no authority to "screw around with ORs signed by the Secretary of the Navy." If the funds weren't immediately restored, I would put on my jacket and start down the hall to the Office of the Chief of Naval Operations for a shoot out. I looked at the clock on the wall and told "Hank" to pass on to the Program Manager that without further ado I was heading down the hall in exactly thirty minutes if he didn't receive a phone call within that time telling him that the dollars were back in the program. "Hank" called me twenty minutes later and told me I didn't have to take that walk after all. So much for guns in Navy fighter planes!

17
THE F-14B

The only enduring tragedy of my thirty-three year flying career is that I never got to fly the Tomcat with the big engine. For a Navy fighter pilot that is a real tragedy!

Very early in the F-14's operational career it became obvious that something had to be done about that godawful Pratt & Whitney engine. Defense Secretary Packard's peremptory engine decision would doom the entire run of F-14As to living with the "interim" engine for decades unless something were done. The new engine would be first, more reliable and second, more powerful. There is an axiom which states that a fighter pilot can never get enough thrust. But, in the case of F-14 pilots, the need for more thrust and much more reliability was critical.

Two early airframes were designated to be fitted out with Pratt & Whitney F-401-P-400 engines which generated 28,100 pounds of thrust at sea level in full afterburner. The engine was a derivative of the F-100-PW-100 engine which powered the U.S. Air Force's F-15A Eagle. Although two airframes had been designated for conversion, only one ever flew. On 12 September 1973 the first F-14B prototype made its first flight. After completion of a series of test flights, the prototype was removed from active inventory and put in storage.

For several reasons the idea of re-engining the F-14A fleet has always been a touchy subject in the Pentagon (both OPNAV and OSD). The first reason was the development debacle over the joint Air Force/Navy advanced fighter engine. The Navy withdrew from the development program after a series of technical problems and cost overruns which one senior official described as throwing money down a rat hole. The second reason the re-engining subject was so touchy was that Secretary Packard had personally identified a new engine for cutting at a particularly stormy session with Navy leadership over program overruns. A third reason, and a particularly aggravating one at that, was the enor-

F-14B prototype at Calverton.

F-14B prototype in flight over Long Island Sound.

CHAPTER 17: THE F-14B

VF-24 F-14B.

mous costs to the Navy for bandaiding the TF-30 engine. Somewhere in the vicinity of one quarter of a billion dollars were paid to the engine manufacturer from 1972 to 1982. The net result of all that money was an engine that was still unreliable.

And, of course, a final reason was simply dollars. Each time the subject of re-engining was raised by the fleet, the bill to do so was increasingly insurmountable. It was an increasingly unpalatable decision and Naval Aviation leadership continued to ignore the problem.

Finally, in 1981, as a result of more and more vocal complaints from the fleet, the first F-14B prototype was taken out of long-term storage. Two General Electric derivative fighter engines (DFE) were installed and were designated F-101-DFE. There were some technical problems matching this smaller, lighter and more powerful engine with the F-14A airframe. These were finally overcome and a short flight test program was conducted by Grumman and Navy test pilots.

The list of Navy candidates to fly the new airplane was submitted to the Pentagon by Grumman for approval. Naturally, there were some senior naval officers names on the list, including the author's who had just completed a tour of duty as the functional wing commander at Miramar. The airplane manufacturer quite naturally wanted those senior people to experience the sparkling performance of that marvelous combination of powerplant and airframe. It was years after I retired that I learned that my name had been put on the list, and also that it had been removed by some unnamed senior naval officer. God help him if I ever find out who it was!

The enormous increase in reliability and the spectacular increase in thrust made the F-14B truly a fighter pilot's dream. Installation of the engines in the other airframe designated eight years earlier had just begun when, in the fall of 1981, the Navy canceled the program and decided to continue with the "interim" engine. The reason given was, simply, affordability. One year later the F-14D program was initiated. Three years later a contract was let to Grumman to install two General Electric F110-GE-400 engines in the F-14B prototype airframe. Two years later flight tests began again as part of the F-14D development program.

So, the F-14B was a unique airplane. Three times it was configured with a bigger and better engine than the one being endured by the fleet. Three times it raised the hopes of fleet pilots who prayed for a good engine. The first two times their hopes were dashed. The third time was the lucky one!

PART IV
FIXING THE TOMCAT

VF-124 F-14D.

As marvelous an airplane as the original Tomcat was, and as well-received as it was in the fleet, it was, nevertheless, stillborn! The interim engine which was never intended to end up at the cutting edge of our deployed battle forces continued to power fleet airplanes for over seventeen years. The Tomcat was an expensive airplane. It was expensive to buy, expensive to operate, expensive to maintain and its losses were very expensive. One might ask whether it was worth the investment. The answer is, "probably, yes." But, a better answer would be that it would have cost a great deal less in the long run to have fixed its problems correctly rather than use bandaids. By my simple calculations, the non-decision which left the interim engine in the airplane for seventeen years cost the Navy almost a quarter of a billion dollars in silly engine fixes and over a billion dollars in engine-related aircraft losses. Never will I forget receiving a telephone call from my safety officer while I was the wing commander at Miramar, that one of the squadrons airplanes had experienced an engine stall followed by catastrophic damage. The airplane limped back to Miramar on its one good engine and made a successful landing.

F-14D prototype at Calverton.

The significant thing about this particular event was that it was the first catastrophic engine failure with an engine equipped with the new protective shroud. The squadron Skipper was ecstatic with the fact that the exploding turbine section had not done any damage to the rest of the airplane. All of the tremendous release of energy had been contained in the protective shroud surrounding it! When I looked into the intake I was shocked at what I saw. All of the turbine blades were sticking at random angles into the turbine shroud where they had lodged after separating from the turbine wheel. Even the engine dome had been torn loose and was lying on the bottom of the engine inlet just forward of the compressor face. It was an unbelievable sight. But, what was more unbelievable was the fact that this event was somehow being considered a success. Here, we had finally conjured up a way to protect the airplane and the aircrew from its engine! Amazing! What was even more pitiful was the fact that the U.S. Navy paid a hefty bill to the airplane manufacturer for coming up with a way to fix a symptom of an illness rather than the illness itself! From that day forward I was convinced that somebody had to fix the Tomcat!

Section of VX-4 F-14Ds.

18

THE FUTURE OF THE F-14

I recall very clearly the day Captain Dave Frost walked into my office in the Pentagon, a sheepish expression on his face and a stack of viewgraphs under his arm. That was the day the F-14D was born. It was early August 1982 and I hadn't been in the building more than a week. As Director, Aviation Plans and Programs I had an awesome responsibility, that of executing all aviation programs and formulating the planning necessary to ensure that execution was responsive to the programming guidance of the Chief of Naval Operations. Still wet behind the ears as OP-50, I naively listened to the woeful tale of neglect which the F-14 program represented since its fleet introduction in 1973.

But, it was not a new story to me. I was just new to the job. No, the F-14 fleet introduction was an event which I had attended and one at which the then Secretary of the Navy performed like someone in show business. As a Commander in Air Warfare Analysis as OP-05W was called in those days, I had bummed a ride in the Secretary's airplane along with twenty or so other naval officers. We went to Miramar and deplaned. The Secretary continued on to Naval Air Station, Point Mugu, a base about forty miles north of Los Angeles. The following day he flew down to Miramar, just north of San Diego, in the back seat of the first F-14A to be delivered to the fleet. It was the 31 of December 1973 and an important day for many people. For the Grumman dignitaries it meant almost a corner on the market for U.S. Navy carrier airplanes. Along with the new fighter the Grumman "Iron Works" also produced the all-weather attack plane, the A-6A Intruder, the KA-6 tanker, the EA-6B, electronic warfare jammer airplane, the E-2 Hawkeye airborne early warning radar airplane and even the C-2 Greyhound, carrier on-board delivery (COD) airplane. Virtually every airplane on the modern carrier except for the Ling-Tempco Vought light attack A-7 Corsairs and the Lockheed S-3 Viking, anti-submarine warfare airplanes was produced by Grumman. Yes, indeed, this was a big day for Grumman. But, it was an equally good day for the Navy because, for the first time the carrier battle group commander could boast of a long range maritime air superiority airplane with a long range air-to-air missile and a multiple shot capability. This capability was what had been so badly needed to counter the increasing threat posed by the Soviet bomber force armed with long range air-to-surface missiles. But, the biggest winners on that day was the Navy's fighter community. This was the day they had been waiting for; because the F-14 represented, even with all of its warts, a quantum increase in capability. It was, hands down the best maritime air superiority airplane in the world and the most lethal fighter in the world.

The sleek F-14 taxied right up to the reviewing stand and the Secretary, resplendent in a specially tailored royal blue flight suit, jumped out of the rear cockpit, sprinted vigorously up the steps to the waiting lectern, grabbed the microphone and made a grand speech (as only he could) about the significance of the moment. He acted as though he were running for the Senate seat which he now holds. As charged as the moment was for all of the people in the audience, what ensued in the next few years can only be described as neglect by a disinterested leadership within the Navy.

As Dave Frost went through viewgraph after viewgraph this sense of neglect was reinforced. I had just come from the fleet. I had just spent two wonderful years as head of the Pacific Fleet fighter community. Nothing Dave told me in the ensuing two hours was news. However, the totality of the neglect came home as though Dave's pitch were far more eloquent than it

CHAPTER 18: THE FUTURE OF THE F-14

really was. As he saw it the F-14's problems were fourfold.

First, and foremost was the engine. It was a disgrace! The first thirty-six airplanes in the production line were to be powered by an interim engine. Never intended to be front line airplanes, these F-14As would be used in a fleet training role and in the RDT&E community until the real engine was ready to be introduced into the production line as front line fleet F-14Bs. But where was the new engine? It was in development jointly with the U.S. Air Force, and the program office at Wright-Patterson Air Force Base in Ohio was having development difficulties. Called the Advanced Technology Engine (ATE), program, its development costs had grown and its ambitious schedule had slipped again and again until finally, in utter frustration, the U.S. Navy backed out of the engine development program entirely; leaving the Navy fighter community stuck with a terrible engine, one never intended for the fleet, and one filled with its own unique development problems. In retrospect, it would have been cheaper to have continued with the development of the ATE engine. When I commanded the fighter wing at Miramar I conservatively estimated that over forty F-14As have been lost to engine related problems. At thirty-five million dollars a copy the total cost of those losses approached $1.5 billion. The ATE was supposed to develop about thirty-seven percent more thrust than the engine it was replacing and offered twenty-nine percent greater fuel specifics. But its most important feature was, of course its resistance to stall. This weakness in the original TF-30 engine was the greatest contributor to the airplane losses. I decided that the engine was the first priority. I made the commitment (though I didn't articulate it to Dave) to fix the engine even if it cost me my career.

The second of the four problems, in order of importance to me, was the terrible reliability and maintainability of the airplane. I recalled the nightmarish problems I had experienced at Miramar as Dave showed me slide after slide of proof. But, this problem would virtually go away with the resolution of the other two problems; avionics and radar improvements. Little thought had been given to the "ilities" when the development of the AWG-9 radar was begun by Hughes Aircraft Company way back in 1958. The weapons system was really old technology by the time the airplane entered the fleet. The improved radar, with designed in reliability and maintainability, would go a long way toward making the new F-14 an easier airplane to keep flying.

The third problem, in order of importance (my priorities) was the radar. The increasing threat posed by supersonic Soviet bombers as well as the security compromise which it was thought occurred in the 1979 overthrow of the Shah of Iran dictated a major improvement in the radar to make it more effective in the electronic warfare environment which was sure to exist in a real shooting war with the Soviets. Furthermore, the Phoenix AIM-54 missile needed to be improved for the same reasons. Of course, the state-of-the-art improvements which both of those programs would incorporate in reliability and maintainability would be the principle drivers in higher availability rates of F-14s in combat.

Last, but far from least was the avionics. The avionics architecture of the F-14A was ancient by 1982, and desperately needed upgrading. All the new tactical aircraft which emerged in the late 1970s and early 1980s had the trappings offered by high speed multiplex digital data busses, multi-function cockpit displays (also called glass cockpits), improved signal processors, higher capacity computers and a host of state-of-the-art gadgetry such as heads-up displays (HUDs), fly-by-wire flight control systems and, in the F-16, a side arm flight control stick. As Dave spoke of these improvements I found myself reminiscing about my flight in three different versions of that marvelous machine. First, a front seat ride in an F-16B, then the prototype YF-16/J79 and finally the F-16XL powered by the superb F-110 engine. That was the engine, I thought, that would make the improved F-14 a world class fighter. But the new class of avionics architectures enabled the aircrew to handle the increased mass of information now available to achieve a level of "situational awareness" (SA) beyond the wildest dreams of fighter aircrews of a decade ago. After all, I thought, SA was the big differentiator, the edge in aerial combat which spelled the difference between winning and losing. As the saying goes in fighter aviation, "There are no points for second place."

Captain Frost's pitch took two hours; much too long for a formal opening thrust at trying, one more time to fix the F-14. But I needed to hear it all. I'd heard all of it before, but only in pieces. The totality of the problem, expressed in dollars, was just what had killed the program in earlier attempts to solve the Tomcat's problems. I blame the engine as the principle culprit. Early aircraft losses generated a great deal of bad press and pressure to fix the TF-30 problems grew especially after the decision was made to back out of the ATE engine development program. Each time a problem arose the engine manufacturer developed a fix and promptly sent a bill. The bills added up but engine performance and reliability did not reflect an improvement effort costing almost a quarter of a billion dollars.

As Dave turned off the overhead projector and began stacking the viewgraphs preparatory to making his exit I began to understand the enormity of the problem; and why the last three Deputy Chiefs of Naval Operation had either failed to try to fix the F-14 or had failed in the attempt. This last ditch effort seemed to face almost insurmountable obstacles. The odds were stacked against us. But, this time the genesis of the attempt was a lowly Captain in OP-506. He was the program coordinator for the F-14. His responsibilities were to coordinate the efforts of the Naval Air Systems Command and the fleet commanders with the Chief of Naval Operations' staff and the staff of the Secretary of the Navy . . . a daunting assignment. It was never intended that a Program Coordinator be the driving force behind any program. Such pressures for change should properly begin in the fleet. But, the fleet had long since given up any hope for the improvement of the F-14. Furthermore, to be effective, programs must have advocacy in high places. The F-14, in 1982, had no support from anyone in a position of influence, either in the Navy or the Office of the Secretary of Defense.

However, we had one thing going for us. It was a new strategy; one that had not been tried before. Each time anyone had tried, in the past, to fix the F-14 they had been stopped dead in their tracks by a simple question. Where are you going to get the Research and Development (R&D) money? There simply wasn't any available. There were too many higher priority programs which were gobbling up all of the money available to Naval Aviation.

Programs such as the tilt rotor JVX (now V-22) Osprey, the F/A-18 Hornet, the HARM anti-radiation missile, the Advanced Tactical Aircraft (ATA, then A-12 then AX), the Advanced Air-to-air Missile (AAAM), the Advanced Medium Range Air-to-air Missile (AMRAAM), and a host of other higher priority programs were already breaking the bank.

The new strategy was a simple one. It was to offer to give up fighter inventory numbers, whatever that took, change the freed up Aircraft Procurement, Navy (APN) dollars to R&D dollars and fund the F-14 improvement program with them. The strategy was a little transparent, I admit, but it seemed to get us past first base. I knew that ultimately, there would be pressure from the fleet to restore those inventory numbers. But, it didn't matter much anyway. Not one of the Navy aircraft programs had sufficient inventory, nor would those inventory objectives ever be achieved.

The problem was simply affordability. Naval Aviation was no longer affordable.

There is a thing called "pipeline." It represents those extra airplanes over that number required to fill all squadron inventories, needed to take care of periodic repair and modification. The pipeline was represented as a percentage of the required inventory needed to keep the fleet up to snuff. The percentage differed from airplane type to airplane type because of differences in the time needed to effect repairs and install modifications. But, the pipeline numbers were updated annually and were constantly changing. The figures generated by this annual updating process were unassailable; annual arguments with the congressional committees having refined the process over the years.

As OP-50, I presided over the annual procurement of new aircraft as well as the repair and modification of existing inventory. In recent years there simply had not been sufficient procurement dollars to buy enough aircraft to fill out inventory plus pipeline. Therefore, the Navy was operating "out of pipeline" in every one of its aircraft programs. The average age of aircraft was always a bellweather to tell whether we were doing well or poorly. I remember one year we artificially lowered the number by "smoke and mirrors." We did so by buying out the T-34C trainer production line, closing the line and then storing the extra airplanes in a dehumidified hangar in Texas. It made sense to buy out the line. The trainers were relatively inexpensive so we were able to buy a large number thereby dropping the average age of aircraft. I recall that we took credit for the new average age number on Capitol Hill but we didn't tell them about the hangar in Texas.

When Captain Frost had gotten his viewgraphs fixed up for the first frontal assault I sent him down the hall to try it out on the "beancounters" in OP-92. In the Pentagon that technique is known as sending up a trial balloon. Dave would come back with some idea of the bean counter's concerns so we could improve on the presentation we made to their Boss. Dave came back with a sour look on his face and as they say, "shot full of arrows." It was the last time I sent him off alone. Beancounters have a habit of heaping a good deal more abuse on a Navy Captain than they would on an Admiral. One in particular, a rotund, balding civilian in his

CHAPTER 18: THE FUTURE OF THE F-14

fifties with an enormous ego had the temerity to tell me that there was no way I could proceed with this program unless I formally renounced the VFMX program. (VFMX was a future study effort for the follow-on to the F-14 and the A-6). He had no authority to make such a demand and we both knew it. On the other hand, I knew that this fat little survivor was extremely skillful at delaying, maiming and even killing programs. He could throw up road blocks faster than we could tear them down. So, I acquiesced and drew the outrage from my own long range research and development planner, another civilian with an equally overblown sense of importance. Oh, Lord, we suffer the bureaucrats and all their foibles! I informed the former that never in the history of the US Navy had an aircraft program been in the fleet a full ten years without a model improvement. He countered with a long litany of obfuscation over the blatant squandering of hundreds of millions of dollars over the futile bandaiding of the F-14's engine problems. The reason he was so familiar with the engine story was because he was responsible for the OP-92 review of all modification (APN-5) expenditures. Without further ado the VFMX was taken out of the Naval Aviation Plan. But, there was a subtlety in the rescinding of the VFMX program which did not escape the Secretary of the Navy. That subtlety was that the VFMX program was intended to be a single airplane which would replace both the F-14 and the A-6. With its cancellation the door was open to a new medium attack aircraft which would become the Advanced Tactical Aircraft. That is precisely what happened and the stealthy medium attack aircraft which came to called the A-12 was born.

Finally, after months of haggling over numbers and words on viewgraphs we were ready to take the formal step of presenting the plan to the two-star admirals review board. I was a member of the board. Our function was to screen the presentation and ensure that it was acceptable for review by the three-star review board. After a scrubbing by the three-star board the program would, presumable, be ready for presentation to the Chief of Naval Operations Executive Board for approval or rejection.

But beancounters are smart. They endure the incumbents until they depart the scene and try similar tactics on their successors. Thus, it was that the months rolled on and long-suffering but determined Captain Frost received orders to bigger, better and less painful duties and was relieved by an equally long-suffering and determined Captain Lee Tillotson. It didn't take Lee very long to get up to speed and the program was once more in motion. Lee briefed the program twice to the two-star board, once to the three-star board and finally to the four star executive board. The niceties of changing procurement dollars to research and development dollars had, however, to be approved by the Assistant Secretary of the Navy (Research, Engineering and Systems). It is interesting to point out that, in 1982, of all the service Assistant Secretaries for Research and Development only the Navy's man had control over the service's RDT&E funds. Several briefings were necessary to the Secretary of the Navy's staff before the final briefing in the "Blue Room" (the Secretary of the Navy's decision center) was scheduled. It is difficult to imagine, but a full three years had elapsed from the day Captain Frost walked into my office until the final briefing occurred in the blue room and the Secretary of the Navy signed the document authorizing the expenditure funds to fix the F-14. From the time it entered the fleet in 1973 until the Blue Room briefing the F-14 limped along on the leading edge of the U.S. Navy's battle forces with an interim engine and no substantial improvement for twelve years. That in itself is a disgrace.

Although the Chief of Naval Operations Executive Board approved the improvement of the Tomcat a great deal more "spin" was applied to the program, some good and some bad. The bad part was that a program called the A-6F was generated by the Secretary's staff and tied directly to the F-14 improvement program. This was amusing to me as OP-50 in that I was told that approval for the F-14 program would be done at the same meeting that would also bless the A-6F. The delay in the F-14 improvement program was incurred while many people scampered about "kluging up" a program in which none of the blue or green (Marine) suiters had any faith. The A-6F saw Captain Lee Tillotson complete his tour of duty and I met, for the first time, his relief, Captain Hank Kleeman. Hank, the hero of the Gulf of Sidra in 1981 would be the one to brief the Secretary in the Blue Room.

The A-6F program eventually collapsed under its own weight. It was a bad program from the outset. When I first flew the A-6 it was called the A-2F1 and its tailpipes could be tilted down for enhanced take-off roll and landing performance. The date in my logbook was 3 November 1960. Since then the A-6 had become a legend for load carrying and all-weather capability. In its time it was unsurpassed by any all-weather attack system in the world. But by 1984, a full twenty-six years after I first flew the machine, its time had come. No one in uniform supported a half billion dollar program to improve, for the fourth time, the venerable A-6.

There was simply no way that the basic engine-airframe combination could be made survivable against the threat of the 1990s. No amount of money thrown at it could make more than small improvement in its ability to penetrate an integrated air defense system, deliver its weapons on target and egress unscathed. Youngsters in the fleet have a great ability to put things in perspective. To optimize accuracy and survivability a strike airplane will ingress a target area, do a pop-up maneuver, execute a dive bomb attack, recover at low altitude and egress the area at high speed. The time of greatest vulnerability is the pop-up maneuver. The F/A-18 Hornet can do the pop-up maneuver beautifully. Its two afterburning engines enable it to complete the pop-up maneuver in a matter of a few seconds. The same maneuver done by an A-7 Corsair II or an A-6E Intruder is called by the youngsters in the fleet, "the climb of death."

I believe the Secretary of the Navy sensed this lack of blue and green suit support and created a "blue ribbon" committee to study alternatives to the A-6F program. The principal alternative studied was an improved version of the F/A-18 Hornet with greater internal fuel and a two-man crew. As Director, Aviation Plans and Programs, I was an obvious choice for the committee. I was not invited. Instead, the Navy two-star member was an aviator who had spent his entire career hunting for submarines. The Marine Corps general officer sitting on the board was admonished at several late night counselling sessions at Marine Corps headquarters against being so vocal in favor of the Hornet. In due course, the committee reported out in favor of the A-6F and we proceeded accordingly. A bright young Captain selectee Bob Wittenberg, the A-6F program coordinator, was picked to do the A-6F part of the dual program briefing in the Blue Room and he set about preparing for the event with characteristic vigor.

But, I mentioned that there was a good side to the impact the Secretary's staff had on the F-14 improvement program. At his direction a matrix of improvements, broken down into major components and expressed both in cost and measures of effectiveness was developed. It was a menu of options from which the decision-maker could select the airplane he thought he could afford and one which would, at the same time do the job. It was clever, especially for a fixed price development program. But, that was another problem. Somewhat arbitrarily, the Secretary established a $700 million dollar cap on the F-14 program and a $500 million dollar cap on the A-6 program. There was no way, not even with mirrors, that the F-14 development program could be executed for that money! At the Secretary's direction a group of costing experts and designers from Grumman and the Naval Air Systems Command sat down together to squeeze the programs costs into those arbitrary limits. In a sense it was a paper drill in which pieces of the development program were written off to other program expenses. Mostly through smoke and mirrors a resolution was reached and the day was set for the Blue Room decision.

19
THE BLUE ROOM

On the appointed day, 13 March 1985, and at the appointed hour, the three of us started down the fourth floor E-Ring corridor to the Blue Room. We discussed programming tactics during the five minute walk. The Blue Room derived its name from its light blue, wall-to-wall carpet. The room was small for a conference room. The long conference table which dominated it was ringed by a dozen chairs. Flanking the table was a single row of chairs flush against the walls. That was it! Around the table sat the Chief of Naval Operations (directly in front of me), several other three and four star naval officers and a few of the Secretary's senior staff members. It was not a large group.

Commander Bob Wittenberg began his briefing with a series of overhead slides citing the dire need to improve the venerable Intruder to survive against the threat of the 1990s. The airplane was to be fitted with a new, composite wing, a new engine (the General Electric F404 which also powered the new F/A-18 Hornet), a new radar and avionics improvements to enhance its all-weather attack capabilities. The total development program, to cost not more than $500 million dollars, would carry the A-6 through the period of time it would take to replace the entire medium attack aircraft inventory with the newer, stealthy Advance Attack Aircraft. Bob did a good job at briefing the program but, it was a preordained understanding that the Secretary would approve it; and he did, signing the implementing order as he waved for Captain "Hank" Kleeman to begin his briefing of the F-14D program.

Since "Hank" was a newcomer, I introduced him to the Secretary and, without further ado, he started. "Hank" didn't use slides. Instead he passed out copies of a brochure, ringed at the top, to the gentlemen seated at the conference table. Then, standing at the Secretary's left side he began talking, reaching down to turn the pages as he went. In a format similar to the A-6F presentation, he made a good case for improving the F-14s engine, avionics and radar to enable it to be effective against the threat of the 1990s.

Unlike the previous brief, it did not stress survivability, but rather put emphasis on being able to counter the threat of a raid of supersonic Soviet Backfire bombers against a U.S. carrier battle force. The Russian bombers, carrying long range anti-ship missiles posed a threat to the battle force so severe that only a dramatically improved F-14 could prevail. "Hank" did a good job of briefing the program and I began to feel confident of success when the Secretary dropped the bomb. Why?, he asked did we need to put a new engine in the airplane. Wasn't the engine it had good enough? After all, the existing engine had powered the F-14 force all these years. Re-engining the fleet would be a very costly project. Of course, he knew the answer, to these questions, and I knew that he did. We had discussed them before. So, a sudden sense of total frustration came over me and I rose. In spite of the fact that I had been told not to open my mouth during the brief, I stood up and the Secretary looked at me. The Chief of Naval Operations, sitting directly in front of me, his back to me, sensed that I had risen and I saw a band of pink begin to rise above the collar of his shirt. I knew I was about to get in trouble but suddenly I didn't give a damn! I was really ticked off! Three years of work was about to go down the drain. Without the engine the F-14D wouldn't be worth the powder to blow it to hell! Everyone in the fleet knew that.

The engine was, in reality, the most important part of the F-14D program (although nobody had ever said so). And now, this little man was about to kill the engine. I couldn't believe it! These bureaucratic bastards were going to give those youngsters in the fleet the same lousy engine that they had been forced to live with for over eleven years. It was too much! Even if it cost me my career, I decided to state the case in unmistakable terms.

I began to tell the Secretary that under peace time conditions with the fleet adhering to the strict throttle restrictions, they averaged one engine stall per week. Quick action prevented any ensuing damage in most cases. But, I reminded him, he knew the youngsters in the fleet better than most of the people in the room. (In a room full of blue uniforms, this comment really appealed to his ego). He knew, I reminded him, that when the battle was joined, when the aircrews saw the enemy at close hand the fangs would come out and they would ignore all those throttle restrictions and let it all hang out! The end result, I predicted, would be more F-14 losses because of engine stalls than as a result of enemy action.

That was the bottom line. If the engine weren't included, the whole program should be canceled and we should get on with the VFMX program. (There was a hidden agendum here. Resurrection of the VFMX program would certainly kill the nascent Advanced Attack Aircraft program since each provided for a follow-on the A-6).

There was an agonizing silence in the room. The Chief of Naval Operations sat in front of me, his back as stiff as a board and his neck redder yet. The silence lasted for probably five seconds but it seemed like five years. I sat down and the Secretary said, simply, "Okay" and signed the implementing document on the table in front of him. The meeting was over and we, in the wall seats, waited respectfully as the gentlemen at the table filed out of the room. No one spoke to us. After it was over, Bob, "Hank" and I gathered our materials shook hands all around and headed back down the hall. The F-14 was about to be fixed after all!

VF-32 F-14A.

20
THE A-PLUS

The plan approved by the Secretary of the Navy for the F-14D program called for the production of 304 new F-14Ds and the re-manufacture of approximately 200 F-14As to F-14Ds. However, when the Navy Advanced Tactical Fighter (Navy version of the Air Force Advanced Tactical Fighter) became an official program new start, the F-14D plan was changed. Now, there would be only 127 new production F-14Ds and 400 F-14As would be re-manufactured to F-14Ds. To fill the fighter inventory gap sufficient F-14As would be configured with the new engine that was scheduled for all F-14Ds, the marvelous General Electric F-110. This interim airplane was to be called the F-14A Plus.

But much of all that occurred long after "Hank" Kleeman and I walked triumphantly out of the "Blue Room." The document which the Secretary signed called for a "not to exceed" unit flyaway cost of $30 million in 1983 dollars. Since the Navy, in that year was already paying $36 million dollars for an F-14A, I didn't have much faith the program would ever achieve that extremely stressing limitation. But, getting the F-14D program approved was such a stunning victory, I chose not to be overly worried about that particular detail for the moment. That could be settled later.

The real haggling began between the Grumman Corporation and the Naval Air Systems Command over the fixed price development contract for the F-14D. Fixed price for a development contract is somewhat of an oxymoron. The word, development, implies a certain amount of risk as new technologies are explored for incorporation into a production line. But the sad experience that the Defense Department had recently with cost overruns and the major emphasis being put on waste, fraud and abuse caused the congress and the taxpayers to view the idea of fixed price development contracts with approval; regardless of how silly they might be. There was a great deal of reluctance on the part of the aerospace defense industry to sign up for such contracts but it was rapidly

VF-14 F-14A Plus (F-14B) carrying two Sidewinders, two Sparrows and two Mk. 83 1,000 lb. bombs.

PART IV: FIXING THE TOMCAT

CHAPTER 20: THE A-PLUS

becoming the only game in town so, for the most part, they signed up, although they did so perhaps a little cynically. In the great debate that followed four things became obvious:

1) The contemplated F-14D development program could not be accomplished within the arbitrarily set fixed price of $750 million.
2) The unit flyaway cost ceiling of $30 million could not be met.
3) The production schedule for introduction of the new F-14Ds could not be met, for a variety of reasons (mostly development problems).
4) There was no way that the Navy could procure that many new F-14Ds and, at the same time, buy new A-6Fs, A-12s, NATFs, V-22s, ATSs, SH-60s, and so on.

The Aircraft Procurement, Navy (APN) appropriation simply could not support the acquisition of so many new and costly systems in the coming decade.

A great deal of scaling down had to be done to the Naval Aviation Plan over, not just the period covered by the five year defense plan (FYDP), but also the expanded planning annex (the following ten year period). Many things occurred during the scaling down including reducing the numbers of air wings, reducing the number of airplanes in each fighter squadron by two and changing the entire composition of the air wing. The acquisition plan for modernizing the U.S. Navy's fighter inventory was also changed. Partly because of a slippage in the F-14D development schedule, and partly because of cost, a plan was put together to re-engine those F-14As not scheduled for re-manufacture and call them F-14A Plusses. So, the fighter inventory of the 1990s would be a combination of old F-14As, F-14A Plusses, re-manufactured F-14Ds and new production F-14Ds. It was not what I had originally hoped for but it was an achievable plan and the fleet would be getting new engines as soon as possible. That was an accomplishment of which I could be understandably proud.

As might be expected the F-14A Plus was received in the fleet with welcome arms. The first airplanes were delivered in November 1987 to squadrons at NAS Oceana, Virginia. They represented a huge improvement in performance. The engines produced over 30 percent

OPPOSITE: VF-211 F-14A PLUS (F-14B) carrying six Phoenix missiles.

greater thrust, had supposedly) improved specific fuel consumption which would increase loiter time on CAP station by a substantial amount but increased combat radius by only a few nautical miles. The results which actually obtained after the fleet began feeding data back from operational experience on combat radius was that it; was minimal.

What the fleet told the engine experts in the Naval Air Systems Command was that, in the real world, an F-14A Plus got off the catapult with about 400 to 600 pounds more internal fuel. This was because they (the F-14A Plusses) didn't need to use afterburner for the catapult launch whereas the F-14As did need it. In addition, the A Plusses reached altitude sooner, with a higher quantity of internal fuel and could loiter at a higher altitude. That was the good news.

The bad news was that, once at loiter altitude, the A Plusses burned about 100 pounds of fuel per hour more per engine than the As. When all was said and done, the fleet operators reported back (to the disappointment of the airplane manufacturer and the engineers at NAVAIRSYSCOM that it was "a wash."

But what was far more important than all of those wonderful statistics was the robustness of the engines. All of those strict throttle restrictions were gone forever. F-14A Plus aircrews could, for the first time, fight their airplanes with a reckless abandon they had never felt before.

Unfortunately the serious military budget cuts of the late 1980s caused some more drastic measures to the fighter inventory programs. As of the writing of this book there are only 37 new F-14Ds and only 18 approved A to D re-manufactures in fiscal year 1991. At issue between the congress and the Department of Defense are 12 more re-manufactured F-14Ds in the fiscal 1992 budget. The Secretary of Defense doesn't want them, and the Congress is telling him to buy them.

I distinctly recall testing the robustness of that wonderful General Electric F-110 engine on 21 March 1984 at Edwards Air Force Base in the Mojave desert. My assignment in the Pentagon as Director, Aviation Plans and Programs gave me the opportunity, once in a while, to sneak away for some interesting flying. On this particular occasion, I was offered the opportunity to fly the F-16XL. It was an experimental version of the F-16 with a bigger, cranked wing, and was powered by the new General Electric F-110 engine. Since that engine was the one to power the F-14A Plusses and the F-14Ds I had asked an Air Force friend to arrange for me to fly

PART IV: FIXING THE TOMCAT

VF-74 F-14A Plus (F-15B) near NAS Oceana, VA.

the F-16XL. Among the many interesting aspects of that memorable flight was what I later described to the Secretary of the Navy as the acid test. At an altitude of thirty thousand feet I reduced the throttle to idle power and slowly raised the nose of the airplane to maintain altitude. When the airspeed stabilized at one hundred forty knots I found the airplane was descending at about two thousand feet per minute with its nose high in the air and in a semi-stalled condition. At that point I did two things almost guaranteed to induce compressor stalls in almost any other engine. I jammed the throttle to the firewall and into the full afterburner detent. At the same time I put in full left stick. The rolling maneuver which followed was a full three hundred sixty degrees complete with a yawing, wallowing, semi-stalled movement that I found hard to describe. And, throughout the roll the engine spooled up from idle power all the way to full military thrust, into afterburner and all the way to full afterburner without so much as a tiny burp! I thought to myself that this was truly a fighter pilot's dream come true!

The first F-14A Pluses were delivered to NAS Patuxent River, Maryland for testing. The first fleet F-14A Pluses were delivered to the Fleet Replacement Squadron (FRS), VF-101 at Oceana, Virginia in November 1987. The first one I got the chance to climb into was a Fighter Squadron TWENTY-FOUR airplane at Naval Air Station, Fallon, Nevada conducting the first F-14 air-to-ground weapons training ever.

21
ELECTRONIC COUNTERMEASURES

There is a basic law of physics, in the field of electronics, which says that the larger an aircraft, the greater the power needed to protect it from the air-to-air and surface-to-air, radar-guided missile threat. I know that is an unscientific articulation of the law . . . but the right thought is there. When an electronic countermeasures suite was first contemplated for the F-14, this law of physics was not as clearly understood as it is today.

The function of the F-14 Electronic Countermeasures (ECM) suite is to enhance aircraft survivability and effectiveness. To achieve this function the generic F-14 ECM suite includes the following:

- **Radar Warning System (RWS) to provide:**
  - Passive detection and classification of radar threats
  - Real-time warning of imminent threats to the aircraft
  - Azimuth angle information on enemy missile tracking radars
  - Missile launch warning to the air crew
  - Semi-automatic control of expendable countermeasures

- **Active Defensive ECM System (DECM) to provide:**
  - Automatic detection, sorting and classification of enemy fire control radar threats
  - Automatic activation of optimized angle/range deception jamming against enemy terminal tracking radars

- **Countermeasures Dispensing System to provide:**
  - Dispensing of chaff, flares and expendable jammers to confuse enemy fire control radars/missiles

During the early F-14 formulation phase, the Navy hoped to have a very robust ECM suite. This suite would have included two ALQ-100 jamming systems (for separate forward and aft protection), four ALE-39 chaff/flare dispensers and a radar/missile Warning system.

When the F-14 program started, however, programmatic and cost/schedule considerations caused the initial ECM suite to be more austere, i.e., only one ALQ-100, two chaff/flare dispensers and the APR-25/27 radar/missile warning system.

With regard to the ALQ-100 ECM jamming system, on 19 May 1971, the OPTEVFOR 18th Partial Report on Project F/O 210 detailed the, ". . . effectiveness, limitations and protection afforded an F4J by the SHOEHORN installation of the ALQ-100. Significant problems were uncovered regarding the degraded hemispherical effectiveness of pulse coverage and of fuselage masking." As a result of the OPTEVFOR report, there should have been fair warning that, in an even larger tactical airplane, such as the F-14, there would be trouble. The degree of protection provided by the ALQ-100 was finally evaluated by Air Test and Evaluation Squadron FOUR and determined to be totally unsatisfactory. One of the realities of the ECM game is that new threats are always emerging, requiring that the ECM suite be continuously updated in response to these new or perceived threats. Indeed, in the 1970s, the emergence of new threats caused the Navy to initiate a QRC (quick reaction change) program called "Charger Blue." This program resulted in the successful development of the ALR-45/50 radar/missile warning systems, as form/fit replacements for the old and obsolete APR-25/27 systems. A similar jammer improvement program led to the ALQ-126 system as a form/fit replacement for the ALQ-100.

In November 1973, the approved Chief of Naval Operations' Electronic Warfare Program included plans for equipping, insofar as was possible, all strike, fighter and support aircraft of deployed air wings with ALR-45/50, ALQ-126 and ALE-29A/39 air EW equipments. However, significant budget deficiencies dictated that certain squadrons and air wings be configured with a mix of ALQ-100 and ALQ-126 equipments. The inadequacy of funding support for equipping F-14 squadrons with acceptable ECM equipments continued for years. Since then, the story of solving the ECM problems on the F-14 has been a true horror story of bureaucratic obfuscation, turf-guarding and ineptitude.

The delay in incorporating new ECM systems is shown in the F-14 ECM suite summary table below. It can be seen, from the table, that even though the ALR-45/50 systems were incorporated fairly early in the game (on aircraft 39 and subsequent), the ALQ-126 jammer incorporation was inordinately delayed until aircraft 395; and subsequently the ALR-67 until aircraft 559. The ASPJ (advanced system programmable jammer) incorporation was delayed until even later on the F-14D program with aircraft 596.

In 1974, a message from the Naval Air Reserves complained stridently about this same lack of an updated ECM suite in the reserves.

In July 1975, Rear Admiral "Swoose" Snead, the functional wing commander at Miramar, sent a blistering message reporting on the end-of-cruise debriefs from the first two F-14 squadrons in the Pacific Fleet; Fighter Squadrons ONE and TWO. His own words are more eloquent than any I could choose: "The ECM/DCM suite in the F-14 is totally inadequate. Known threat capabilities dictate that we be ready to fight our equipments in highly sophisticated environments. But, we are not nearly ready to do so with our current ECM suit . . ."

In early 1981, the Navy came to realize that when the F-14 performed its TARPS (reconnaissance) mission, its capacity of chaff dispensers was woefully inadequate to protect the airplane. On August 5 of that year, the Grumman Aircraft Division was tasked to develop an Expanded Chaff Adaptor that could be mounted on one of the fuselage weapons stations. What began as a quick fix turned out to be a very desirable capability when, in 1983, the F-14 was tasked to conduct reconnaissance flights over Lebanon. So, from the late 1970s and on, it became popular to accept the proposition that the Tomcat would never be sent "over the beach." I overheard the Secretary of the Navy, say it many times during this timeframe. It was this solecism which tended to perpetuate the notion that the F-14 would be limited to a "fleet air defense" mission rather than to "maritime air superiority", as it should have been. This attitude, coupled with a general disinclination on the part of the fighter community to exploit the air-to-ground capabilities of the F-14 (which had been designed in from the start), was ultimately to spell the demise of the F-14D program and, in the longer run, the F-14 program itself. The ridiculous contention, over the years, that the F-14 was a single mission airplane has had a singularly deleterious effect

F-14 Electronic Countermeasures Suite Incorporation

System	F-14A	F-14A	F-14A	F-14A+	F-14D
A/C No.	5,6,11, 13-38	39-394	395-558	559-595	596 and sub.
Jammer (ALQ-?)	-100	-100	-126	-126	-165 (ASPJ)
Threat Warning	APR-25/27	ALR-45/50	ALR-45/50	ALR-67	ALR-67
Expendables	ALE-29	ALE-29A/39	ALE-29A/39	Same	Same

CHAPTER 21: ELECTRONIC COUNTERMEASURES

VF-1 F-14A.

on the whole Navy fighter community. This fallacy was finally overcome in the late 1980s by the realization of some forward thinkers in the community, that its future lay in the adoption of the strike fighter mission, a role which had been inherent in the design of the airplane from the day it was first conceived. That is the real tragedy in the F-14 story. As of the writing of this book, almost twenty years after the fleet introduction of the Tomcat, the bureaucratic battle is still raging. A single naval officer was placed in charge of a Radar Homing and Warning Receiver (RHAW) development program intended to satisfy the requirements of all new Navy tactical aircraft. That office has successfully kept the program from introduction into the F-14 program. Despite technical problems which were encountered in adapting the equipment to the F-14, the charter of the office has been vigorously invoked. Meanwhile, the F-14 community, desperate for a solution, had found a new U.S. Air Force ALR-56C Radar Homing and Warning Receiver scheduled for introduction into the F-15 fleet. An informal evaluation by Air Test and Development Squadron FOUR (VX-4) showed that it would do well in the F-14. This evaluation so enraged the RHAWS czar that internecine warfare broke out with the testing community and the fleet on one side and NAVAIRSYSCOM and the Department of Defense on the other. The time-honored shibboleth of "service to the fleet" became a lost cause which took second place behind bureaucratic feifdom. The fleet lost!

In 1992, the decision by the Secretary of Defense to terminate the F-14D program in its infancy had rendered any further serious efforts to secure an adequate ECM suite for the F-14s remaining in the fleet, moot. Like the engine issue, the ECM issue also lacked the support of Naval Aviation's leadership and, as is always the case, the youngsters in the fleet have had to pay the price!

22
THE RESERVES

I can recall very clearly the day the Chief of Naval Reserves came to the Pentagon to plead his case for starting up the first reserve F-14 squadron.

As the Director, Aviation Plans and Programs (OP-50), I was experiencing serious problems modernizing the tactical air assets of the regular Navy. The fact that the Secretary of the Navy was a bombardier navigator (B/N) in the reserves didn't make my job any easier. He had already directed that, with the fleet introduction of the F/A-18 Hornet, I should also do what he called a "horizontal integration" of the airplane into the reserves.

What this meant was that as I introduced the new Hornet into the regular Navy light attack community, I would also introduce it into the four light attack reserve squadrons. The idea was that when the regular Navy's light attack community completed its transition to Hornets and became the strike fighter community, the reserve squadrons would also have completed the same transition. Certainly, the reserve modernization program was getting a great deal higher priority than it had enjoyed in the past. I viewed my next priority in reserve modernization to be the transition to the A-6 Intruder

VF-301 F-14A.

CHAPTER 22: THE RESERVES

VF-302 F-14A.

into a reserve force medium attack community. The airplane least able to be introduced into the reserves at that point in time was the F-14. The reasons for this were manifold.

Principal among those reasons was assets. The fighter community had fewer assets with which to juggle the transition than any other community. Also, we were buying fewer of them each year than was called for in the regular Navy modernization plan.

The two fighter squadrons on the forward deployed carrier (*U.S.S. Midway*) still operated F-4s and would continue to do so until they could be replaced by F/A-18, strike fighters. This was driven by the fact that Midway would need substantial ship modifications (like bigger jet blast deflectors) to handle the F-14 whereas a transition from F-4s to F/A-18s would be simpler and cheaper.

Another argument against transitioning the reserves to F-14s, at that time, was that we were in the middle of expanding naval aviation by adding two more air wings. New F-14s were very expensive. Therefore, I could never afford to buy as many per year as I wanted to comply with the regular force modernization called for in the newly approved naval aviation plan. Each year, the putting together of the sponsor program proposal (SPP) for the annual budget drill was growing more difficult. So, when Rear Admiral Bob Dunne showed up in the spring of 1984 to talk my boss, OP-05, into transitioning four reserve Phantom squadrons into the F-14, I felt a strong reluctance to take on this additional commitment.

At the end of Dunne's session with OP-05, I was called in and expressed my reluctance to take on the reserve transition at that time. I was over-ruled and we pressed forward with a modification to the plan to include four reserve fighter squadrons. Had I been in Dunne's shoes I would have done the same thing. So, there were no hard feelings. We were both just doing our jobs as best we knew how. The carrier-based reserve squadrons are organized into two reserve air wings; CVWR-20 home-based at NAS Cecil Field, Florida (as of the writing of this book) and CVWR-30 home-based at NAS Miramar, California. Both of these fields fell victim to the base realignment commission (BRAC) in 1993, so the reserve headquarters of both air wings may

VF-201 F-14A firing a Phoenix missile.

VF-202 F-14A.

CHAPTER 22: THE RESERVES

move. The same force reduction movement in the Clinton Administration which spawned the BRAC also recommended the reduction of the carrier-based reserve forces from two to one air wing.

Each reserve air wing consists of nine squadrons; two fighter squadrons, two strike fighter squadrons, one attack squadron, one airborne early warning squadron, one tactical electronic warfare squadron and whenever mobilized or deployed aboard a ship, one helicopter antisubmarine squadron. Although the reserve air wing headquarters are located at Cecil and Miramar air stations their component squadrons are located at sites up and down both coasts where the demographics and logistic considerations dictate.

Reserve fighter squadrons 301 and 302 (elements of CVWR-30) are stationed at Miramar. Reserve fighter squadrons 201 and 202 (elements of CVWR-20) are stationed at NAS Dallas, Texas. The first reserve unit to receive the F-14 Tomcat was Reserve Fighter Squadron THREE ZERO ONE, the Fighting Infernos, stationed at NAS Miramar, California. This occurred on 1 October 1984. The squadron has truly achieved some remarkable milestones in its history. It won the Admiral McCain trophy as the best naval reserve squadron three consecutive years. It also received six CNO safety awards, five Noel Davis Battle "E" awards and has accumulated more than twenty-three years and 69,000 hours of mishap-free flight operations; a record unsurpassed, to date, by any other Navy fighter or attack squadron in aviation history.

In 1987, VF-301 became the first reserve squadron to successfully fire an AIM-54 Phoenix air-to-air missile. Reserve Fighter Squadron THREE ZERO TWO, the other reserve fighter squadron at Miramar has an equally fine record and received its F-14s in the year following the first arrival of the airplane in the reserve fighter forces. The Stallions of VF-302 have gone on to set records in use of the TARPS reconnaissance pod in winning aerial reconnaissance meets and also in the application of the F-14 in the attack role by delivering air-to-ground munitions.

In October 1986 the first F-14s arrived at NAS Dallas and were assigned to the Hunters of Reserve Fighter Squadron TWO ZERO ONE. In March of 1987 the other reserve fighter squadron at Dallas, the Superheats of Reserve Fighter Squadron TWO ZERO TWO received their F-14s. Since that time both fighter squadrons of Reserve Carrier Air Wing TWENTY have set records as distinguished as their Miramar counterparts. Contrary to the grim predictions by many aviation experts that the reserves would never be able to operate airplanes as complex and sophisticated as the Tomcat, that airplane has been successfully integrated into the reserve forces.

VF-302 F-14A.

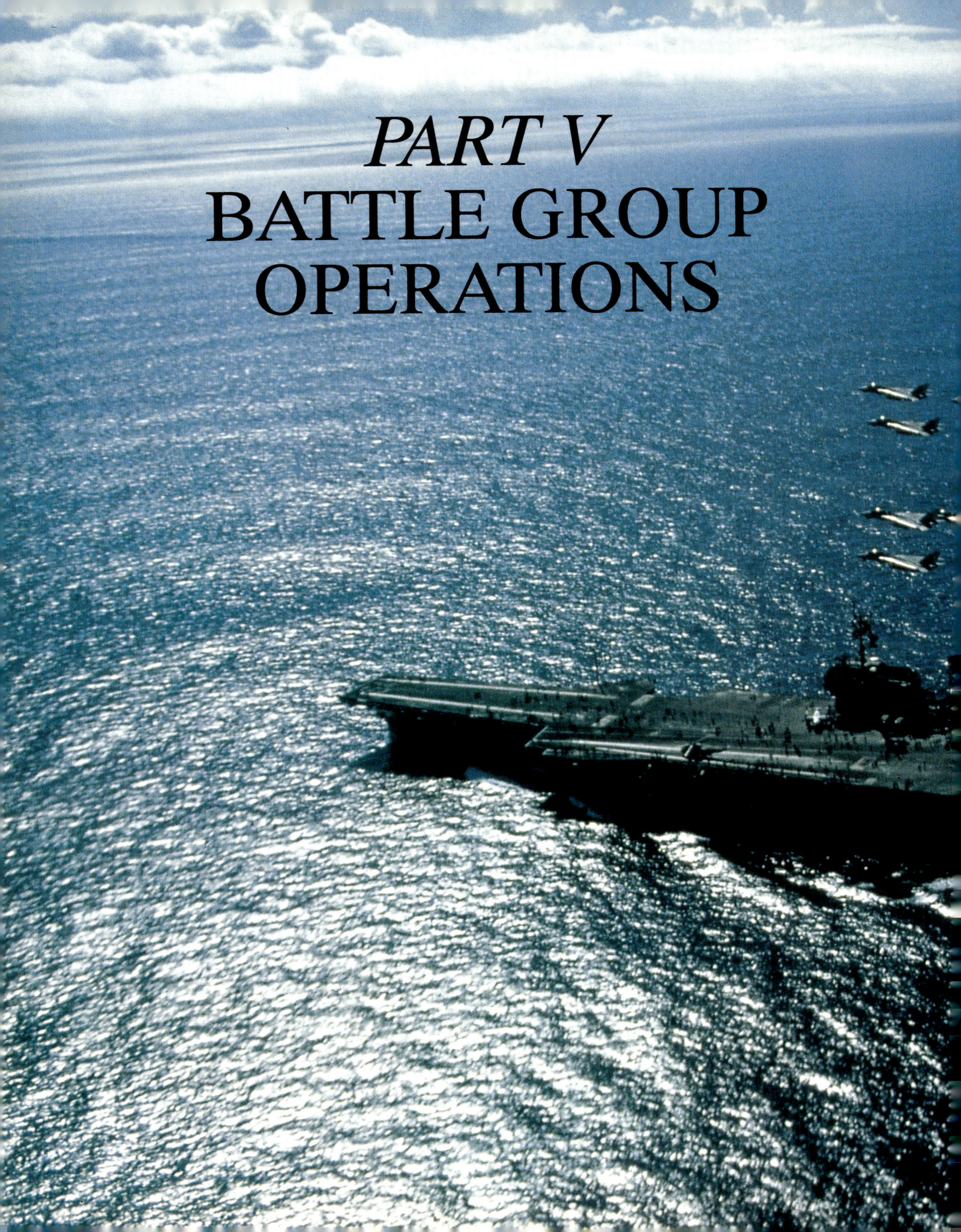
PART V
BATTLE GROUP OPERATIONS

The mode of operations of a U.S. Navy carrier battle group depends almost entirely upon where it is, where it is going and what it is going to be asked to do when it gets there. Cold weather operations in the northwest Pacific Ocean, for example, may place very different constraints on the composition of the embarked air wing, the way its aircraft are configured and how they operate when compared to operations, say, in support of the invasion of Panama.

Once a battle group chops (reports) to a numbered fleet it goes prepared for battle. Its aircraft, for the most part, are armed when airborne and its aircrews are certified fully trained for hostilities. Whenever a deployed battle group can do so, it trains. It schedules exercises within its own forces or with friendly foreign forces. It even mixes it up once in a while with forces which are not so friendly, (witness the periodic missile exercises in the Gulf of Sidra, off the Libyan coast). It schedules and executes fleet exercises and expends live ordnance in those exercises. A deployed battle group at sea is either conducting combat operations or training for them.

Battle Group commanders, out of necessity, become very resourceful in finding new and unique ways to hone the combat skills of their aviators. Each air wing has both new and old aircraft to work with. There is a constant learning process going on, in finding out the very best ways to employ the newer machines and always an ongoing effort to improve on ways to operate the older ones. This constant evolution is probably the strongest aspect of carrier aviation. It is not the development community, nor is it the test and evaluation community that figures out the best way to operate aircraft from carriers . . . it is the fleet aviators! It has always been that way; and I suspect it always will! In subsequent pages in this part of the story, former battle group commanders have been interviewed on how they learned to operate all their aircraft in their particular part of the world. Specifically, they have described how they optimized the strong points of the Tomcat.

PREVIOUS: Twenty-one F-14s overfly the USS Constellation in the Indian Ocean – the photo was taken from the twenty-second F-14. To the author's knowledge, this is the greatest number of F-14s airborne from a carrier air wing at a single time.

OPPOSITE: USS Constellation (CVA-64) Battle Group in the Indian Ocean, December 1974.

23

OFF LEBANON

From 1983 until 1986 the United States kept a naval presence in the eastern Mediterranean Sea in the immediate vicinity of the coast of Lebanon. This was to support U.S. nationals in Lebanon as well as diplomatic personnel in the presence of civil unrest. It was during this period that battle group commanders were tasked with aerial photo reconnaissance requirements using organic assets. As a result of this tasking, periodic aerial reconnaissance missions were flown by F-14As configured with the tactical airborne reconnaissance pod system (TARPS). There were two airplane configurations used during these missions. Each included two external fuel tanks and the expanded chaff adaptor (ECA). The differences were solely in the weapons suite. One weapons configuration consisted of two AIM-7 Sparrow air-to-air missiles and two AIM-9 Sidewinder air-to-air missiles. The other configuration featured four Sparrows and two Sidewinders. In each configuration, the ECA was carried in the after fuselage missile station.

As discussed in the previous chapter, due primarily to its large size, the problem of providing the F-14A adequate coverage with electronic countermeasures suite was technically difficult. Since tests of the ALQ-100, ALR-67 and the ALE 29A/39 on the F-14A proved this to be so, the expanded chaff adaptor was fabricated at the Naval Avionics Facility in Indianapolis, Indiana. This adaptor, when fitted onto the after fuselage missile station increased the airplane's chaff capacity by over 200 percent. Various chaff dispensing techniques were employed by fleet aircrews on reconnaissance missions over Lebanon.

In addition to the two TARPS equipped F-14s flown on each mission at least two more fighter configured F-14s were placed on combat air patrol station over the water but in the vicinity of the objective area of the particular reconnaissance mission.

Although the missions flown over Lebanon during this period were not technically combat missions, they were flown as such because there were folks on the ground who were hostile; and who had weapons which could down an F-14 if it were not careful.

As a consequence, all photo reconnaissance missions were carefully planned and executed. Support aircraft were positioned to provide assistance should the reconnaissance airplane be taken under fire. The response capability included fighters on CAP station just off the beach in case hostile fighters from Iraq should challenge the mission. There was also a response cell of strike aircraft on patrol in the vicinity should the reconnaissance airplanes be fired upon.

The experience acquired by fleet operators proved itself to be quite useful in the development of expertise, procedures and tactics. This experience was put to good use in the rather extensive use of TARPS F-14s in the Persian Gulf war ten years later.

24

INDIAN OCEAN

The U.S. Naval presence in the Indian Ocean was, up until about 1979, only a fleeting one characterized by the passage of battle groups through its vast expanse enroute to and from the Suez Canal. Unlike any other ocean the Indian Ocean has characteristics which make carrier operations particularly perilous.

When the U.S. embassy in Teheran was seized by rioting Iranian radicals a naval response was immediately ordered and what became known as "Gonzo Station" was institutionalized as a naval commitment . . . forever. Until Iran returns to the family of nations as a moderate nation state with conventional national interests, I am afraid, an Indian Ocean battle group presence will be a fact of life. The uniqueness of the Indian Ocean stems, purely and simply, from the monsoons. The annual winds which flow southward from the high recesses of the Himalayas cross the Indian peninsula as an enormous air mass gathering up the surface of that huge body of land in the form of dust . . . a fine powdery substance with a high clay content. This red sediment rises in a huge cloud-like formation as high as ten thousand feet and drifts across the Indian Ocean. It deposits upon anything in its path a clinging clay-like film which, when salt water is added turns to a horrible slimy mud. Airplanes and ships become caked with the foul stuff. With the cloud comes the enormous sea swells which are produced by the movement of the air mass. Ninety thousand ton aircraft carriers roll, heave and pitch in the enormous swells and the red clay mud makes carrier flight and hangar decks as slick as a bar of soap.

Excruciatingly painful lessons were learned as fully fueled F-14s slid across slick steel decks, rolling over the side pulling their tractors along with them. Special procedures were adopted and the difficulties were finally overcome. But, it was observed by thoughtful analysts, that the only ships operating aircraft in this daunting environment were U.S. aircraft carriers. The Russians headed for safe ocean anchorages. The Brits, French and other carrier navies found good reason to be elsewhere. Only the crazy Americans stayed . . . and flew.

One incident comes to mind which the mention of Indian Ocean will always call to my recollection. I can still see his face clearly. He was Lieutenant Blake Stitcher, and his call sign was a very apt one. It was "Horse." We played racquetball half a dozen times. He was good, adept, well-coordinated, well-built and a quiet, sort of self-effacing guy. He stood only about five feet ten inches in height. His physique was medium, but he was quick and powerful. He had close-cropped dark brown hair and the palest of blue eyes. He sported a small, well-groomed moustache and was fairly close-mouthed. I liked him. He also turned out to be something of a hero to me. He had that self-assured, gutsy character which I have found in certain people who, when the chips are down, always come through.

His squadron deployed to the Indian Ocean on one of the *Nimitz* class carriers. They were almost finished with the six month deployment when the message came across my desk. I was absolutely astounded. The event described in the message was difficult to believe. An F-14, on combat air patrol on "Gonzo" station, experienced a flight control malfunction and, after some fairly incredible out-of-control maneuvers, recovered back aboard its parent carrier. The unusual thing about the incident was an apparent disinterest on the part of the squadron to elaborate on it or to pursue any further elaboration.

I called in my operations officer and told him I thought there was the makings of an award for the aircrew involved. From what I had read in the first message I was sure there were all the ingredients of an Air Medal. What sheer guts! What airmanship! I had recognized the name of my racquetball opponent.

The sense of my enthusiasm was transmitted to the squadron commanding officer but the response was far less than I had anticipated. So, I decided to wait for the squadron to return to Miramar and talk to the principal players in the incident. The event occurred on the last week of the last line period on "Gonzo" station. The ship was headed home. It could wait.

Presently, the squadron was back at Miramar and I asked to have a meeting with the Skipper. He was on leave, I was told, and would be back in three weeks. Could the executive officer help? No. I decided to speak with my racquetball player friend and asked the aide to set it up. On schedule he showed up without his back seater (RIO). I noticed immediately, that his eyes were still a little blood-shot even though it had been almost a month since the incident. He sat down on the overstuffed chair in my office and began one of the most incredible stories I have ever heard in naval aviation!

He was on combat air patrol in the northern Arabian Sea. He and the other F-14 were doing practice intercepts against each other under the positive control of the radar controller on the carrier. They alternated being the bogey and the fighter. My racquetball opponent described just finishing up a simulated firing run against his wingman and they were about to separate for another run when his airplane suddenly tucked under and began to pitch down towards the surface of the Arabian Sea twenty thousand feet below.! His first reaction, he told me was to reduce power to idle and to thumb out the speed brakes. The pitch rate increased rapidly and he found himself hanging from the lap belt with his helmet jammed against the top of the airplane's canopy. He shifted his left hand to the control stick to assist in hauling back on it with both hands while both feet were locked against the rudder pedals. He lifted weights for conditioning and told me he was pulling back on the control stick with a force that he estimated was over two hundred pounds when the stick broke off in his hands. The resulting negative "g" force almost incapacitated both of them.

The pilot told me he fully expected the wings to fail under extreme negative load factor. The extreme negative "g" prevented them from doing anything effective for the first several excruciating seconds. By the time the two aviators recovered their composure the airplane was in a dive angle passing through the vertical. It con-

VF-24 F-14A landing on USS Nimitz.

USS Carl Vinson on station in the Indian Ocean.

tinued past the vertical and the nose of the airplane began an agonizing inverted climb to the horizon when the pilot, still holding the broken stick in his hand, lunged for the stabilization augmentation system (SAS) switch and turned it off. The airplane immediately stopped the nose down pitching motion in an inverted climbing attitude. Reaching down to the stub of the broken control stick, the pilot pushed it to the left and the airplane surprisingly rolled upright. It was behaving normally but control of the F-14 with the stub of the control stick was, at best, minimal and chancy.

The pilot found it extremely awkward reaching down between his knees and attempting to control the airplane. The two aircrewmen talked about the likelihood of success of attempting a carrier arrested landing in these circumstances and concluded that even if they were able to fly it into the arresting wires, there was a good chance that a hook skip or bolter would put them in an unrecoverable position requiring an instant ejection attempt at low airspeed and, essentially, at sea level. The record books give an unacceptable probability of survival from such endeavors. Nonetheless, the two young men decided to try to return to the carrier advising the landing signal officer of their problem. The approach was rough. Pitch and roll control were horrible, but the two intrepid aviators came through like troopers resulting in the salvage of an otherwise lost airplane. I was extremely gratified.

But, something was definitely wrong and the young man was not enlightening me as to why his own Skipper was not too enthusiastic about his performance. Two days later, when the Skipper returned, he enlightened me. It seems that our two intrepid aviators, when they were preparing for the catapult launch, went through the routine pre-launch checks with the squadron maintenance trouble shooters and were informed of a horrible grinding noise emanating from the horizontal stabilator hydraulic actuators in the aft fuselage. The chief petty officer informed the pilot and recommended that the airplane be "downed" for inspection. They talked about it on the intercom system and the pilot convinced the RIO that they should take the airplane, overrule the maintenance crew and go flying.

The Skipper explained to me that their judgement was grossly flawed in taking the airplane; and their performance was magnificent in saving it. The two aspects, when added up, provided justification for both a courts-martial and an air medal. They canceled each other out in the Skipper's view and I agreed.

25

THE ACHILLE LAURO INCIDENT

At 4:45 on the afternoon of 10 October 1985 a cluster of aircraft were catapulted from the U.S.S. Saratoga (CV-60) in the eastern Mediterranean. The carrier had been participating in the NATO exercise, Display Determination during the past two weeks. Two days earlier, on 8 October, the ship had been directed to withdraw from the exercise and conduct two days of long-range flight operations in support of the Achille Lauro incident.

The missions were combat air patrol flights ostensibly in with the purpose of preventing terrorists, in small boats, from approaching the Achille Lauro from the seaward side as she was tied up at Port Said. For this reason, the F-14 combat air patrols were loaded with a full bag of twenty millimeter ammunition including tracers. The grueling five hour missions included using KA-6D tankers for in-flight refueling support. Long range reconnaissance missions were also flown using S-3s equipped with cameras. After two full days of this, Saratoga was released and had turned toward their intended port of call at Dubrovnik, Yugoslavia. It is noteworthy that the alert aircrews had been stood down to a 60 minute alert status. It was the first time that the fighter alert had been relaxed beyond a 30 minute status in the two previous deployments. (Alert 60 means sixty minutes to get into the air from sound of alarm). In fact, the entire E-2 early warning squadron was in formation on the foc'sle conducting a memorial service for a young Lieutenant (junior grade) who had been killed in an automobile accident in Italy.

It was in this relaxed conditioned that the ships crew were stunned by the announcement over the I-MC (public address system), "Now, launch the alert E-2. Now, launch the alert F-14s!"

At the time of the incident, Commander, Task Force SIXTY (CTF-60), was Rear Admiral David Jeremiah, who was also the embarked Battle Group Commander. Reporting directly to him was the Captain of Saratoga, Captain Jerry Unruh, and the air wing commander, "Bubba" Brodsky.

Information had been received that a chartered Egypt Air Boeing 737 would shortly take off from Cairo carrying four hijackers of the Achille Lauro cruise liner and two Palestinians. The airplane had been chartered by the Egyptian government and was being flown by an Egyptian crew. Saratoga launched four F-14A fighters, one E-2C airborne early warning airplane, two KA-6D tankers and one EA-6B electronics warfare airplane. They were about to participate in a team effort which would dramatically highlight the most sophisticated anti-terrorist operation ever conceived to date. Ultimately, another E-2C, three more F-14s, and two electronic intelligence airplanes would be added to the cast. The two electronic intelligence airplanes, one a carrier based EA-3B and the other an Air Force EC-135 carried Arab speaking intelligence experts to listen in on radio transmissions to and from the 737. The airliner was on a flight plan to Tunis when it was intercepted and ultimately escorted to the Italian NATO air base at Sigonella on the island of Sicily.

This dramatic episode had begun on 7 October when terrorists seized the Italian cruise liner Achille Lauro while it was on a short pleasure cruise between the Egyptian ports of Alexandria and Port Said. During the three day highjacking incident the terrorists murdered an American citizen, wheel chair bound Leon Klinghofer, one of several American passengers, and then dumped his body overboard. The corpse later washed up on a

CHAPTER 25: THE ACHILLE LAURO INCIDENT

VF-84 F-14As with VAW-124 E-2C . . . "The Team."

Syrian beach. This senseless act of savagery outraged Americans the world over. But what outraged them even more was the attempt by the Egyptian government to sequester the perpetrators out of Egypt by airplane after the liner docked in Cairo. It was the tip-off of this event which caused a rapid series of communications from Washington to United States Commander-in-Chief, Europe (USCINCEUR) in Vahingen, West Germany, to his next in line, Commander-in-Chief U.S. Naval Forces, Europe (CINCUSNAVEUR) in London. Next came the communication from London to the Sixth Fleet Commander in Gaeta, Italy, and on to Commander, Task Force SIXTY (CTF-60) at sea.

White House approval to execute the plan developed by the Carrier Air Wing Commander Robert "Bubba" Brodzky was received and its execution began with the afternoon launch of the eight airplanes, all Grumman built. The E-2C was positioned off the coast of Egypt and its radar scanned the sky for the lift off of airplanes from the airport at Cairo. The F-14s were positioned in a barrier combat air patrol (BARCAP) in a north-south line just north of Benghazi/Labraq, Libya across the central Mediterranean.

The electronic intelligence airplanes listened to all electro-magnetic emanations from each radar contact, listening as well to radio transmissions and were able to identify the airplane carrying the terrorists. It was now the job of the electronic warfare airplane, the EA-6B to enter the operation. The newly installed Tactical EA-6B Mission Support System (TEAMS) on *Saratoga*, a computer assisted planning and analysis system, had been a major player in the development of the intercept plan. The EA-6B's job was to jam all transmission from the 737 when it attempted to communicate with other agencies. The airliner was selectively isolated from the outside world except for the four F-14s being vectored by the E-2C to intercept it, the EC-135, the EA-3B and the EA-6B, all of whom were tied together with a data link from the E-2.

The intercept was a "lights out" evolution so that the aircrew of the airliner would be unaware of its being intercepted. The intercepting airplanes had already completed an intercept of another "large airplane" and had nearly had a mid-air collision with the unsuspecting airplane. Identification was made with a hand-held flashlight from a vertical separation of only fifteen feet . . . a dangerous business.

Fighter Squadron ONE HUNDRED THREE airplane, side number 205 made the positive identification of the Egyptian airline by approaching from the rear and below. Again, it was necessary to get as close as fifteen feet to read the airplane's markings. Upon completion of the intercept, just south of the island of Crete at an altitude of 34,000 feet and a airspeed of 400 knots, the E-2C completed the same intercept of five other F-14s who joined the silent, blacked-out formation. The airliner's aircrew were still unaware of their presence.

From this point on all communications with the Egyptian airliner was done by the E-2C using a very high frequency radio channel which the fighters did not have. It was only after a considerable period of time during which the airliners crew, intimidated by the terrorists, adamantly refused to turn toward Sigonella, that the E-2C decided to move to the next step in the plan. Although the F-14s were loaded with tracer ammunition and were prepared to "fire across the bow" if necessary, the next step in the plan was called the "lights on" step. The E-2C directed all seven of the airplanes to move up forward on either side of the airliner to be in full view. Then, at the command, "Lights on, now", all aircraft turned on all their external lights. It must have looked like an armada of airplanes surrounding the poor airliner. Several of the intercepting aircrewmen reported seeing some scampering going on through the airliner's windows. Heads were seen at several of the windows staring out at all the anti-collision lights, navigation lights, running and formation lights. There followed more radio communications between the E-2C flight leader and the airliner, informing them that, one way or the other, they were going to land at the Italian NATO air base at Sigonella on Sicily. There were attempts by the airliner to contact Tunis and then Athens requesting permission to land. The flight leader was finally able to convince the Egyptian crew that they had no alternative but to follow orders. As another part of the plan, a reconnaissance equipped F-14 took overhead infra-red imagery to document the landing at Sigonella, and accidentally discovered that the Egyptian airliner nearly had a runway collision with two C-141 aircraft.

Meanwhile permission had been obtained through diplomatic channels for a landing at Sigonella and Italian authorities to take custody of the terrorists and to allow the Egyptians to return to Cairo. The intercepting aircrews were whisked off to London under tight security for debriefings. To this day, their names are kept classified for their own protection. The final chapter in the drama came when the Italian government fell after the uproar over their having let the terrorists go free.

This nighttime drama, enacted high over the Mediterranean, came to characterize the professionalism of the team of over a dozen U.S. military aircraft, most of which came from an aircraft carrier, in carrying out an extremely complicated operation on very short notice. It was a perfectly executed operation with the Tomcat as the centerpiece. As the Commanding Officer said to me, "You don't get to practice these kinds of special operations; but you've got to do it right the first time. The full value of the second pair of hands, eyes and the unique skills of the radar intercept officer came home to me.

One of the aircrewmen told me, "The night time intercepting, identifying and redirecting of a specific airplane at Presidential direction is a realtime, multi-faceted and monumental operation."

26
NORWEGIAN SEA

The vast and forbidding body of water separating Norway and the eastern coast of Greenland is one of the most challenging places on planet Earth to operate an aircraft carrier and conduct flight operations. The southern exit from this mighty sea is called the GIUK (Greenland, Iceland, United Kingdom) gap. Perching directly in the narrowest spot between the southeastern tip of Greenland and the United Kingdom is the tiny island nation of Iceland. Just like a cork in a bottle, the Commander-in-Chief of the Atlantic Fleet was quick to observe. It is through this narrow choke point that the Soviet Northern Fleet would pour in the event of a global war between the Soviet Union and the United States. For this reason, over the forty years of the cold war, the United States has maintained a military presence on the island. NATO Patrol plane forces under the NATO command of Commander, Iceland Defense Force, operating out of the NATO air base of Keflavik, have patrolled this narrow gap watching the passage of Soviet surface and submarine forces to and from the North Atlantic. Also from Keflavik, NATO fighter interceptors watch the passage of the awesome bombers of the Soviet Long Range Naval Air Arm departing for, and returning from their regular deployments to places like Cuba and Africa. The U.S. Navy doesn't routinely operate aircraft carriers in the Norwegian Sea. When carrier battle groups

VF-51 and VF-111 F-14As on USS Carl Vinson (CVN-70). (Official U.S. Navy Photograph)

PART V: BATTLE GROUP OPERATIONS

Another photo of VF-51 and VF-111 F-14As on USS Carl Vinson (CVN-70). (Official U.S. Navy Photograph)

do enter that forbidding body of water they do so as part of a North Atlantic Treaty Organization (NATO) exercise and usually with more than one carrier battle group. Given these facts, the operations involving the aircraft carrier *U.S.S. John F. Kennedy* are worthy of note in that the operation of F-14s were unusual, to say the least.

For *Kennedy* and her crew, what started out to be a routine 30 day NATO exercise ended up being a 90 day ordeal. She sortied from her home port in Norfolk, Virginia in the fall of 1976. In the words of Captain John Mitchell, the weather turned bad about the time they arrived in the North Sea and just stayed that way. Air operations consisted principally of A-6 tanking missions, S-3 ASW missions and E-2s and F-14s for air defense. Initial operations north of Scotland ended up with a brief port visit in Edinburgh, then another brief operating period in the North Sea with a subsequent port visit in Willemshaven before heading North. Their mission was to transit to the northern Norwegian Sea, within about 400 miles of Murmansk and well above the Arctic circle to "taunt the Russians." A Soviet AGI intelligence vessel tailed them from the moment they entered the Norwegian Sea until their departure. It tried to keep station about 8 miles off the port quarter. *Kennedy* played games with the AGI. Once the Soviet skipper thought he had the behavior pattern of an American aircraft carrier conducting flight operations figured out, he began to anticipate the carrier's turn into the wind at the commencement of each hour and three quarters cycle. *Kennedy* threw him a wringer by faking a turn into the wind and then reversing course, accelerating to high speed for a launch cycle downwind. This was followed, for example by a recovery into the wind and a subsequent full cycle downwind. The AGI would fall far behind *Kennedy* and belch black smoke while mightily trying to keep her quarry in sight. Various combinations were tried to keep the Soviet off guard. One of the most dangerous aspects of operations in the Norwegian Sea was the frequency of unexpected fog banks. On one particular period *Kennedy* remained in a fog bank that seemed to stretch forever, for several days. It was so bad that the Captain couldn't see the bow of his own ship from his perch on the bridge. Nonetheless, they felt compelled to maintain a combat air patrol airborne to respond to daily visits by Soviet bomber reconnaissance flights. The sea was perfectly calm and as smooth as a sheet of flat, black glass. There was no surface wind at all. No seaman in his right mind would enjoy roaring around in the middle of a fog

CHAPTER 26: NORWEGIAN SEA

bank at twenty-five knots. But that is what it took to generate enough wind over the deck to launch and recover aircraft. The visibility was so critical that the only airplanes launched were triple cycled E-2s and a section of F-14s. Not even tankers nor S-3s were launched. The catapult into a fog bank was extremely uncomfortable for the aircrews but not excessively dangerous. What was extremely hazardous was the recovery. The aircrews knew without being told that each pound of fuel in their tanks was a small increment of life. They were extremely careful how they moved their throttles, knowing that getting back aboard was going to take every bit of skill in their bag of flying tricks. Over a period of several days flights of two F-14s came down the glide slope with the aid of the radar controllers in the Carrier Air Traffic Control Center (CATCC). Both controllers and air crews knew that they would have to put their airplanes exactly in the center of that tiny keyhole above the ramp of *Kennedy*'s flight deck that would permit a last minute stab at a carrier landing. The pilots never did see the "ball" of the optical landing system. The landing signal officer first saw the landing light on the nose gear of each F-14 as it appeared out of the fog bank. He had to make an instant decision, yes or no. If it was yes, he had to make the right call, like, "Drop your nose, and come right a little." It had to be instantaneous and correct and the pilot's response also had to be instantaneous and correct. If the answer were no, then an immediate wave-off signal was given on the optical landing system and over the radio. The wave-offs were frequent and the landing traps only occasional. It was a hell of a way to conduct flight operations. The fact that there were no losses during this period is a tribute to the exquisite skill of every member of that marvelous *Kennedy* team. The conclusion drawn by the Skipper of the *John F. Kennedy* was that one operates aircraft carriers in the Norwegian Sea with a great deal of caution.

27
NORTHWESTERN PACIFIC

One of the most hostile environments in the world for aircraft carrier operations is the northwestern Pacific Ocean. Beginning in the fall of 1982 U.S. Pacific fleet carrier battle groups began making periodic forays into the northern reaches of the Pacific just southeast of the Kurile Islands. The Kuriles are a string of islands which extend from the tip of the Soviet Union's Kamchatka Peninsula.

The principal purpose for these excursions was to exercise the Navy's sophisticated weapons systems in the cold weather which characterizes that area for most of the year. But, it was not just cold temperatures which affect carrier operations in that area. Of even greater concern for carrier aviators were the monstrous swells and foul weather. Frequent and unpredictable fog banks extending for hundreds of miles have given U.S. carrier aviators grey hair since the inception of what are now called NORPAC (northern Pacific) exercises. The first of these is worth describing for it contained elements of adversity in all of the above categories.

The two aircraft carriers which made up the carrier battle force were *U.S.S. Midway* and *U.S.S. Enterprise*, an odd combination for a number of reasons. *Enterprise* is nuclear powered and operated an air wing including F-14s. *Midway*, one of the oldest carriers in the fleet, operated an air wing with a different aircraft composition, particularly it's fighters which were F-4 Phantoms. The weather was not too favorable for flight operations but the two carriers steamed on parallel courses and about fifteen miles apart through biting cold wind and heavy seas launching and recovering aircraft. Suddenly, and without warning, the battle force steamed into rapidly deteriorating visibility, and finally a dense fog bank. Captain McGrail, caught with an entire twenty plane gaggle in the air, reversed course one hundred eighty degrees and ordered his chief engineer to fire off all twelve boilers.

Now, steaming downwind, the ancient carrier accelerated at a painfully slow rate, gradually developing some wind over the deck by virtue of its own speed through the water. As the wind over the deck increased *Midway* began recovering her airborne orphans who by now were dangerously low on fuel. Unfortunately, the airplanes lowest on fuel, the F-4s, were also the ones needing the greatest wind over the deck (thirty knots). For that they had to wait a long time. Finally, the doughty *Midway* was chugging along at thirty-four knots with the Skipper and the chief engineer literally holding their breaths for the ancient power plant to blow a gasket. It didn't, and the Phantoms finally recovered. By this time *Midway* was quite a distance downwind of *Enterprise* and, reversing course again, reduced speed to maintain an optimum thirty knots wind over the deck, once more time steaming into the wind and paralleling *Enterprise*'s course. *Midway*'s sprint downwind had brought her back out of the cloud bank and she enjoyed substantially better weather than *Enterprise*. The latter had gotten into progressively worse weather ceilings and visibility to the point at which she could no longer continue flight operations.

The normal peacetime minimum ceiling for carrier operations is one hundred feet. *Enterprise* had one A-6 tanker and two F-14s stranded in the air with no place to go. Nor were they equipped with the capability to make automatic carrier landings all the way to touchdown. When informed of their plight *Midway* offered to take the three airplanes aboard.

Up to this time F-14s had never operated aboard *Midway*. This was because she did not have the kind of JBDs (jet blast deflectors) required by the Tomcat. These devices lift hydraulically up from the flight deck just behind each catapult. Their purpose is the protect aircraft on the flight deck from the jet blast of airplanes on the catapult at full power in preparation for flight. In due course, *Midway* recovered the three airplanes from *Enterprise* and catapulted them off later for their return flight. However, to do this, *Midway* having only two bow catapults, had to clear almost the entire flight deck of airplanes and then catapult the two F-14s without the use of JBDs at all. This meant launching a larger than normal number of her own aircraft and stowing the rest of them behind the island and on the hangar deck. The launch was successful but represented a famous first for carrier aviation.

Two points can be drawn from the episode. Carriers operating in hostile environments should, if possible, enjoy commonality of equipment and aircraft. The second point merely highlights a known characteristic of carrier aviation; it enjoys a high degree of operational flexibility!

It was some time later that the two carriers again were caught in a fog bank that extended for hundreds of miles. This time they were not so lucky. With about twenty airplanes airborne, the weather again turned sour. It was deemed wise to terminate air operations because of a mean combination of very heavy swells (meaning a pitching deck), low ceiling and very restricted visibility. To further aggravate the situation, the carrier was unable to launch the helicopters; making the recovery of a downed aircrew in the freezing water the sole responsibility of the escorting destroyers . . . a time consuming and chancy evolution. The carrier was able to trap an airplane on about every fourth landing attempt. The landing signal officer was forced to wave off other attempts simply because the deck was pitching up and down in such large excursions (as great as sixty feet) that a landing attempt would be too dangerous. The carrier configured as many airplanes as it could into tankers and began launching them as needed to keep the waiting airborne planes refueled. It became a process of diminishing returns and the situation was fast becoming critical. Just about then an Air Force KC-10 happened to be passing by and checked in with the battle force. Although he indicated he had another mission to perform he delayed

VF-114 and VF-213 F-14s on the USS Enterprise. (Official U.S. Navy Photograph)

VF-111 F-14A tanking from an Air Force KC-10A . . . Tomcat view at left . . . tanker's view at right.

long enough for a few frantic flash (top priority) messages to be sent to higher authority.

Permission was granted to use the KC-10 and its precious cargo of fuel to execute the longest "bingo" in history. The KC-10 tanker headed for the nearest base at Misawa, Japan on northern Honshu with twenty airplanes and the evolution was eminently successful. So much for the vagaries of weather in the northwestern Pacific.

But, weather was not the only hazard to routine peacetime operations in the northwestern Pacific; as evidenced by a NORPAC exercise in 1986 involving an even larger battle force than in any previous exercise. The *U.S.S. Ranger* battle group rendezvoused with *U.S.S. Constellation* battle group and a battle group with the battleship *U.S.S. New Jersey* as its centerpiece. Enroute to this large rendezvous the *Ranger* battle group's airplanes became involved in an extended "engagement" with a large number of Soviet fighters staging out of the naval facility at Cam Rahn Bay, Viet Nam. (this was the huge naval installation built by the U.S. in what was then South Vietnam). The "engagement" was nothing more than a series of approaches by fully armed MiG-23s toward the battle group during which they were intercepted and escorted by F-14s while in the vicinity of the battle group. It was the greatest show of force by Soviet aircraft against a U.S. Naval force ever. The sinister aspect of the evolution was that it was out of character in several ways from all previous Soviet behavior. For one thing, the MiGs flew a long way out from the beach, over two hundred miles. This is something single engined Soviet fighters never do. It had thus far been totally foreign to their past behavior patterns. The second unusual aspect of the operation was the large number of Soviet aircraft and the duration of the engagements.

For nearly forty-eight hours the engagements continued, most of them during daylight hours. In nearly all of the engagements, the F-14s joined with other single stationed fighters into sections of two during the approach so that the "merged plot" (final stage where the

CHAPTER 27: NORTHWESTERN PACIFIC

airplanes come together) always involved two F-14s versus two to four MiG-23s.

In all cases the F-14s maneuvered to control the geometry of the intercept to put the U.S. fighters in a favorable position with respect to the MiGs. In other words the merged plot found the F-14s sitting behind the MiGs, fully prepared to shoot them down without hazard to themselves. That has always been standard policy in the fighter community. Naturally, the early warning provided by the E-2 radar planes was critical to all of this. There is a message buried in this particular operation which was not lost on the observers. During fleet operations there is a tendency to fill a combat air patrol (CAP) station with a single rather than a section of fighters. A single carrier can keep outer air battle CAP stations filled around the clock for extended periods over a limited threat arc. Depending upon how far out the CAP stations are positioned a threat arc of say, 120 degrees can be maintained for an extended period by one carrier. However, this is more easily done by using single F-14s on each station. Strategists and planners need to be reminded that single carrier battle groups are not nearly as effective as two carrier battle groups. One carrier can stand down and rest while the other carrier operates. Again, it is a matter of not having enough assets to do the job; whether it be fighters or carriers involved in the commitment. The bottom line is still; when the battle is joined the basic combat element for a successful aerial engagement is a section of two fighters.

On occasion, NORPAC carriers get rewarded for their efforts in such frigid environs by a port visit to Australia. That makes it all worth while for everyone in the battle group from the sailors to the Admirals; submariners to carrier aircrews. The opportunity to socialize with the friendly Aussies and to enjoy their wonderful country has always been the high point in carrier deployments to the western Pacific. Of particular note was the deployment of *U.S.S. Enterprise* in 1978 to Australia. Naturally, multi-national training opportunities are always highly sought after and regarded by deployed carrier air wings. Training opportunities are always less during deployments than when home-based in the continental U.S.

The initiation of a joint U.S./Australian operation which came to be known as Beacon South, occurred with *Enterprise*'s visit that year. But, it was a very important visit in terms of the long term effect it had on the future operational employment of the F-14.

The first Beacon South exercise essentially pitted the Australian Air Force's F-111 against the U.S. Navy's F-14. Certainly, there were other elements involved in supporting roles, but the big question was whether or not the F-111s could get through the air defenses and hit the carrier. The Australian F-111 aircrews were an extremely professional and talented group of aviators and they flew their machines with precision and panache. Furthermore, they knew the capabilities and weaknesses of the F-14 AWG-9 weapons system and exploited the weaknesses with great effect. For example, the AWG-9 radar employed in the doppler mode tends to lose lock-on when an approaching target turns ninety degrees and reduces closing velocity to below the doppler limits of the system.

USS Ranger, USS Constellation, and the USS New Jersey Battle Force in the northwestern Pacific.

The incoming F-111s would arc around the outer perimeter of the battle group then turn in on different sectors in a coordinated way to present a difficult multi-directional threat. Then, after being acquired by the F-14's radar they would close to a point just outside missile range, execute the ninety degree turn causing a radar break-lock. This maneuver was combined with the employment of electronic countermeasures and decoys and was very effective. The combined efforts of the battle group's surface to air radar, the E-2's early warning radar and the F-14's air to air radar was able to counter these determined airmen in most cases except one significant event.

This incident caused a frustrated battle group commander to finally allow the fighter community to employ a tactic they had developed which essentially used the F-14's radar in autonomous search. This tactic also permitted the fighters on CAP stations, armed with a matrix of target parameters and clearance to fire conditions, to mutually support one another in coping with such a sophisticated raid. The particular event which triggered permission to use the tactic known then as "vector logic" came when an NTDS operator manning one of the ship's radar consoles gave instructions to an F-14 radar intercept operator named Tom McPherson. His Tomcat had radar contact on an F-111 which had very expertly executed the above-mentioned tactics. The final part of the attack was commenced with the wings fully swept back, the plane at seven hundred knots (the speed of heat) and as close to the wave tops as the courage of the pilot dictated. In this case the pilot was both skillful and courageous. Mc Pherson was also skillful as a radar intercept officer.

Anticipating the F-111's tactics, he had managed to maintain radar contact and was in the process of directing his pilot to a successful air to air missile kill solution when the ship's radar operator intervened. The operator had observed a bogus target displayed as a synthetic contact and directed that they turn to a heading to intercept it. Being a good naval officer the Tomcat's pilot turned away from the real target towards the bogus one much to McPherson's dismay. The result was a thunderous boom as the supersonic Australian Air Force F-111 passed directly over the *Enterprise* a few feet over the masthead. That was the moment when "vector logic", changed from a proposed tactical memorandum (TACMEMO) to fully authorized fleet operational tactics. An embarrassed Admiral can sometimes do more for combat effectiveness than all the smart aviators in the fleet!

CVW-14 fly-by over Perth, Australia.

28

"NAVY FOUR, LIBYA ZERO"

On 15 January 1989 two F-14As roared down catapults of the *U.S.S. John F. Kennedy* (CV-67). The time was about eleven thirty in the morning. The place was the Mediterranean Sea southwest of the island of Crete and about one hundred twenty miles off the coast of Libya. As far as the four aircrewmen, two pilots and two radar intercept officers (RIOs), were concerned it was going to be a routine combat air patrol mission, a little boring except for the carrier landing that would terminate it. Little did any of the four think that in the next few minutes events would accelerate into a flurry of real combat culminating in a few missile shots that would ring around the world and fire the imagination of airmen everywhere.

Unfortunately, a new policy, aimed at protecting the families of the aircrew from terrorism, convinces me that their names be omitted from this book. So be it! Those are the consequences of naval operations in the 1990s. As we watched, in January 1991, the unfolding of the air war against Iraq I came away with a vague foreboding that war would never be the same again. The electronic media, for better or worse, had brought the horrors of war for the first time into the living rooms of America, in real time and in living color. Sooner or later, I warned my wife, we are going to watch a clean cut American boy or girl die . . . in real time and in living color. And worse, some eager reporter is going to thrust a microphone into his face and, as the last seconds of his life tick away, ask him if it was really worth it! The American psyche may not be able to stand the horrible impact.

Fortunately, back in the late 1970s, the Navy approved the issuing of high quality miniature tape recorders to tactical air crews. These recorders were hooked up to the wires leading to the aircrew's headsets and microphones so that if they wanted to record anything said over the intercom or radio, all they had to do was turn on the recorder. This occurred when I was the fighter wing commander at Miramar, California. I still have some memorable tape microcassettes and derive some nostalgic pleasure listening to, for example, a radar intercept officer, describing, in nauseating detail, my ineptitude during my first attempt to do night aerial refueling in an F-14. The dialogue was uncensored and contains frequent use of four letter words between us as I vented my spleen in frustration for missing the basket time after time. When I finally got the hang of it and poked the basket several times in a row successfully, I informed him rather acidly that I didn't need his incessant commentary anymore and asked him to shut his frigging mouth! Such vignettes represent priceless moments.

But, now a real time video and audio record can be made and kept of what an F-14 aircrew is saying and hearing in the cockpit, while at the same time video recording what the aircrew is seeing on either the heads up display (HUD) or the television camera system. Such systems are priceless in analyzing a dogfight. No amount of lying in the bar at happy hour can change what has been recorded forever on video tape. I have an edited video tape of the engagement which occurred on this day in the Mediterranean Sea. It is a priceless bit of primary source material. I only wish I could put at least the audio portion into this book for the reader to hear. No words I could put together can capture the excitement of the next seven minutes. The four letter words and some classified numbers have been expunged. But the emotional, heart-pounding exhilaration of aerial combat is all there in living sound. The heavy breathing of aircrewmen straining under the enormous exertion of functioning at six and one half times the force of gravity only adds to the authenticity. The sheer exuberance at seeing their missile strike the enemy airplane just behind the cockpit is recorded in unrehearsed war whoops and bleeped epithets. This is the tape that was carried by the four airmen on up the chain of command until they found themselves describing the engagement to the Chairman of the Joint Chiefs of Staff in the Pentagon. It took him but a few moments to recognize the importance of the tapes. Still enlargements were immediately made clearly showing live missiles mounted under the wings of both MiG-23s. It was these enlargements which were displayed to the United Nations Security Council by the U.S. Ambassador and which encouraged him to denounce the Libyan Ambassador as "a liar." The Libyan statesman had stated that the MiGs were unarmed.

The eighteen ship *John F. Kennedy* battle group was in its fifth month of a six month deployment. Four times before it had steamed past the Libyan coast and each time, according to current U.S. policy, the battle group had exercised its "right of innocent passage." This simple means that the freedom of the seas, enjoyed by all nations beyond the territorial limits on any littoral country, needs to be constantly exercised to be a viable principle of international law. On their four previous passages there had been the usual air activity by the Libyan Air Force. A minor show of interest by Libyan fighters and electronic surveillance produced no incidents. However, on this passage the battle group commander felt uneasy.

Colonel Khadaffi was extremely sensitive about all of the recent bad publicity regarding his chemical weapon production plant at Rapta. The battle group commander later confided that if there were going to be an international incident, it would occur during this passage. Accordingly, he was very specific in his briefing on the "rules of engagement" (ROE) to the air crews just before beginning the flight information region (FIR) operations in early January 1989. Fresh in his mind must have been the incident in March 1986 in which the U.S. Navy destroyed four Libyan surface combatants. Or, perhaps he was thinking of the incident the following April of the famous raid on Khadaffi's headquarters.

Rules of engagement are terribly important to men of arms when they go in harm's way. They govern how they conduct themselves in combat. The problem with ROE is that they are subject to some degree of interpretation and they are always classified (and properly so). In this case, the battle group commander wisely decided to clarify the existing ROE with a degree of specificity which had the effect of putting the aircrews into the decision process. Put simply, the battle group commander promised that he, personally, whenever an incident became imminent, would advise the air crews that the likelihood of an incident had increased. Therefore, the aircrews, armed with that declaration, were permitted to defend themselves if they believed they were threatened. For our four aviators that enlightened policy became a very important factor in determining the outcome of the events of 3 January 1989. The battle group commander had good reason to be anxious. For some reason, not explainable, the Libyans had recently moved more MiG airplanes to both the base at Al Bumbah and, farther east, at Gabal Ab Al Nassar. It was for this reason that until this flight a standard air wing policy had been for Libyan flight information region (FIR) operations to be flown only by experienced air crews. In a moment of impulse, the battle group commander suggested to the airwing commander and his squadron COs that they throw in a nugget aircrew once in a while for experience. So on this particular mission one section had a nugget pilot and an experienced RIO and vice versa. Now, he was a little uneasy about the suggestion.

A few words are appropriate here about FIR operations. The entire airspace over the Mediterranean Sea is divided up into segments called flight information regions for purposes of a rudimentary air traffic control. The FIR off the coast of Libya was routinely entered by U.S. Navy carrier air crews for training while their carriers transited the region. In the Libyan FIR they exercised special precautions because of the history of Libyan fighters venturing out to reconnoiter the battle group. On this particular day our four fighters were manning two combat air patrol (CAP) stations just 30 or 40 miles inside the Libyan FIR. VF-14 had the CAP on the western station and VF-32 was CAP one the eastern station. Several flights of A-6 Intruders were going to do practice bombing on smoke flares.

The plan for this day called for the A-6 flights to enter the FIR in sequence, drop a smoke in the vicinity of one of the CAP stations, drop their practice bombs, depart the FIR and be followed by the next flight of Intruders. Each time a new flight entered the FIR one of the CAP sections would establish a patrol overhead the A-6s while the other section was free to do practice radar intercepts against one another. When the A-6s changed, so also did the Tomcats switch CAP duties. The lead pilot in the eastern CAP section was the Com-

CHAPTER 28: "NAVY FOUR, LIBYA ZERO"

manding Officer of VF-32, the lead pilot on the western station was the Executive Officer of VF-14. The eastern station leader was also the most senior officer of the four airplanes when a call came in from the airborne E-2 radar early warning airplane that a flight of two bogies had taken off from Al Bumbah and crossed the beach headed their way. The flight leader was given a vector to intercept the bogies and the A-6s turned north and departed the FIR. The lead aircrew had experienced some difficulties earlier in the flight with their radar and elected to turn it off for a while. As so often happens in the Tomcat, if the system is turned off for a while and then recycled it will work perfectly. During the post-launch tanking and enroute phase of the flight this very thing had happened. Fortunately, just prior to entering the FIR the lead radar intercept officer (RIO) had been very relieved to see a good scope and a good inertial navigation presentation when he cycled the radar back on. Now as they turned toward the bogies the aircrew sensed an immense feeling of relief. They had several Sparrow radar-guided missiles and several Sidewinder heat-seeking missiles strapped on with a good bag of fuel (having just topped off from the tanker before entering the FIR). What more could a fighter aircrew ask? They were about eighty miles off the beach when the E-2 call came. The bogies were seventy miles away and at an altitude of approximately 8,000 feet. The lead RIO (who happened to be the CAG Operations Officer) got an immediate radar contact. It was air wing policy to lock up the radar contact as early as possible to give the bogies the opportunity to turn back toward land. The knowledge of being locked up by an armed F-14 was usually sufficient motivation to cause the Libyans to turn away. But this time they did not!

The lead pilot's pulse quickened as he simultaneously turned toward the bogies and, leaving the throttles set at a medium power lowered the nose starting a descent from 20,000 feet during which the speed built up to a comfortable 450-475 knots. There was a cloud deck below them and they wanted to get below it before they got too much closer. The two flights were closing at a rate of over a thousand miles an hour so there was a sense of urgency in their descent. There was another reason for the descent. They wanted to be looking up at the enemy fighters and force the opponents to be looking down at them. This would give the F-14s a distinct advantage because their radar wouldn't be bothered by the radar clutter presented by the surface of the water while the opponents would have to contend with it. To be sure their Sparrow was substantially superior to the enemy's Apex missile. However, it did have the capability of looking down and shooting.

The advertised range of the Apex missile, about a dozen miles, had already established their agreed upon tactics. If the enemy actions were determined to be definitely hostile by that difference then that would be the shoot, no shoot decision point.

The seven minute segment of their lives began at exactly 11:55 AM when the radar controller in the E-2C early warning airplane informed them that two aircraft had taken off from the Libyan air base at Bumbah. It was on the Libyan coast about halfway between the seaports of Tobruk and Benghazi. Sure enough, there on their radar screens were two small radar returns at a range of 72 miles at about seven thousand feet and headed right at them at a speed that ensured they were Libyan tactical airplanes. The two F-14s, flying in a combat spread formation executed a thirty degree turn away from the enemy airplanes but observed on their tactical information display that the bogies had countered with a turn of their own which placed them again on a constant line of bearing and, therefore, a collision course; and closing fast. The first turn executed to the left was to give them an offset and some radar intercept aspect. This had two purposes. The first was to ensure a favorable attack position. The second was that it would enable them to convert the intercept geometry to a join-up from astern and an escort position until the bogies departed the vicinity of the battle group.

At 11:58:43 the flight leveled off at about three thousand feet and 475 knots, noting that their bogies were now closing on a collision course at a range of fifty-three miles and descending.. The RIO was now doing all the talking, announcing his intentions at the beginning of each jinking turn to the E-2, knowing full well that back at the ship the Admiral was listening and his operations officer doing the talking. The two jinking turns had been made also to keep the F-14s between the bogies and the carrier. There was some rapid conversation between the pilot and his RIO as they attempted to get the television camera system (TCS) on line. An earlier system check had determined that the camera and audio recorder were operating correctly but the video recorder was not. Fortunately, at the most critical point in the engagement it began working correctly enough to provide the graphic proof the MiGs were armed. The ammunition which the U.S. Ambassador to the U.N. needed to prove their case to the world. By making the second

CHAPTER 28: "NAVY FOUR, LIBYA ZERO"

F-14A dropping flares.

turn he hoped again to offset them from the bogeys to gain a tactical advantage. A head-on engagement with an enemy who had a forward quarter, radar guided air-to-air missile was not the engagement of choice.

The time was 11:59:16. The bogies again responded with a countering turn back toward them, obviously being controlled by their own ground controlled radar. Still the bogies were beyond visual range but were closing at close to one thousand knots closure rate. It was getting a little dicey! After the first turn the air warfare commander on *Kennedy* (called Alpha Whiskey) broadcast to them the coded signal "weapons yellow and weapons hold" which meant that the Alpha Whiskey believed that a hostile incident was imminent and action in self defense was authorized. That was exactly what the pilots needed to know. The outcome of the impending incident was now under their control . . . a scary thought in a way, but a wonderful position to be in. It was also a wonderful reinforcement of the special trust in which the battle group commander held them. It was, furthermore, a reassuring statement of how qualified he thought they were not only to make the right decision but also to defend themselves.

The time was 12:00:08. Each time he had "jinked" (turned) the flight lead RIO had announced the fact to the controller in the E-2C. Time was rapidly running out and the flight leader strained his eyes to pick up the two bogies visually. He knew they were two small black specks inside the small but bright diamond on his HUD.

The time was now 12:00:53. Finally, the lead RIO said, "Bogies have jinked back at me for the fifth time. They're on my nose, now inside of twenty miles." He directed the section to turn on the master armament switches. The wingman acknowledged the call. If either of them pushed the launch button a missile would come off the selected station and there would be no recalling it. The pilot had the Sparrow air-to-air radar guided missile selected, the radar was locked on the number two airplane when the lead pilot maneuvered slightly to place the diamond symbol on his heads-up display in the center of the firing circle . . . the heart of the firing envelope.

Anticipating that his RIO was going to suggest shooting at any moment, the pilot said, over the intercom, "Wait a minute", and broadcast, "Alpha Whiskey, this two zero seven, over." It was a last minute, desperate attempt to get "Snake" Morris's approval to fire. The range was about 16 miles. There was no response. At exactly a range of 12.9 miles the RIO fired a Sparrow missile and the pilot immediately executed an F-pole maneuver (thirty degree turn) to the left. "Aw, Jesus", was all the lead pilot could think of saying over the intercom. The wingman followed suit with an F-pole maneuver to the right. Shortly thereafter the section of F-14s turned back into the MiGs and a second Sparrow missile was fired by the lead RIO. The range now was about 10 miles. The lead RIO called on the intercom, "Bring it back, bring it back" to the pilot. He responded by reversing his turn and roughly centering the dot in the circle of his radar symbol on the "heads up display (HUD). The time was 12:01:20.

"Fox one, fox one", was the transmission which had come out of his tightened throat sounding strangely like someone else's voice. The second Sparrow missile came off the rails and sailed off into the blue space in front of him. The pilot still couldn't see the MiGs when he noticed that his wingman, off to his right, had fired a Sparrow. At the same time the wingman called, "Tally-ho, eleven o'clock high. They are turning into me."

Somewhat casually he told his RIO on the ICS, "They got one off." The lead RIO misunderstood who the "they" were, assumed that the MiGs had fired and frantically began punching off round after round of defensive chaff bundles with his manual release button.

Meanwhile, the lead pilot was following the flight of his wingman's missile and, lo and behold, it exploded as it flew into the right intake duct of the second MiG. That was the first time the lead pilot saw the airplanes. It is worth freezing the picture for a moment in order to give the reader a word picture of the relative positions of the four airplanes as viewed by the lead pilot. He was seeing the two MiGs through the forward left windscreen looking slightly up at them with a target aspect of about sixty degrees (the angle made by the intersection of the aircraft vectors). The F-14 wingman was spread to the right of his leader. The MiG wingman was spread to the right of his section leader and the two planes had begun a left turn toward the lead F-14's wingman.

The time was 12:01:57. The F-14 flight leader initiated a hard right turn and a slight high yo-yo calculated to put him above and to the six o'clock position of the lead MiG which was passing directly in front of him from left to right. The damaged airplane, streaming black smoke, entered a steep right turn and was lost from view just after its pilot ejected. The F-14 wingman executed a similar high yo-yo maneuver to put himself in support of his leader. The lead pilot was starting down in a firing run at the six o'clock position of the first MiG which

CHAPTER 28: "NAVY FOUR, LIBYA ZERO"

had begun a descending left turn. The flight leader, knowing it was a kill, shouted on the radio.

The time was 12:02:06. "Good kill, good kill, I've got the other one," he grunted as he yanked the airplane into a hard right descending turn feeling the painful squeeze of his anti "g" suit trying to combat four and one half times the force of gravity. The flight leader flicked the control switch on his stick to select Sidewinder. There was no familiar growl from the missile's seeker head on his own head set. There should have been because his F-14 was pointed directly at the airplane's tailpipe. Frantically, he stepped to another Sidewinder station.

All the time the RIO was screaming on the intercom. "Select Fox 2, (meaning Sidewinder), Shoot 'em, Fox 2, Fox 2, shoot Fox 2." Still no tone. In desperation the pilot shifted back to the Sparrow mode and tried for a PLM pilot lock-on to no avail. By now the MiG was perilously close and they were overtaking him fast. Again in desperation the pilot shifted back to Sidewinder mode and, glancing down at his left console, seized the Sidewinder tone volume control knob twisting it clockwise. The roar of the Sidewinder tone drowned everything else out as he realized that some how in the melee it had gotten turned off. The fog of war struck again!... almost. But there was still time and as he heard the Sidewinder come on in his headset he squeezed the trigger and the Sidewinder came off the left wing station. There was an instant of doubt as it appeared not to be guiding. He thought to himself, oh Christ, not again. Then the missile began a long beautiful arc towards the descending MiG-23 striking it in the fuselage just behind the cockpit. Just as the missile struck, the canopy flew off and the pilot ejected. Beautiful!

The time was 12:02:36. The total elapsed time from the first call from the E-2 to the impact of his Sidewinder was less than seven minutes; seven minutes of his life that they would never forget. There was a sudden urgency to get the hell out of there and the pilot engaged afterburner for the first time in the engagement and headed the flight for the deck. The MiG-23 for all its faults has one huge advantage over most other tactical airplanes, eye-watering speed and acceleration. He didn't want to give the Libyans a chance to run them down with another flight of MiGs which could appear at any moment. The flight leader reported to the E-2C that they had, "splashed two Floggers and that there were two good 'chutes in the air." Rounding out their descent at about seven hundred feet over the water the two Tomcats in a combat spread with their wings fully swept back did what F-14s do so well booming along at six hundred fifty knots headed back to the ship. When I asked if they did a victory roll back at the ship the pilot's face took on a sheepish look as he replied with artless candor, "Hell no, Admiral, I boltered!"

The Skipper, Captain Denny Wisely, and the CAG Jerry Norris were all there to greet and congratulate before the more formal and exhaustive intelligence debriefings began. As they climbed out of their flight gear in the squadron ready room they noted that someone had written in large letters on the blackboard in the front of the room a score which took into account the two Libyan SU-22s in 1981 and today's kills. It said, "NAVY FOUR, LIBYA ZERO."

VF-143 F-14A shooting an AIM-9 Sidewinder missile.

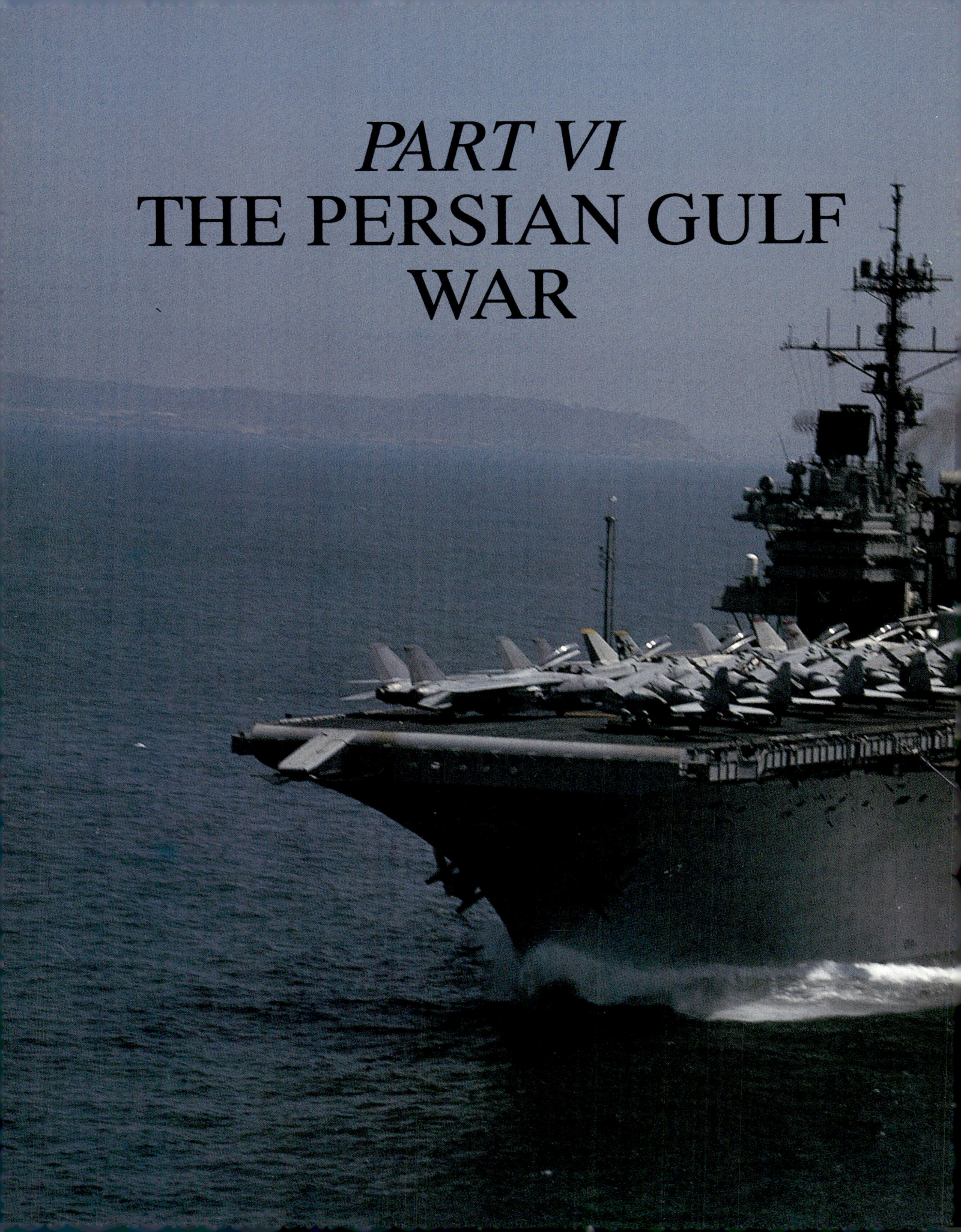

PART VI
THE PERSIAN GULF WAR

USS Ranger (CV-61) en route to the Persian Gulf.

No carrier battle group commander would be crazy enough to go into the Persian Gulf. That statement probable reflects the generally accepted wisdom up until the remarkable events of January and February 1991. It is a very restricted body of shallow water. A surface-to-surface missile attack by, for example a Chinese-built Silkworm missile would first be detected only minutes before impact.

Never in my wildest dreams could I ever imagine one (much less four) carriers operating in the northern reaches of that body of water conducting full-blown combat operations against targets in Iraq and Kuwait. But, that is what happened, though it was only made possible because of the neutrality maintained by Iran and the cooperation of Saudi Arabia and other Arab states. Furthermore, two other aircraft carriers were operating in similarly restricted waters on the other side of the Arabian Peninsula, in the Red Sea. In an effort to describe how the F-14 was employed in the Persian Gulf War it would be useful to describe briefly the build up of carrier based aircraft first in the northern Arabian Sea, then into the Persian Gulf and the Red Sea.

At the time of the Iraqi invasion of Kuwait the two closest carrier battle groups were the one led by USS INDEPENDENCE (CV-62) which was in the Indian Ocean near the strategic island of Diego Garcia and the one led by USS EISENHOWER which was in the central Mediterranean Sea. INDEPENDENCE began an immediate high speed transit to the northern Arabian Sea and on 5 August could have begun long range strikes from the Gulf of Oman. EISENHOWER proceeded immediately to the eastern Mediterranean, transitted the Suez Canal and was in position to begin strike operations from the Red Sea by 8 August.

Between then and 15 January carrier battle groups began deploying from both the Atlantic and Pacific Fleets in what was to become the largest assemblage of naval forces since World War II. On 15 January strike operations began from the decks of USS SARATOGA (CV-60) and USS JOHN F. KENNEDY (CV-67) from the Red Sea against targets in western Iraq. At the same time strike operations began from the decks of USS TEDDY ROOSEVELT (CVN-71), USS AMERICA (CV-66), USS RANGER (CV-61) and USS MIDWAY (CV-41) from the Persian Gulf against targets in Kuwait and eastern Iraq.

A fighter force of ten F-14 squadrons and twelve F/A-18 strike fighters squadrons had been assembled for sea based strike operations in that remarkable short time. Add to that force squadrons of Marine Corps F/A-18 operating from Saudi Arabia alongside the US Air Force F-16s and F-15s; and a total US force of aircraft capable of taking on the almost 700 aircraft in the Iraqi air force in aerial combat. There was a small number of Arab coalition fighters arrayed against the Iraqis as well as some fighters from the NATO air forces which participated. The war was conducted in four phases:

- *Communications, Command and Control*
- *Air defense suppression*
- *Battlefield preparation*
- *Ground offensive*

In the first phase, key points in the Iraqi communications, command and control networks were taken out by manned and unmanned aircraft. The Tomahawk missiles fired from battleships and precision guided weapons dropped by the F-117 stealth airplane under cover of darkness and heavily supported by other aircraft were effective in "putting their eyes out." All of this was accomplished in a matter of hours of intense assault. The second phase began with intense day and night air strikes by Air Force, Navy and coalition strike aircraft. Extensive use was made, during this phase, of anti-radiation weapons targeted against surface-to-air missile and radar sites. Again, within a matter of hours air superiority was achieved against Iraqi air defenses. The third phase was nothing more than a mass of pinpoint strikes with precision guided weapons and "dumb bombs" against airfields, revetted aircraft, bridges, Scud missile sites, Iraqi armor and other targets whose destruction would make the coming ground offensive easier. This included "carpet bombing" by B-52s against Iraqi troop concentrations in and around Kuwait.

The final phase, the ground offensive was very intense and short. A target rich environment for tank killers of all sorts (A-10s, helicopters, F-16s, F/A-18s, F-15s and A-6s) was created when dug-in Iraqi armor was flushed out of cover and then bottled up on the roads north out of Kuwait. It was the largest turkey shoot in history. The Tomcat was employed in several missions during the different phases of the war.

VF-143 F-14B over Kuwaiti oilfield. (Official U.S. Navy Photograph)

29
PERSIAN GULF

When the first U.S. aircraft carrier steamed into the Persian Gulf on 3 January 1990 there was an almost audible intake of breathe among my retired naval officer friends. One of them referred to it as "trolling." In the narrow confines of that strategic body of water any sensible carrier battle group commander would be extremely uncomfortable with the territory of a potentially hostile country only a few flying minutes away. He would feel much more comfortable in "blue water" surrounded by deep water for five hundred miles in any direction. U.S.S. Ranger (CV-61) with Carrier Air Wing TWO embarked, completed its Advanced Training Assessment (ATE) the day Iraq invaded Kuwait. The carrier's Commanding Officer, Captain Ernie "Ratchet" Christensen knew that no U.S. aircraft carrier could be better positioned to fight the coming war. The air wing commander, Captain Jay "Rabbit" Campbell felt the same way. The Executive Officer of one of the air wing's two fighter squadrons, the "Bounty Hunters" of Fighter Squadron TWO had similar feelings when he heard the news. Commander J.J. Quinn was also ready to go to war.

Ranger sailed from its homeport in San Diego on the 8 December tide. There was a brief stop in the Subic Bay naval base in the Philippines and then a sprint across the Indian Ocean to get to the war zone in time. Ranger aircraft were the first Navy airplanes to strike Iraqi targets. J.J. Quinn recalls the odd feeling of being able to see both land masses on his first combat mission of the war. On the right was Iran, menacing in its quiescence. On the left was Saudi Arabia. Ahead was Iraq . . . "Indian Country."

Um Qasr was the first target for Ranger's air wing. It was a small airfield. The air wing commander believed in giving strike planning and leading responsibilities to all of his squadron commanding officers. The first strike was planned and lead by an A-6 squadron commanding officer. The second strike was assigned to the other A-6 squadron commanding officer.

It is noted that Ranger was one of two carriers which had what was often an "all Grumman air wing." The carrier John F. Kennedy was the other carrier. There were two A-6 medium attack squadrons, two fighter squadrons and no light attack (strike fighter) squadrons. The "Grumman Air Wing" also called, simply, the Kennedy air wing, was the brain child of former Secretary of the Navy, John Lehman. The relative combat effectiveness of a Kennedy air wing as compared to a standard air wing (one A-6 squadron, two fighter and strike fighter squadrons) has yet to be adequately measured. Both have good and bad aspects. The third strike was planned and lead by the commanding officer of the "Bounty Hunters", Commander Jackson. From then on, the "Bounty Hunters" led the all the squadrons in both the Red Sea and Persian Gulf in a number of categories:

- they flew 96 flight hours on the first day
- they flew 1,176 flight hours in February
- they flew 1,904 flight hours in the 43 day war
- they flew 557 sorties in the 43 day war

The kinds of missions which Persian Gulf battle force F-14s flew were essentially the same as those flown by counterpart F-14 squadrons in the Red Sea. The first strike missions were long ones since the carrier was initially positioned in the southern reaches of the Persian Gulf. However, as the battle force commander grew less uneasy with his surroundings, the launch point for strikes against Iraq moved deeper into the Gulf and closer to the targets. On 25 and 26 February, when a large percentage of total Iraqi armor became trapped on the routes leading out of Kuwait, the target rich environment caused Ranger to move within 180 miles from the beach. This permitted her strike aircraft to make the short (280 mile) run to the killing fields more often each day. Combat air patrols were gradually moved closer and closer to Iraqi territory and at the end of February were positioned forty miles from the target. Complete dominance of the skies over Iraq was the key to the U.S. success in the war.

CHAPTER 29: PERSIAN GULF

VF-32 F-14A escorting an A-6E.

PART VI: THE PERSIAN GULF WAR

Tomcat night aerial tanking from a KA-6 tanker.

VF-32 F-14A over Iraq.

VF-24 F-14B over the burning oilfields of Kuwait, April 1991.

CHAPTER 29: PERSIAN GULF

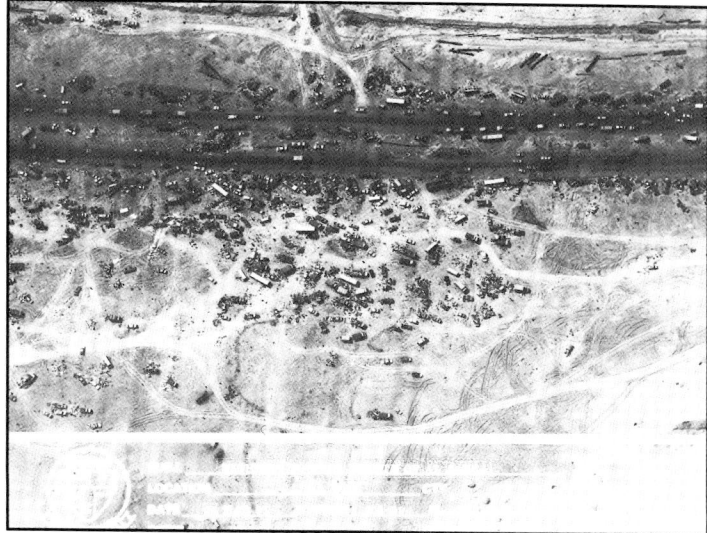

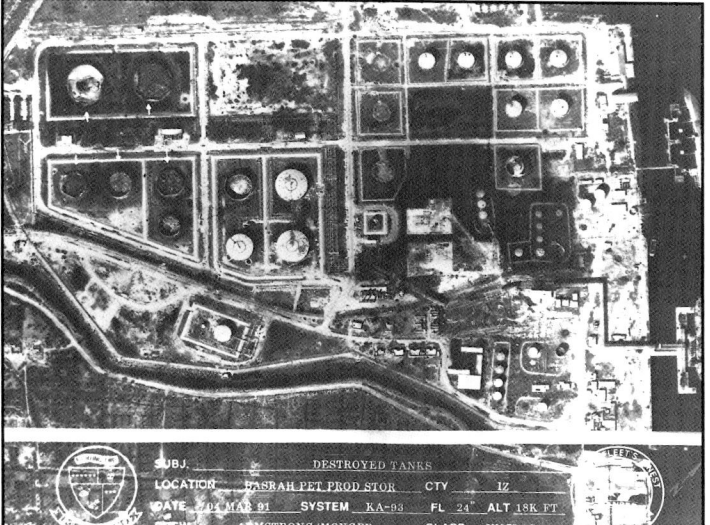

Four photographs from a VF-2 TARPS reconnaissance mission.

On average, strike escort missions were three hour missions and required at least one aerial tanking. The combat air patrol missions averaged from five to seven hours and required at least two aerial refuelings. The tankers were their own organic air wing tankers (KA-6s) or U.S. Air Force KC-135s or KC-10s. On one particular flight, the "Bounty Hunters'" commanding officer Jackson flew what he called a "ball-busting" eleven hour mission. Knowing how excruciating it can be to sit strapped to an ejection seat for more than two hours, I asked how that aircrew felt. The now commanding officer, J.J. Quinn told me they were "grapes" when they got back. If there is a footnote to the role played by F-14s in the Persian Gulf War it would have to be this. It represented the last opportunity for the F-14 to prove itself in the air-to-ground role in actual combat. Many leaders in the fighter community had been warning for years that the F-14 must get active in the strike mission or die. People like "Hoss" Pearson, "Spike" Prendergast, Phil Anselmo and a host of others were simply not listened to. If allowed to go unchallenged, Defense Secretary Cheney's decision to kill the F-14D and replace it with an upgraded version of the short legged Hornet spells the end of the Tomcat . . . a premature passing which it does not deserve.

30
RED SEA

The same feeling of discomfort that a carrier group commander would feel steaming around in the Persian Gulf would also be felt in the narrow confines of the Red Sea, and for the same reasons. The only difference in the Red Sea is that the ship would have friendly territory on both flanks, Saudi Arabia on the east and Egypt on the west. However, at the outbreak of war the three carriers which made up the Red Sea battle force began launching combat strikes against targets in western Iraq.

The principal targets were fixed and mobile Scud missile launch sites, generally in western and northwestern Iraq. There was a great deal of unease in coalition leadership circles over the importance of keeping Israeli forces from retaliating against Iraq for their unprovoked Scud attacks against Israel. As a consequence, an inordinate amount of military resources was expended in locating those sites and eliminating Iraqi missile assets. F-14 photo reconnaissance missions were flown using the tactical aircraft reconnaissance photographic system (TARPS) pods mounted on one of the airplane's external store stations. Once the Scud site had been located then F-14 fighter escort missions were flown with the strike aircraft. After the dust settled F-14 photo reconnaissance missions were flown to the target to assess bomb damage. These escort missions continued to be flown throughout the war. However, the fighter assets committed to this mission were gradually reduced as Iraqi air activity decreased.

For the first three days of the war there had been considerable Iraqi air activity observed. However, it appeared that Iraqi pilots had a healthy respect for the beyond visual range (BVR) air-to-air missile capability of the F-14. Whenever the Iraqis were in a position to detect an AWG-9 (F-14) radar signal on their electronic countermeasures equipment they turned tail and ran. Some of this respect doubtlessly stems from their experience with Iranian F-14 confrontations in the past.

Also, in the early stages of the war the Red Sea battle force experienced its only F-14 combat loss. Although considerable effort was expended to recover the radar intercept officer (RIO), the pilot was captured and spent the rest of the short conflict as a prisoner of war (POW). The rules of engagement imposed by the staff at Riyahd were very restrictive for beyond visual range missile attacks against aerial targets. F-14s possessed the capability to identify friendly targets and the F/A-18s, using their non-cooperative target recognition system, could identify hostile targets. Nevertheless, the rules of engagement required confirmation from an E-2 early warning radar airplane or from the E-3 AWACs before a missile could be fired against a target that couldn't be visually identified. At the outset, the senior naval officer, Vice Admiral Stan Arthur, Commander, Naval Forces, Central Command, attempted to get Lieutenant General Horner to relax that particular rule, but to no avail. In defense of the staff at Riyahd, there were two to three thousand combat sorties per day launched from the two battle forces and from airfields in Saudi Arabia. Merely keeping track of them was an enormous task. To have managed traffic to avoid "conflictions" as safely as they did was a minor miracle. The fact that "blue on blue' aerial engagements did not occur is almost unbelievable. Much of the credit for the remarkable safety record set by coalition aviators in that war should go to strict adherence to a stiff set of rules of engagement.

Another mission was flown by Red Sea F-14s which could not be revealed until a recent relaxation of security. This was the B-52 escort mission. Flights of B-52s launched from Barksdale Air Force base in Louisiana and, assisted by aerial tankers flew non-stop to the combat zone and launched air launched cruise missiles (ALCMs) against targets in Iraq. F-14s from the Red Sea battle force would fly out, rendezvous with the bombers and provide fighter escort while they were vulnerable to enemy air defenses.

CHAPTER 30: RED SEA

VF-33 F-14A from USS America (CV-66).

Red Sea F-14s also routinely flew combat air patrol (CAP) missions to provide support for pop-up missions. These were short notice missions against mobile Scud missile sites. Often, there would only be minutes after a Scud missile attack before the launcher could be moved. Rapid response was necessary. F-14 CAP flights were able to escort strike missions diverted for that purpose.

The TF-30 engine in the F-14As in both Red Sea and Persian Gulf battle forces continued to plague the fighters. There were several instances when F-14s escorting strike forces experienced compressor stalls while aerial refueling. On at least one occasion an F-14 experienced compressor stalls followed by an engine flameout which was subsequently re-lit. The performance of the F-14As with heavy missile loads limited their ability to aerial refuel above about 23,000 feet. Above that altitude it often became necessary to tap afterburner during a tanking attempt. This, of course, became an exercise in futility. On the other hand, the F-14A Plus (with the big engine) represented an enormous improvement in reliability.

The geography of the Red Sea battle force's station required a great deal of long range combat. The requirement to fly through Saudi Arabian air space enroute to and from Iraqi targets made for four and five hour missions. The distance along that route to Baghdad was over twelve hundred miles. All in all, the F-14s on the Red Sea battle force performed all those difficult missions with a high degree of professionalism and resourcefulness.

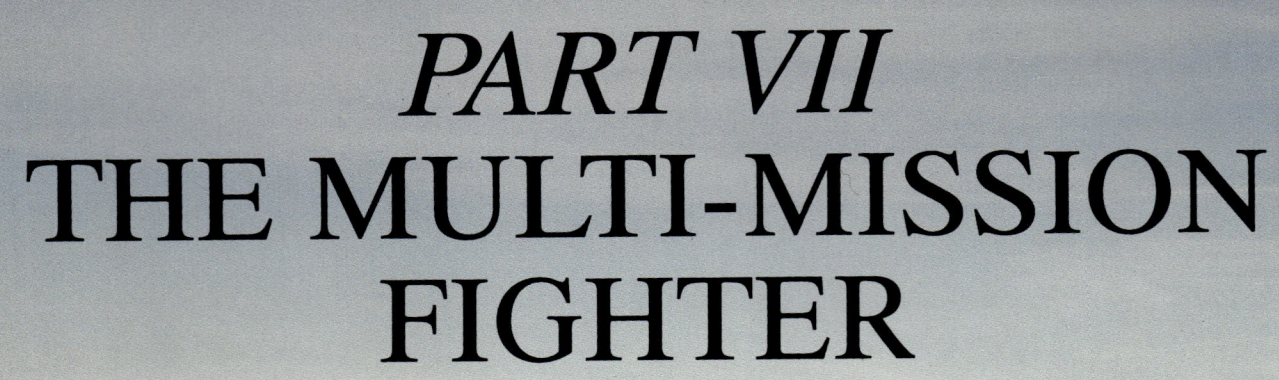

PART VII
THE MULTI-MISSION FIGHTER

VF-51 F-14 carrying four Mk. 83 1,000 lb. bombs.

When the expression, "multi-mission fighter" is used nowadays it is something of a misnomer. What it really means is a fighter which also has an attack mission. Fighters have, more often than not, always had secondary missions like photo reconnaissance, MiG sweep and strike escort. But they have not always had a credible attack mission capability. The F7U, F4D, F3B and F11F come to mind as a few examples. The F-14A had a significant air-to-ground capability, but it was never made credible. That is because the funds set aside to do the required air-to-ground testing were spent for other tests, considered to be of higher priority. As a consequence, the Tomcat, by default came to be considered a "single-mission" fighter.

Of course, that is an over-simplification of a much more fundamental fact of military aviation; for as long as I can remember fighter pilots have tended to look down their noses at the crude business of dropping bombs; or, for that matter, anything from their airplanes. Somehow, the business of cracking open the canopy so that the end of one's silk scarf can trail in the slipstream of one's Spad biplane seems so much more glamorous than dropping something on a bridge. Furthermore, it has always seemed to me more interesting to match my wits and aeronautical skill against another aviator who is out to kill me. There is a personal aspect about aerial combat which has always captured my imagination. Knowing that eventually you will meet the pilot who is as good as, or even better than, you adds to the thrill of the "sport of kings." Each time a fighter pilot squares off for a one-on-one engagement with another pilot, he must wonder, "who is this guy? Is it possible that he is the one fighter pilot in the world who can clean my clock?" By the way, the U.S. Air Force avoided falling into this trap by calling every tactical airplane a fighter plane. Therefore, any Air Force pilot who flew tactical airplanes was a "fighter pilot" (except for the "Warthog" pilots).

But there is even a more fundamental reason why the F-14 never was used as a bomber. As mentioned earlier in this work, the unique air-to-air capability of the F-14 was a factor in the outcome of the enormous battle over the relative cost of land-based versus sea-based tactical air forces. The issue has reappeared over the years as an internecine war between the roles and missions of the U.S. Air Force and the U.S. Navy. It is going on again as the Persian Gulf war fades into the past and military spending is being cut again. Now it is a question of whether the B-2 can replace the aircraft carrier. It is an absurd issue but it keeps on rearing its ugly head.

However, when the issue arose in the late 1960s as the Viet Nam war was winding down it looked as though the then premier U.S. fighter, the F-4 Phantom, could no longer protect the carrier from the increasingly threatening Soviet air-launched anti-ship missile. The development of the F-14 was a major factor in the winning of the battle. That very fact made it absolutely imperative that the Navy demonstrate, with-

VF-33 F-14A, "Starfighter 200," dropping high-drag Mk.-83 bombs.

out a doubt, that the F-14 could really do what it was purported to do. The insistence on demonstrating its effectiveness against a very daunting air-to-air threat, over and over, lead to an attitude within the Navy fighter community which totally focussed on the air-to-air threat and ignored the air-to-ground mission.

In the early 1980s when the Navy strike fighter community (Hornet pilots) began to replace the light attack community (Corsair pilots) some farsighted leaders in the fighter community foresaw the need to demonstrate the air-to-ground capability of the F-14. But, too many fighter pilots dragged their feet, and the inevitable happened. Secretary of Defense Dick Cheney, acting on bad advice from his own Hornet advocates, canceled the F-14D program in favor of an upgraded version of the Hornet. One could say that the Navy fighter community did it to themselves!

31

THE F-14D "SUPER TOMCAT"

The F-14D finally arrived in the fleet in 1990 at NAS Miramar. It was an event that was much too long in coming but nonetheless welcome. It brought to the fleet a new airplane, so great are the improvements in virtually all measurables.

The new radar gave it an enormous increase in effectiveness against small, stealthy targets as well as against stealthy aircraft. In addition, its capability against all types of targets in an electronic warfare environment has been vastly improved. This facet alone may well be the most important single enhancement it brings to fleet maritime air superiority. As an adjunct to the active radar sensor comes an even more important feature especially against stealthy foes. This is the infra-red search

VF-31 F-14D launching from Cat #3 from the USS Carl Vinson (CVN-70).

CHAPTER 31: THE F-14D "SUPER TOMCAT"

VF 51 F-14A dropping four Mk. 84 2,000 lb. bombs on target at Fallon, Nevada.

PART VII: THE MULTI-MISSION FIGHTER

F-14A front cockpit.

F-14D front cockpit.

F-14A rear cockpit.

F-14D rear cockpit.

CHAPTER 31: THE F-14D "SUPER TOMCAT"

F-14A rear cockpit at night.

F-14D rear cockpit at night.

and track systems (IRST). It represents a major improvement and one which gives it an enormous edge in the air-to-air arena over any other fighter in the world today. Since the IRST is a passive sensor its employment will introduce major changes in fighter tactics. The IRST currently operates in the three to five micron wave length. Further development will give it an ability to operate in the eight to twelve micron wave length. This will, quite literally, render stealth irrelevant since it permits very long detection ranges against high altitude, high speed targets.

The new engines give the F-14D a thirty-two percent increase in thrust over the F-14A which currently makes up the bulk of the fleet fighter inventory. The increase in agility stems from a combination of increased Ps and the advantage of variable geometry which gives it an edge over all free world fighters. But the new engines bring other benefits to the outer air battle as well as the close-in combat arena. Both range and loiter time are increased making it a dramatic improvement over current fleet fighters.

The new glass cockpit and avionics give the aircrew a quantum increase in combat effectiveness by raising their level of situational awareness as well as making better use of a huge increase in data now available to them.

In addition to fighter improvements, the F-14D now possesses the capability to be what the F-14 was initially designed to be; a multi-mission aircraft. With a small investment in software changes the F-14D has the capability to perform the long range strike role as well as the highly touted air force F-15E. The airplane is uniquely configured to excel in that role. With four 2,000 pound bombs semi-submerged in the tunnel between the engines it represents such a low drag configuration that it can run in at low altitude at 650 knots in basic engine. The variable geometry wings give it remarkable range with that large bomb load as well as an impressive attack agility. The benefits in susceptibility and survivability are also substantial. A carrier air wing employing F-14Ds in both the fighter and strike roles could field five squadrons of the best fighters in the world when needed in the maritime air superiority role. Then that same air wing could field five squadrons of long range, deep strike aircraft.

Finally, and of equal importance, the F-14D represents the absolute state-of-the-art in reliability and maintainability improvements. The synergism which this would represent in that all F-14D air wing would be equally enormous especially in terms of logistics.

32
TOMCAT 21

There have been countless combinations of capabilities, which when added to the F-14A, give it a new life and a new name. The number of permutations has been almost infinite. Just a few of those ideas were dignified with a name. "Super Tomcat 21" was the last and the most capable. The 21 stands for the 21st century. Although just an idea, a paper airplane, the packaging of it was done with thought given to helping the Navy solve its aircraft problems. What are those problems? In the early 1980s it was becoming painfully obvious that, as airplane costs continued upward, the number which could be bought each year with a level and then a diminishing budget grew smaller.

It had become almost a crippling problem by the mid-1980s. The analysts say that for an air force to remain credible it must maintain the average age of its airplanes at about seven years. As the older airplanes attrite from the force, newer ones are bought to replace them. When it had become clear that there wasn't enough money in the Navy's annual procurement budget to replace the aging airplanes with new ones, the Navy began fixing up the older ones instead of retiring them. A buzz phrase entered the lexicon called "force modernization by service life extension program" or, simply, SLEP. This was done with modification money and became, in short order, a huge appropriation, over half a billion dollars by 1985 and increasing annually. It remains an expensive way to achieve force modernization because such overhauls never buy the airplanes a complete new life, but rather a part of a new life. It was a band aid solution to a growing problem.

That year the average age of the four thousand aircraft in the Navy's inventory was eleven years and growing. That same year it had also become obvious that the Navy would not be able to buy enough aircraft to equip the highly touted 600 ship navy. As a result a new strategy was developed which came to be known as the level force readiness policy. The way it worked was that as

Above and opposite: Tomcat 21 model.

new airplanes were developed to replace older models, they would go to the fleet and also to the two reserve air wings. The reserve air wings, once modernized, were identified as the ones which would go onto the two aircraft carriers which were in SLEP and major overhaul. The theory was that in a major conflict those two carriers would be brought out of overhaul on an emergency basis and pressed into service. It would take quite a while to accomplish this major undertaking; long enough for the two reserve wings to whip themselves into shape.

To be sure, they maintained a reasonable state of readiness through weekend training, but carrier qualification training was not something they could do on weekends. This trick of identifying the two carriers in overhaul as dedicated reserve wing carriers did several things for the navy. It allowed them to cancel the purchase of the fourteenth air wing (and later the thirteenth air wing) while at the same time justifying the funding for several new *Nimitz* class nuclear powered aircraft carriers. Congressmen can count. When they approve new carriers they make sure there is adequate aircraft to go on them.

They were quick to perceive the difficulty being experienced by the navy in buying enough planes to keep their average age level. I had always questioned whether the two carriers in overhaul would ever get into a war before the war ended. Therefore, I was really questioning the credibility of the idea of putting brand new airplanes into reserve squadrons while the fleet squadrons continued to grind around in seriously aging aircraft.

Indeed, the speed with which new airplanes were integrated into the fleet was greatly reduced. The F/A-18 was a case in point. The second thing the total force concept did for the Navy was to ultimately put more new airplanes in the total force. Those critical of the total force concept were walking on thin ice because its principal advocate was the Secretary of the Navy, himself a U.S. Navy reserve commander who flew, as an A-6 bombardier-navigator both with reserve squadrons and fleet squadrons on a regular basis. Before the total force concept, the two reserve air wings were given the oldest airplanes as they fell out of the fleet inventory. It was a policy clearly understood by everyone. The fleet got the

PART VII: THE MULTI-MISSION FIGHTER

CHAPTER 32: TOMCAT 21

Above and opposite: Tomcat 21 model.

new stuff and the reserves got the cast-offs. That way of doing business made sense to me then and it still does today. Long range planners at the Grumman Corporation recognized the difficulty that the new advanced tactical fighter program was experiencing. Since it was the fighter that would eventually replace the Tomcat, and since the Grumman Corporation was not in the ATF competition, it made good sense to have an advanced design of the basic Tomcat waiting in the wings.

Super Tomcat was a whiz bang airplane with new engines, greater internal fuel capacity, new avionics and radar, a new fly-by-wire digital flight control system and a new all glass cockpit with multi-function displays and situational awareness enhancements. But the active duty (blue suiters) viewed the unsolicited design work as capable of threatening the naval version of the ATF and made it abundantly clear that the gentlemen from Bethpage should not go running around town peddling such ideas. The design work was down played in 1986 and then resurrected in 1991 when the Navy took all funding out of the NATF program. Now, that there is no follow-on to the F-14 program there is more interest in some form of major modification. Early in 1991 the Navy took all of the funding (all R&D) out of the program. It was now officially dead. Earlier the Secretary of Defense canceled the F-14D program.

But there remained within the blue suit ranks enough credible aviators who knew that the decision to replace F-14Ds with F/A-18Es and Fs was stupid. The congress was aware of this. The Hornet mafia in the Department of Defense teamed up with the Hornet mafia in the Navy to bring about this decision which was acceded to by the Navy decision makers because, as submariners, they simply didn't understand that the Hornet was not just a cheap Tomcat. That battle is not quite over as the first draft of this book is being completed. There are long memories on capitol hill. Some of the members of congress remember well that day a dozen years ago when a feisty little Vice Admiral had the guts to speak his mind. He wouldn't roll over for the Secretary of the Navy nor for the Secretary of Defense, for that matter. That was the day the F-111B died and the Tomcat was saved. Such things can happen again.

33

THE ADVANCED STRIKE FIGHTER

There is a very fundamental responsibility for any military organization which takes priority over all other missions. That responsibility is to do everything possible to reasonably guarantee its survival in combat. Some of the things it must do, therefore, are to acquire the tools necessary to survive, and to win. Adequate equipment, trained personnel, the proper logistics and good leadership are all elements for ensuring survival and victory in combat. It is what is called combat readiness.

An aircraft carrier battle group is about as complex a weapons system as can be found . . . anywhere. Like any other military organization expected to fight, its first responsibility must be to provide the means for surviving and winning in combat. To do this in today's world, the battle group must provide a bubble which I will call maritime superiority. That bubble extends outward from the center of the battle group in all directions; on the surface of the sea, under it and above it. Exactly how far the bubble extends in all directions can be debated; but it would be determined, to a large degree, by the threat. One could say that the depth below the surface that the bubble should extend ought to be, perhaps, the crush depth of the latest Soviet attack submarine. By the same token the bubble above the surface should extend upwards to about 80,000 feet and a distance from force center equal to the launch-and-leave range limit for the newest air-to-surface missile from a Soviet Backfire bomber. These are merely examples of how the dimensions of the bubble have been determined in the past. But, regardless of its dimensions, the battle group must achieve and maintain maritime superiority inside that bubble. This must come as first priority above all other missions for a very good reason; without it all other missions are irrelevant. Others may choose to call this sea control. That's fine. I believe my term, maritime superiority, is more descriptive.

In today's world, maritime superiority is achieved under the sea's surface by the combined efforts of the battle group's direct support submarine forces, the surface ships' anti-submarine warfare sensors and weapons, and the fixed and rotary wing anti-submarine warfare assets of the embarked air wing assisted if possible by shore-based air assets.

Where the bubble extends along the sea's surface, maritime superiority is achieved and maintained by the combined efforts of the surface combatant's anti-surface sensors and weapons; the anti-surface weapons and sensors of the direct support submarine force; and the anti-surface weapons and sensors of the battle group's air assets.

Finally, maritime superiority above the sea's surface (maritime air superiority) is achieved and maintained by the surface-to-air weapons and sensors of the surface combatants; and the air-to-air weapons and sensors of the battle group's embarked air wing. For years the United States Navy has tailored its forces to defeat an increasingly dangerous Soviet threat whose capabilities have demanded an enormous investment, on our part, in high technology platforms, sensors and weapons to achieve and maintain maritime superiority in all three dimensions of that bubble. A concomitant investment has been necessary to enable the battle force commander to integrate and coordinate all of these complex systems available to him. Now, we see the trend of much of this Soviet high technology weaponry migrating to third world nations much more rapidly than a few years ago. The highly capable MiG-29, for example, is now being exported to a number of those countries. There is little reason to suspect that this trend will reverse itself in the

CHAPTER 33: THE ADVANCED STRIKE FIGHTER

Lockheed/Boeing's Advanced Strike Fighter proposal. (Illustration courtesy of Lockheed)

near future. Indeed, recent events in the Soviet Union may suggest that increased transfer of weaponry to the third world may become an economic necessity. The lesson here is that the United States will still need high technology weaponry despite the end of the Cold War.

However, the increasing costs of these high technology weapons systems clearly dictates that something has to give. No longer can the United States Navy afford the luxury of single mission tactical aircraft on its already crowded carrier flight decks. In 1982, when I reported to the Pentagon as the new Director, Aviation Plans and Programs I became very familiar with the Navy's aircraft procurement problems. It was very clear then to the long range planners that a strategy to replace two single mission airplanes with one multi-mission airplane was sorely needed. The decision to embark on a program to replace the F-14 fighter and the A-6 long range, all-weather strike airplane with a single airplane was approved at the highest level in the Defense Department. The program, called VFMX, was approved and initial funding for trade studies, feasibilities studies and concept evaluation was approved. The initial operational capability (IOC) of the VFMX at that time was to be about 1997. At the same time the urgency to improve both the A-6 and the F-14 as interim measures to counter the increasing Soviet threat was also clearly understood.

In 1982 the A-6 had been in the fleet almost twenty-two years and had seen several modifications during that time. The F-14 had been in the fleet over ten years and had yet to see any modifications. In fact the airplane was still flying on the cutting edge of the fleet with the interim engine which was originally only to go into the early block of airplanes. It was not until 1989 that the first modification to the original F-14 arrived in the fleet; an incredible seventeen years. Four years earlier the F-14D and A-6F programs had been officially approved, but only after the funds for VFMX were zeroed. It was believed by some of the bureaucrats in OPNAV that the two programs would have a better chance of success if VFMX were taken out of the picture.

The logic of that concern escaped me at the time; but it seemed a small price to pay to get the two modification programs moving through the acquisition wickets. Among the operational naval aviators in OPNAV there was limited support for the A-6F program since it represented considerably older technology than the F-14. The operational requirement (OR) for the A-6F program was created in the office of the Secretary of the Navy, not from the fleet which should have been its source. I personally did not believe that anything could be done to the basic A-6 platform that would give it even marginal survivability against the threat of the 1990s. Nonetheless, the A-6F program received the necessary blessing from a "blue ribbon committee" who felt under considerable pressure to approve it. The Director, Aviation Plans and Programs, who should have been a principal player, was specifically excluded from this committee.

In retrospect, I suspect that the "blue suiters" were out-maneuvered by the office of the Secretary of the Navy. By agreeing to zero the funding for the VFMX program, we had opened the door for yet another single mission airplane.

The emergence of a relatively new technology called stealth was all that was needed to formulate the Advanced Tactical Aircraft (ATA) program. It was to be a single mission strike aircraft. Again, the operational requirement (OR) was dictated by the office of the Secretary of the Navy. Clearly stipulated in the document were the requirements that it be a two place, side by side airplane, that it be subsonic and that it should have a range of no less than that of the A-6. When it was learned that instructions to the several contractors doing the trade studies did not rule out a supersonic platform there was great outrage from the Secretariat until that was changed. I was personally designated to ensure that this correction was implemented.

The winner of the ATA competition was selected and the designation assigned was A-12. This occurred in about 1989. In 1990 the F-14D program was cancelled by the Secretary of Defense on the grounds of affordability. In 1991 the A-12 program was cancelled by the Secretary of Defense on the grounds of cost overruns, technical difficulties and mismanagement. Through these two cancellations naval aviation had gone full cycle and was back to square one. Since the inventory dilemma which faced naval aviation in 1982, only two things had changed. Everything else was exactly the same. The cost of tactical aircraft was still increasing at the rate of 9 to 12 per cent per pound per year. The annual aircraft procurement (APN) plan was becoming increasingly unexecutable and naval aviation's share of the budget was not going to increase. The two significant things which made the inventory dilemma different in 1991 from what it was in 1982 were stealth and the end of the cold war. We have already discussed the negligible effect that the end of the Cold War will have on the Navy's need for high tech weaponry. As for stealth, since it had already been shown by the U.S. Air Force's Advanced Tactical Fighter (ATF) program that supersonic performance and the internal (stealthy) carriage of a substantial weapon load were not mutually exclusive requirements, the natural fallout should have been a resumption of the VFMX program. There was even greater need now for a multi-mission airplane. Both the A-6 and the F-14 inventories needed to be replaced by a new multi-mission aircraft program. The Navy was now even less able to afford the luxury of single mission airplanes.

How then did the Navy come up with the AX program? The first version of the AX tentative operational requirement (TOR) stipulated a subsonic airplane with an air to air capability on a "not to interfere" basis with the airplane's primary mission of deep, all-weather strike. Subsequent versions relegated supersonic performance to a "nice to have" category. The request for proposals (RFP) which came out in August 1991 stipulated the airplane have a "respectable" air-to-air capability. The AX is, in effect, a single mission airplane. To be sure, it might be made into a tanker version and fill some other supporting missions. But, it could never be a fighter; as long as a requirement for supersonic performance is not clearly spelled out. The answer to the opening question in this paragraph is; "a combination of economics and flawed logic."

CHAPTER 33: THE ADVANCED STRIKE FIGHTER

The official Navy position on the dilemma is that a new airplane, the F/A-18E and F will satisfy the Navy's maritime air superiority requirements for the foreseeable future. The reason given is that it is the only affordable alternative to the costly F-14D since the AX is going to absorb such a large portion of future aircraft procurement (APN) budgets. This is where the flawed logic shows up. At the time of this writing, there is about $5B of R&D in the fiscal year 1992 five year defense plan (FYDP), with more certain to come, in order to increase the wing area and internal fuel capacity of the F/A-18. There can be no solid estimates as to development and procurement costs until the design matures. Nevertheless, in early September I listened to a senior naval officer try to prove (?) with slides that a completed design with virtually all of the R&D dollars already spent (F-14D) would, without question, have higher life cycle costs than a paper airplane just starting development (F/A-18E and F). If that isn't comparing apples and oranges, I don't know what is! He may be right; but he certainly didn't prove it with those slides. But, even if he is right, two more questions need to be asked; "by how much?", and, "so what?" If the F/A-18E and F doesn't adequately do the job, maritime air superiority is not achieved and the carriers might just as well tie up at the pier. There is no such thing as partial or qualified or even "respectable" maritime air superiority. You either have it or you don't! As the saying goes, in aerial combat, "there are no points for second place."

As for the AX program, the tentative operational requirement (TOR) stipulated $11B for R&D, $41B for procurement, and a unit fly-away cost of not more than $63M. These numbers are expressed in 1991 dollars.

Except for minor software changes to the avionics, the R&D dollars have already been spent to make the F-14D an interim replacement for the A-6 and still provide for the survival of the carrier battle force. By comparison, the unit fly-away cost for an F-14D in 1991 dollars would be about $50M. Priorities have clearly gotten mixed up in this decision forced upon the Navy by the Secretary of Defense.

Before proceeding further in this line of thought it is important to understand the phenomenon we call stealth. There is no questioning the fact that so-called stealth represents an enormous potential increase in the combat effectiveness for military aviation. However, there is so much misunderstood about the observability of military platforms that a few words of background (all drawn from open literature) are appropriate.

Myths and Realities - There is the wide spread belief that stealth makes airplanes invisible to radars. Not so! All that stealth does is reduce detection range. This is very important to keep in mind when considering LO (low observable) and VLO (very low observable) characteristics to be stipulated for military platforms. A corollary to that first misconception is that stealth technology applies to the full spectrum of radar frequencies. Not so, again! In fact, the new over-the-horizon (OTH) radar which just received rave reviews from Commander, Operational Test and Evaluation Force (COMOPTEVFOR) operates in the low frequency (LF) range which makes most current stealth techniques relatively ineffective.

Another myth that needs to be exorcized is that stealth is new. Not so! As far back as World War II the Germans experimented with placing radar absorbent carbon material in the leading edge of the wing of one of their bombers. The famous U-2 was a stealth airplane although stealth features were added to it only after one was shot down over Russia. Its successor the YF-12 was the first airplane to have stealth features designed into it. The B-1A/B bombers are stealth airplanes. There has been the suggestion that the supposedly stealthy F-117 of Persian Gulf fame was visible to the radar operators of a British warship in the Gulf simply because the ship's ancient radar operated in a frequency much lower than today's ship's radars. If this turns out to be true the same could be said for the highly touted B-2 bomber.

Stealth is also presumed by many to apply only to radar cross section. Not so. The camouflaging of ship, tanks and airplanes in World War II was an effort to achieve stealth in the optical part of the spectrum. Infrared (heat) reduction techniques have already proven to be successful against heat-seeking missiles and sensors using the infra-red spectrum. Acoustic stealth has long been practiced by submarine forces the world over; but should not be limited to that particular arena of warfare. Indeed, a quiet airplane was developed during the Vietnam War. Finally, and perhaps most important, stealth can be practiced in the operational employment of forces by reducing or eliminating electromagnetic emanations of equipment. This last element of stealth, when combined with cover and deception can be a powerful operational tool for field commanders. It was shown to be enormously effective in the Persian Gulf War in 1991.

Observations - Stealth technology is also being applied to weapons. But, stealth technology is a dynamic and rapidly evolving engineering discipline. If one chose to represent the YF-12 as a first generation stealth airplane, the F-117 could be called second generation and the B-2 third generation. There will doubtlessly be more. The ATF is certain to go a step beyond B-2 in stealth design and concept. But, it should be noted from previous comments that there is such a thing as counter-stealth; and several major powers are hard at work developing counter-measures to thwart this remarkable technology we call VLO. It is only a matter of time until counter-stealth becomes a reality in terms of techniques, tactics and hardware.

Conclusions - One thing is clear. We do not know just how effective stealth really is. The experience of the Persian Gulf War should be taken with a grain of salt. The Iraqi command, control and communications systems were reduced to a shambles early in the air phase of the war. Much of the initial damage was inflicted by unmanned aircraft. The effectiveness of the F-117 should be examined with that cold hard fact as a backdrop. In incorporating stealth into platforms, concessions are necessary to other air platform characteristics, such as speed, payload, range and agility. So great are these concessions in the case of the F-117 and B-2 bombers (the F-117 is not really a fighter) that if these two highly touted airplanes are detected by any sensor (including the human eye), even the most third rate air force can easily run them down and attack with weapons as simple as guns. They are virtually defenseless, being unable to outrun, out-maneuver or (perish the thought) out fight their enemy. Kissing off a half billion dollar B-2 bomber to a 3,000 dollar Stinger type missile in the hands of a teen age insurgent is a trade-off which the National Command Authority will carefully consider before committing that asset to a third world contingency action.

We need to know much more about what stealth really does for us before America begins the enormous investment in stealth hardware represented by systems such as the B-2, Advanced Tactical Fighter and the AX. The U.S. has the ability to do this measurement and to conduct the necessary evaluations. An operational evaluation along the lines of the highly successful AIM/ACEval of the 1970s in which the operational effectiveness of front line weapons systems was rigorously tested in realistic scenarios, is certainly in order before this country enters into production of any of them. Perhaps the four ATF prototypes, now in mothballs, could be employed somehow in such an evaluation.

In reviewing the realities of stealth technologies and the requirements of the navy battle force commander, it is abundantly clear to me that the Navy cannot afford a new single mission tactical airplane. There are any number of knowledgeable experts both in and outside the Navy who understand and agree. Unfortunately, the adamant position of the Defense Department in cancelling the F-14D program has forced the U.S. Navy to accept a less capable maritime air superiority airplane (F/A-18E and F) and to continue pursuing the AX program.

There is a subtlety here that must not be overlooked by Navy planners. For as long as I can remember the Navy has been forced to battle for its carriers against those who claim they are vulnerable. In the late 1960s this criticism became extremely vocal at a time when the existing Navy maritime air superiority assets were being outstripped by Soviet bomber developmental successes. The battle was with the Air Force and the Defense Department over the relative costs of land-based versus sea-based tactical air forces. The F-14 appeared in the nick of time, and became the most powerful argument in favor of keeping the carriers as an essential part of the national defense strategy.

The decision, at this critical juncture, to kill the F-14D program in favor of a less capable maritime air superiority airplane may well prove to be a fatal judgement for aircraft carriers. Those active duty dissenters to this decision who understand its true implications do not wish to be quoted. Although I understand and appreciate their reluctance to speak up, they have already been overtaken by events. Recently, a large number of "ballsy" and highly regarded young officers put their naval careers on the line by signing an open letter to the Secretary of Defense taking him to task for the rather short-sighted decision to cancel the F-14D program. More taxpayers should read that letter. One spurious argument for the present strategy is that the "robust anti-air-warfare capability" of the AX will assist the F/A-18E and F in achieving maritime air superiority. The notion that the AX will perform "respectably" in the role of a missileer is just as much nonsense today as it was in the 1960s when Secretary of Defense McNamara's "whiz kids", pushing the F-111B program, advocated putting the performance in the missile rather than in the airplane. With all the battle force's eggs (missiles) in a few baskets the missileers would become primary targets and could never survive a close-in engagement. Besides, it defies the laws of physics to expect a subsonic platform (AX) to influence the geometry of a forward quarter

CHAPTER 33: THE ADVANCED STRIKE FIGHTER

engagement against a Mach 3 bomber at eighty thousand feet. It would have to be in the direct line of approach even if a missile existed to do the job. The second law of physics which is being defied is the one about the size of a fighter's radar dish, peak power and radar aperture. It is silly, for example, to contend that the smaller dish in the F-18 E and F can do the same job as the F-14D somehow, with lights and mirrors.

The technology is here now, today, to develop an advanced strike fighter (ASF) which could satisfy both the long-range, all-weather strike and the maritime air superiority missions. The United States Navy needs this aircraft program now! It certainly does not need a very expensive single mission AX! As a matter of fact, an ASF could easily satisfy the joint requirements of the F-15, F-16, F-111, F-14, F/A-18 and the A-6 replacement programs. The potential savings from economy of scale alone would be enormous. This is the direction toward which the defense department ought to be moving.

Fortunately, the solution is simple. The AX Operational Requirement needs to be rewritten only enough to ensure that the AAW mission gets equal billing with the Strike/ASUW mission by requiring, at least, a supersonic dash capability. Now, in doing the Concept Exploration and Development trade studies in this first phase of the AX program design drivers such as weapons bay volume or range can be traded off yielding an improved AAW capability. Any fleet operator knows that the AX is going to conduct combat operations in two different modes: stealthy and not stealthy, otherwise known as "truck." The initial combat operations would doubtless be stealthy. Depending on the threat the whole panoply of survival mechanisms are available to ensure mission effectiveness and survivability. ECM, DECM, jamming, penetration aids, cover and deception, and all the rest might be considered. Munitions employed would be precision guided weapons exploiting stand-off and the targets, as we learned in the Persian Gulf, would be the enemy's eyes . . . his communications, command and control nodes. At the same time, depending on the enemy's air-to-air capability, enemy fighters would be taken out on the ground with appropriate weapons and in the air by exploiting the maritime air superiority built into the AX. Once air superiority has been achieved as it was in the Persian Gulf, all AXs are turned into trucks simply by carrying large payloads of cheaper, free fall ("dumb") bombs internally and externally. This could be called the "ass kicking" phase of the war. The true multi- role capability of the AX (I would call it the advanced strike fighter) would be evident as the airplane changes into the configuration most suited for the phase of carrier operations at hand. This is operational flexibility as the Navy has always known it. This is what Naval Aviation needs!

In 1992 the AX program was changed to AFX. In 1993 AFX was canceled and a program called JAST (Joint Advanced Strike Technology) was created. JAST, a modest technology development program, is looking at what the next joint advanced strike aircraft will look like.

Much of what the U.S. Navy has learned in the last fifty years about maritime air superiority can be summed up in a few simple truths. In order to tackle a sophisticated air-to- air and surface-to-air threat from the deck of an aircraft carrier, a fighter plane needs to be big. This is so that it can carry a large and capable radar, a large internal fuel capacity and a lethal quiver of diverse weapons. It also needs the combination of engine and wing geometry to loiter efficiently on combat air patrol (CAP) station. Finally, it needs the agility, supersonic speed and staying power to be deadly in the fight when the plots merge. Unfortunately, the F-14D is the only airplane in the world which possesses all of these critical characteristics. The F-14D decision is one that puts naval aviation in a position where there will soon be no options. Ever since the war in southeast Asia U.S. Naval fighter aviation has been the leader in fighter developments, tactics, hardware and training for all other fighter forces in the world. Now, with the stroke of a pen, that leadership has been abdicated on the basis of false economy. Baron von Richthofen was right. The purpose of a fighter is to fly, fight and win. All else is rubbish!

34

THE LITTLE FIGHTER THAT CAN'T

There simply is no way that the story of the Tomcat can be told without reference, however brief, to the airplane which killed it . . . the F/A-18 E and F . . . the Super Hornet!

In early February 1992 an internal memorandum written by an officer in the then (Op-05) organization fell into the hands of one of Washington's more unscrupulous lobbyists. Authored by the F/A-18 project coordinator, it attempted to put into context (his context) the real issues in the F/A-18E and F debate. It also recommended a course of action for the Deputy Chief of Naval Operations (Air Warfare) to follow, and a strategy to pursue.

The summary contained in the first paragraph is such a shocking indictment of the F/A-18E and F program that the memo was recalled and orders issued for all copies to be destroyed. Alas, it was already too late. The memo's author learned a bitter lesson of Washington politics. "If you don't want something you have written to be seen; don't write it!" Here is what the first paragraph said:

> "The debate is quite simple – are the improvements in the E/F worth the cost increase of $20M per aircraft as compared to the cost of a C/D? (P-1 cost sheets for E/F at 48/year are $70M/ aircraft-then year $. P-1 cost sheets C/D's at 48/year in the same time frame are $50M/aircraft then year $). Can these improvements be defended on the Hill?"

The second paragraph, even more damning, summarizes those improvements:

> "A review of the improvements:

> - Range - 80nm (24%) radius increase (internal fuel only, no tanks) in Fighter Escort mission
> - 50nm (12%) radius increase (330 gal tanks) in Interdiction mission
> - Payload - 22% increase. 11 stations vice 9.
> - Bring back - 50% improvement. 9000# vice 6000#.
> - Survivability - CN + one order of magnitude.
> - Growth Potential - 15 years capability, hardware and software."

The memo tries to make the case that the combination of all of the above factors must be stressed to sell the E/F:

> "Individually range, payload and bring back are not worth the money . . . The only rebuttal for the statement, 'the price of the E/F is not worth the 50nm increase in range', is, 'That's correct. But the range increase coupled with the payload and bring back capability is worth the price.'"

Lest the reader come to think that the author is somehow anti-Hornet; it is worth remembering that, as Op-50 from 1982-1984, I fought hard to save the Hornet. The forces of the medium attack community and the Office of the Secretary of the Navy were allied in a powerful effort to kill the entire program. It took the concerted efforts of a number of dedicated naval officers in OPNAV (led by me), Naval Air Systems Command and the U.S. Marine Corps to save the Hornet from being summarily canceled on the basis of the initial unfavorable COMOPTEVFOR report.

My motivation was then, and still is, that the light attack community deserved a better airplane than the A-7 to handle the threat of the 1990s. The F/A-18 A/B and the C/D are good airplanes. Yes, they could use a little

CHAPTER 34: THE LITTLE FIGHTER THAT CAN'T

more internal fuel. But, as the low end of the high-low mix, the Hornet was not a bad decision. However, having said that; it is also abundantly clear that no amount of R&D$ can make either a maritime air superiority fighter or a long-range, all-weather, deep interdiction strike airplane out of the Hornet. It simply does not have the growth potential to be any more than a low cost strike fighter.

The subject of unit cost has been given more smoke and mirrors than an other aspect of the program. The memo states that "P-1 cost sheets for E/F at 48/year are $70M/aircraft-then year $." All one has to do is look at past procurement practices to see that, for expensive airplanes (I submit that $70M is expensive), the Navy has never bought at a rate anywhere approaching 48 per year. It would break the APN bank to buy that many in one year! I predict that the Navy will be lucky to procure more then 24 per year with 12 to 18 a more likely figure. At that rate the unit fly-away cost of the airplane will be considerably higher. I estimate that, conservatively, the Navy will pay over $100M per airplane in then year dollars the first and second years of procurement!

In 1992, when I was invited to write an article for *Seapower* magazine, I submitted a paper titled "The Advanced Strike Fighter." In that paper I predicted that the R&D bill for the F/A-18E and F (which was then agreed to be about $3B) would easily exceed $5B. The above memo admits, in February 1992 to an R&D bill of $6B. Present estimates exceed $9M. Mark my words, it will continue to rise. The only place where R&D money was available to keep the program moving was from the AFX program. In short order the AFX program was killed. That was definitely the wrong thing to do for the future of Naval Aviation.

When the F/A-18A was first undergoing the scrutiny of the acquisition process the Navy made a decision regarding internal fuel capacity. We all knew that the design needed at least another two thousand pounds of internal fuel to be a useful carrier-based strike airplane. Unfortunately, we also knew that adding that additional fuel would probably cause the airplane to fall short of the contract specifications for acceleration and for carrier approach speed, as a minimum. The Hornet was at that critical point in the development process where exceeding two basic specifications such as acceleration and carrier approach speed could well be fatal to the program. All of us felt that would kill the Hornet. So, the decision was made not to put in that internal fuel capacity.

In 1984, an unsolicited proposal was made by the McDonnell-Douglas Corporation to the Assistant Secretary of the Navy, (Research, Engineering and Systems) to put additional internal fuel capacity in the basic airframe by adding a "hump" in the fuselage just aft of the rear cockpit. The non-recurring engineering was then estimated to be $60M. The Secretary of the Navy rejected the proposal, since he had just finished "going to the mat" with the Congress over the issue of adequate combat radius. In the final session with the Congress this gentleman had conceded that a combat radius of only 450 nautical miles in the strike configuration was "good enough." Based on that frank admission, the Congress gave its approval to continue the Hornet in the development process.

Now, ten years later, a program has been initiated to put, (guess what?) more internal fuel capacity into the airplane. This time, the additional 3,800 pounds of fuel will go into a small extension in the fuselage. This plug naturally will add considerable weight and therefore a bigger wing (100 more square feet) is needed. The bigger wing naturally dictated that a stronger empennage be designed. Of course, all of this added weight (6,200 pounds) would require that the engines generate greater thrust. The ability of the engine manufacturers to provide that increase is still considered a "high risk" part of the program.

The airplane which has evolved from all of this tinkering with the original design is a brand new airplane. All the smoke and mirrors in the world can't change that fact! The result, generally conceded by most engineers I know will be "a dog" . . . a ten billion dollar dog! Somebody ought to be taken to task!

One last point. By law, new development programs may not be started without the approval of the Congress. "New Starts", as they are called, require the blessing of the acquisition system before funds may be authorized and obligated. The F/A-18E and F program, a $6B development program by the Navy's own admission, was never given that blessing. It has, thus far, been funded as nothing more than a modification program.

There is no way that this program, no matter how it is dressed up, can be described as anything less than a massive collaboration. The Navy, the contractor and the Department of Defense have joined forces to subvert the express desires of the Congress in pursuing this program. This is probably one of the biggest scandals of the century. It is certainly the stuff for which people ought to be held accountable.

PART VIII
"QUO VADIS?, NAVAL AVIATION"

As eastern Europe rolls back the iron curtain and the American voter reevaluates his priorities, thinking statesmen the world over are reviewing the basics to see how the United States fits into the new world order. The likelihood of a major armed conflict between the USA and any other nation has all but vanished. Indeed, the very phrase super power is assuming a new definition. Economic power is becoming the reality of the 1990s; and it can be just as intimidating as its predecessor, military power, if not more so. As a maritime nation America needs to be able to protect its economic livelihood as much, if not more, than it does its sovereign territory and its people. That economic livelihood depends, to a great extent, upon free access to resources it does not possess in sufficient quantity, or, for that matter, at all. As examples, oil comes to mind along with a host of semiprecious metals as those commodities which need to flow freely to us along vital lines of communication, the sea lanes, from their sources. To protect those lines, one needs a navy adequate to the task.

Just as the likelihood of World War III between NATO and the Warsaw Pact nations is gone; the forecast of lesser, low intensity conflicts between lesser powers is on the upswing. One only has to look at the feisty demands for autonomy from the third world nations to predict, with fair assurance, their stepping on one another's toes in the process. So, the U.S. Navy of the 1990s must necessarily do the same policing of the same lines of communication, but against a different threat.

One needs only to acknowledge the growing rapidity with which high technology weaponry is migrating to the third world nations to conclude that the maritime policing will be no less difficult; at least from a technical standpoint.

Naval engagements, in those circumstances, will be quick, surgical, decisive and will involve only those forces at the scene of the action at the moment. This means that new thinking is needed on the importance of two of the important pillars of maritime strength; sustainability and force levels. The employment of limited naval forces; and U.S. naval commitments to our allies, become critical issues which will dramatically affect the shape of future navies. The United States Navy, in general, and carrier aviation, in particular, will most likely remain important instruments of national power for the foreseeable future. The new technologies embodied in future aircraft carriers and their aircraft need to be closely examined for their true impact on mission effectiveness. In the case of the carriers, characteristics such as speed, range, observability, sea-keeping qualities and survivability need to take advantage of new materials, designs, propulsion, stealth and electronic countermeasures. New naval aircraft such as the naval version of the advanced tactical fighter (NATF), the joint advanced strike technology aircraft (JAST), the tilt rotor V-22 and the advanced tactical system ATSS are all taking advantage of new technologies. Characteristics such as stealth, high thrust-to-weight propulsion, new materials, digital fly-by-wire flight control systems, very high speed integrated circuits, skin arrays and a host of other breakthroughs in electronic warfare and weaponry are being incorporated. All of these, in my view, need adequate assessment before the massive procurement commitment is begun. We guess, but don't know for sure, that stealth and supercruise will be important features for the advanced tactical fighter in the air battle, for either the Air Force or Navy version (if there is one). There can be no guesswork. These questions need to be demonstrated and resolved in prototype programs before the huge investment of limited procurement resources begins. The same must apply in other new weapons programs.

The 1991 decision by Secretary Cheney to kill the F-14D program presented a serious problem to Navy planners. They had earlier, in a separate action, zeroed all funds in the NATF program. This was the Naval variant of the US Air Force Advanced Tactical Fighter program. Now they were in the awkward position of running out of fighters with nothing on the horizon. Not only was it an awkward position, it was also very stupid. The solution they came up with was really no solution at all. It was a paper airplane which will (as of 1994) require somewhere between eight and ten billion dollars in development and would be nothing more than an under-powered F/A-18 Hornet with more internal fuel and a weapons system which, at best, could be called questionably effective in a 1997 combat environment.

To review the bidding, it is worth while to reiterate that in 1982 there was a program called the VFMX. This was nothing more than an R&D program to examine the possibilities for an airplane to replace both the long-range precision bomber, the A-6 Intruder, and the F-14 Tomcat fighter. The VFMX would be a single airplane which would carry out both missions. Some planners thought it was nothing more than a pie-in-the-sky dream. Others thought it was "do-able." I belonged to the second group. Why not? Why couldn't a single airplane do both missions? Certainly, the idea of multi-missions was not new. Indeed, the multi-mission idea is essential to the airwing of the twenty-first century if carrier aviation is to remain a viable element of U.S. foreign policy. When Secretary of Defense Cheney killed the F-14 program he set the stage for a search for a follow-on fighter to the F-14. When he also killed the A-12 (follow-on to the A-6) he also set the stage for a search for a follow-on to the A-6. Such a program is now underway. It was called the ATA, then the A-12, then the AX, then AFX, and now JAST. Unfortunately, it has been given some topspin which is driving it in the wrong direction. If one puts any credence on the operational requirement (OR) for the AFX, as it is being superseded by the new Joint Advanced Strike Technology program, it is going to be a long-range, all-weather bomber, and nothing more. It will be a sub-sonic airplane with virtually no anti-airwarfare (AAW) capability. This will be a terrible mistake, one from which the U.S. Navy may never recover. Several studies (notably one done by Captain Phil Voss of the SPAG) show very clearly that what the Navy needs to develop is not an AFX, or even a JAST but an advanced strike fighter. In other words, a VFMX. Unfortunately, the rising cost of tactical airplanes and the diminishing procurement budget drive me to the conclusion that there will not be enough money in the defense budget for both an F-22 (ATF) and an AFX. Since the AFX initial operational capability (IOC) would have been 2010 it would have arrived in the fleet a good 5 to 10 years after the F-22 reaches operational units in the Air Force. Fiscal realities will drive the American taxpayer to demand that a serious effort be made to develop a Navy derivative of the F-22. That possibility has been greatly diminished by a conscious Air Force decision to remove all carry-through structure in its design that would be absolutely essential for a Navy derivative. Such a derivative (if one were possible) would certainly evolve into an Advanced Strike Fighter rather than an AX (Advanced Strike Aircraft). As this manuscript is being written (1994), the window of opportunity has probably already closed. Unless some forward thinker in the defense department or in the Congress starts the ball rolling now, this will never happen; and what the end product will be, no one can guess. But, for sure it will not be optimum for the Navy's maritime superiority or strike missions. For as long as I can remember U.S. Navy carrier forces have been transitioning. As the cost of weapons systems has gone up, so also has the length of time it has taken for the transition to be completed. The transition to a fighter force of all F-4 Phantoms, for example, took over fifteen years and was finally overtaken by the appearance in the fleet of the F-14 Tomcat in 1972. This transition occurred during a parallel aircraft carrier transition which saw the phase-out of *Essex* class carriers to a combination of *Midway* and *Forrestal* class carriers. F-4s couldn't operate from *Essex* class decks. F-14s could not operate form *Midway* class decks; only *Forrestal* and subsequent *Midway* class carriers.

With the early demise of the last of the *Midway* class carriers the transition to an all F-14 fighter force will have taken nineteen years! The same trend can be noted for strike and other mission aircraft. Clearly, the transition to an all NATF fighter force and an all A/FX medium strike force will take much longer. It may not even be completed before carriers are obsolesced by some other, more effective, instrument of national will. Heresy? . . . perhaps not!

The aircraft carrier's main battery, its air wing, has always been tailored to the task at hand. This phenomenon was clearly evidenced in World War II, Korea, Vietnam and the Persian Gulf; and will always be the case. Therefore, "buying an air wing", as some congressmen are wont to say, is not the same as buying a pound of butter or a dozen eggs at the corner market. An air wing is really a set of capabilities; across a broad spectrum of naval warfare. The air wing need not even have to "all fit onboard the carrier at the same time." This has been the case for twenty-five years. There is still a "shore tail" for deployed carriers of the ninety-thousand ton, *Nimitz* class.

By congressional direction, the U.S. Navy is examining all possible alternatives and sea platforms for a follow-on to the nine *Nimitz* class carriers now in service, or completing construction. This follow-on platform will enter the fleet and carry out the mission of sea-based air power beginning in the year 2015 through, at least the year 2050. Will it, and others of its class be more of the same? Will it be another 90,000 ton monster which cost over four billion dollars in 1990? Probably not!

Contrary to countries like France, Spain, Russia, the U.K., Brazil, and Italy, the U.S. has made little effort to operationally evaluate alternatives to the conventional methods of operating fixed wing tactical aircraft at sea. Except for a brief and half-hearted operational experiment with AV-8A Harriers on *U.S.S. F.D.Roosevelt* (CVA-42) in 1975, the U.S. Navy's efforts in this regard have been greatly over-shadowed by lesser navies.

An experiment in ski-jump launching was conducted by the U.S. Naval Air Test Center, Patuxent River, Maryland in 1985. Although the results were encouraging, no operational follow-up occurred; this, despite some notable success by other navies.

Of particular note is the testing done by the Soviet Navy on board the Soviet aircraft carrier *Tblisi* in 1989-1990 with "marinized" versions of the Sukoi (Su-27) Flanker and the Mikoyan-Gurevich (MiG-29) Fulcrum. Clearly, the United States Navy's R&D efforts in this regard were being dramatically eclipsed by those of the Soviet Navy. The motivation behind these Soviet naval research and development efforts is threefold. First, the cost of a ninety thousand ton *Nimitz* class type aircraft carrier will become prohibitive in the new Council of Independent States which now controls much of the former Soviet navy. Secondly, and more importantly, is the operational flexibility which accrues to the carrier which does not have to accede to the constraints imposed by conventional catapulting and arresting techniques. Thirdly, and most importantly, are the vulnerability and survivability benefits which accrue to the battle force commander who does not have to steam into the wind to launch and recover aircraft; and whose carriers can sustain major battle damage and still inflict decisive damage to the enemy. This, most important, ability to sustain damage and continue to fight has always, and will always, be the ultimate determinant in the outcome of naval engagements for the foreseeable future.

Naval warfare is an evolving art. But, it is not a pretty art form. It is raw, bloody, painful, shocking, demanding of the highest of human heroics and always conducted "in harm's way." Capitulation is not simply a waving of the white flag. The raging sea is the ultimate winner of all naval engagements. The losers have, historically, succumbed to the crushing depths of the ocean and the voracious denizens which abound in them. At sea, defeat is not a pretty picture, because the sea is the ultimate enemy!

The decade of the 1990s presents to U.S. naval aviators a dilemma far more serious than the ones they survived after World War II, Korea, Vietnam or during the Carter Administration. During those trying watersheds there was one thing constant, a polar star which buoyed up the naval development efforts of all the navies of the free world, even in the most difficult fiscal circumstances. That polar star was the military build-up of the Soviet Union. In the 1990s that build-up has stopped. A new world order is sorting itself out in the aftermath of the collapse of the Soviet Union. The threat of World War III in central Europe has vanished. In its place is the ever-growing clamor of third world nations to redress the wrongs imposed and institutionalized by the Cold War. As the free nations of the world strive to make collective security work, there is still the threat imposed by rising expectations of newly freed ethnic groups all over the world. But, the need for a strong U.S. Navy, "adequate to the task" of protecting the national interests remains, in my view, virtually unchanged!

APPENDIXES

APPENDIX I:
F-14 TECHNICAL DATA

Statistic	F-14A	F-14A(Plus)	F-14D(R)	F-14D
Length	62' 8"	62' 8"	62' 8"	64' 1½"
Wing span (swept)	38' 2½"	38' 2½"	38' 2½"	64' 1½"
(25%)	64' 1½"	64' 1½"	64' 1½"	64' 1½"
Wing area	565	565	565	565
Height	16'	16'	16'	16'
Internal Fuel Cap.	16,000 lb.	16,000 lb.	16,000 lb.	16,000 lb.
Gross weight:				
Empty	40,104 lb.	41,780 lb.	43,735 lb.	43,735 lb.
Ext. fuel	4,000 lb.	4,000 lb.	4,000 lb.	4,000 lb.
Six AIM-54	6,000 lb.	6,000 lb.	6,000 lb.	6,000 lb.
Max. T.O.	72,000 lb.	72,000 lb.	72,000 lb.	72,000 lb.
Power plant (two)	TF-30-P414A	F-110-GE-400	F-110-GE-400	F-110-GE-400
Mil. thrust	21,750 lb.	27,600 lb.	27,600 lb.	27,600 lb.
Max. thrust	34,154 lb.	55,200 lb.	55,200 lb.	55,200 lb.
T/W ratio	.64	.96	.95	.95
Wing loading	92psf	94psf	96psf	96psf
Ferry range (2 Tks)	1,730NM	2,050NM	2,050NM	2,050NM
Ceiling (service)	50,000'	53,000'+	53,000'+	53,000'+
Max. speed NM/Hr.	1,544	1,544	1,544	1,544
Mach	2.38	2.38	2.38	2.38

APPENDIX II:
F-14 MILESTONE DATES

Date	Event
1961	Approval of the TFX development program by Defense Secretary McNamara.
1965	Grumman and McDonnell Douglas commissioned by NAVAIRSYSCOM to evaluate the F-111B and propose options.
1966-1967	Flight testing of the F-111B.
1967	
Summer	U.S. Air Force considers replacement for the F-4.
Oct.	Grumman brings unsolicited proposal to VADM. Connolly
Oct.	Jules Bergman television special on the F-111.
Nov.	Secretary McNamara announces his resignation.
4 Nov.	*New York Times* story alleging opposition of the CNO to the F-111B.
1968	
Jan	Concept definition work begins at NAVAIRSYSCOM on a new airplane.
1 Mar.	Defense Secretary McNamara leaves his post.
4 Mar.	VADM. Connolly testifies to the Senate Armed Services Committee on the F-111B.
Apr.	Senate votes to kill the F-111B and authorizes the VFX Program. NAVAIRSYSCOM opens VFX office.
21 Jun.	VFX Request for Proposals (RFP) is released.
17 Jul.	VFX Concept definition contracts were awarded to five contractors.
1 Oct.	Initial proposals were submitted.
13 Dec.	Proposal evaluation completed.
17 Dec.	DoD announces the down selection to Grumman and McDonnell Douglas.
1969	
4 Jan.	Grumman submits best and final offer of $2.781 Billion, a reduction of $474.4 M from 1st proposal.
14 Jan.	DoD announces Grumman the winner.
3 Feb.	RDT&E contract signed.
23 May	Airframe mock-up completed.
Sept..	Grumman informs NAVAIRSYSCOM of coming financial difficulties.
1970	
Jun.	Grumman discusses financial issues with Navy program manager, Captain Mike Ames.
Sept.	Ames writes memo on Grumman's anticipation of difficulties.
Oct.	Grumman picks up option for Lot III.
6 Dec.	Successful first flight of the F-14 on schedule.
29 Dec.	First airplane crashes on its second flight.
1971	
Jan.	Grumman meets with DCNO (Air) to discuss financial problems.
Mar.	First production Pratt & Whitney engine delivered as TF-30-PW-412.
17 Mar.	Navy informs Grumman of special program status assessment team.
22 Mar.	NAVAIRSYSCOM requests Grumman to submit statement of problems to NAVAIRSYSCOM.
31 Mar.	Zarkowsky responds to NAVAIR request
8 Apr.	First *New York Times* article Grumman's problems.
12 Apr.	Ames conducts press conference.
23 Apr.	Navy program manager testifies to Senate Armed Services Committee (SASC). Heavy media coverage suggests "buy-in."
12 May	Proxmire-Hartke press conference; Members of Congress for Peace through Law attack the F-14 program.
27 May	Defense Systems Acquisition Review Conference (DSARC) chaired by DepSecDef Packard. OSD seeks ways to help Grumman
12 Jun.	*New York Times* reports that Snead replaces Ames as F-14 program manager.
16 Jun.	House eliminates $801M appropriation for the F-14 in FY 1972.
23 Jun.	Packard reports failure of negotiations with Grumman.
7 July	Packard commissions study of F-14 program costs
6 Sept.	SASC restores the $800 million previously cut by the House in fiscal year 1972 dollars and directs order of 48 airplanes from Lot IV.
11 Sept.	Navy places order for Lot IV and Grumman agrees.
Nov.	First Navy Preliminary Evaluation (NPE) team begins (slipped from April).
1972	
20 Jan.	Grumman CEO Evans sends indicating that Lot V is invalid.
Mar.-Apr.	TACAIR subcommittee hearings; Towl reveals Grumman's loss of line of credit.
Apr.	GAO report asserts that F-14 will be inferior to F-4.
May	First production airplane delivered (scheduled for January 1972).
Jun.	Grumman engages Lavi brothers as agents in Iran.
Jul.	Second NPE begins (scheduled Oct. 1971).
Jul.	Proxmire alleges unit cost of airplane is $20.8M.
8 Aug.	USN and Grumman conclude agreement for $10 M in advance payments.
Oct.	Fleet introduction; Readiness Training squadron activated (scheduled Nov. 1972).
Nov.	Board of Inspection and Survey trials begin (scheduled June 1972).
16 Nov.	Grumman requests $40M in additional advanced payments.
8 Dec.	Assistant Secretary of the Navy approves $18M in additional advanced payments.
11 Dec.	Navy announces it will hold Grumman to terms of contract on Lot V.
12 Dec.	Grumman announces withdrawal from contract.
Christmas	Grumman pays $17M in employee bonuses.
1973	
3 Jan.	Third installment of advanced payments transmitted to Grumman.
Jan.	TACAIR Subcommittee hearings.
Jan.	Shah of Iran informally requests information on F-14 and F-15 from DoD.

APPENDIX II: F-14 MILESTONE DATES

Date	Event
Feb.	Grumman suggests eliminating Phoenix missile from F-14.
13 Feb.	Warner and Clements visit Grumman headquarters.
8 Mar.	Grumman agrees to produce airplanes; Navy agrees to renegotiate contract after Lot V.
27 Mar.	Grumman agrees to implement management changes.
April-May	Flax study compares F-14 and F-15.
May	Marines agree to buy F-14s.
7 Jun.	Clements directs Navy to stretch out F-14 purchase
July	Shah of Iran visits U.S.; watches demonstration of F-14.
August	Iranian government formally requests information about F-14 and F-15.
August	Grumman and Navy agree to a new contract.
4 Oct.	Shah of Iran receives U.S. permission to purchase both F-14s and F-15s.
Nov.	Static tests completed (scheduled Oct. 1972).
Dec.	First squadron fleet operational (scheduled Oct. 1972).
Dec.	Iran signs order for 30 F-14s.
1974	
Jan.	Navy support date.
2 Jun.	Senate Armed Services Committee charges that Navy covered up Grumman's demand for $125M advance payment before proceeding on Lot VII.
25 Jul.	SASC hearings investigate Grumman investment of advanced payment funds; Goldwater expresses frustration.
31 Jul.	Navy changes terms of loans to Grumman.
13 Aug.	Senate rejects Navy agreement with Grumman; approves Proxmire advanced payment agreement resolution.
Aug.	Bank Melli offers credit to Grumman; DoD disapproves relationship.
4 Oct.	Grumman negotiates commercial line of credit from 9 American banks and Bank Melli.
Oct.	Grumman and Navy deliver $52M check to Clements.
1981	
19 Aug.	Shootdown of two Libyan SU-22s in the Gulf of Sidra.
1982	
Dec.	Department of navy strategy board decision to develop F-14D vice a new airplane.
1983	
Jul.	SECNAV memo to CNO establishing F-14D cost, schedule, and performance constraints.
Sept.	NAVAIR concludes single FFP contract is the only viable approach to achieve SECNAV direction within cap.
Dec.	GFE, repair of repairables and GFE/GFP support excluded from cap.
1984	
May	SECNAV/NAVAIR/President of Grumman reach agreement on F-14D and A-6F program scope and cost.

Date	Event
Jul.	Full scale development contract signed.
Oct.	MSIP radar incorporated vice older technology.
Dec.	Dual chin pod for IRST and TCS incorporated.
1985	
Feb.	GASD submits FSD proposal.
Mar.	DNSARC review milestone II.
Jun.	Critical design review (hwdr).
Aug.	Critical design review (sftwr).
Oct.	SECNAV directs production NTE prices be included in FSD definitization.
Nov.	Stop work on DTDMA JTIDS.
1986	
Jan.	Unable to obtain ASN (S&L) approval to sign definitized contract because of latent defects clause.
Mar.	GASD identifies major problem with SDEX.
Apr.	NAVAIR requests proposal for conversion to USAF JTIDS.
Sept.	First General Electric F-110 engine test flight.
Nov.	Revised program developed. Five month delay to first avionics flight.
Dec.	GASD identifies costs well in excess of NTE price.
Dec.	Contracting officer unilaterally established FFP of FSD contract.
1987	
5 Feb.	SECNAV approves program restructure/approach to handle cost growth and obtains GASD agreement.
Apr.	F-14D advance acquisition contract award.
1988	
Jan.	First avionics/radar flight.
Mar.	Pilot production approval.
Oct.	Milestone III A 1 (Limited production approval).
1989	
15 Jan.	Shootdown of two Libyan MiG-23s in the Gulf of Sidra.
1990	
Jan.	Milestone III A 2 (Limited production approval).
Mar.	Delivery of first production F-14D.
May	Techeval completed.
Dec.	OPEVAL Phase I (OT-IIC) completed.
1991	
Sept.	Delivery of first F-14D (remanufactured).
Dec.	Milestone III A 3 (Limited production approval).
TBD	Delivery of last F-14D.
TBD	OPEVAL Phase II (OT-IID) complete.

APPENDIX III: GLOSSARY

AAA Antiaircraft artillery.
ACLS Automatic carrier landing system.
ACM Air combat maneuvering (dog fighting).
AIO Air intelligence officer.
Air boss Nickname for air officer. Head of air department on aircraft carrier; runs control tower.
Air wing The complement of aircraft on a carrier. It normally comprises eight or nine squadrons, three or four aircraft detachments, 80 to 90 aircraft, and 3,000 to 4,000 personnel.
Alpha strike Term derived during southeast Asian conflict by U.S. Navy for simultaneous strike on pinpoint target by multiple airplanes.
Angels Fighter direction brevity code word meaning altitude in thousands of feet (e.g., "angels twenty" means an assigned altitude of 20,000 ft.).
Anoxia A condition of lack of oxygen supply to the brain. Leads to loss of vision, coordination, consciousness, and leads ultimately to death.
APC Approach power compensator (automatic throttle).
API Armor piercing incendiary. A 20mm round designed to penetrate armor and cause secondary fire to combustibles.
APT Armor piercing tracer. A 20mm round designed to penetrate armor with a pyrotechnic tail which permits shooter to visually observe round in its trajectory.
ASW Antisubmarine warfare.
ATU Advanced training unit in U.S. naval training command.
Balanced formation Three or more aircraft in formation with equal (or nearly) numbers lined up in identical echelons on either side of the flight leader.
BARCAP Barrier combat air patrol.
BDA Bomb damage assessment.
Bingo Term used to describe a flight from the carrier to a shore base for any reason (usually occasioned by some emergency that prevented an airplane's normal recovery on board).
Bolter A missed carrier arrested landing attempt.
Break The position in the landing pattern (field or carrier) directly over the point of intended touchdown where individual members of the flight break out of the formation and turn to the downwind leg for separate approaches.
Buster Fighter direction brevity code word meaning the power setting to be used on an intercept. Buster calls for full military power.
CAG Carrier air group commander. This term of address of the wing commander continues even after air group was changed to air wing.
CAP Combat air patrol.
CATCC Carrier Air Traffic Control Center. That space where radar control is maintained of all aircraft on final approach to the ship.
Charlie Radio transmission meaning "return to the ship for recovery." The term is derived from the signal flag of the same name (designating the letter "c") which means carrier flight operations are being conducted.
Clara Radio transmission from the pilot to the landing signal officer meaning "I do not have the (optical landing system) 'ball' in sight." This transmission, if necessary, is normally made after the pilot has been told by his final controller to "check ball."
COD Carrier onboard delivery. Refers to any fixed-wing airplane designated to transport material and personnel to and from the carrier.
CV Designation of aircraft carrier dedicated to multipurpose warfare. Conventional powered. (CVN is nuclear powered.)
CVA Designation of aircraft carrier dedicated to the strike mission. (No longer in use.)
CVS Designation of aircraft carrier dedicated to the role of antisubmarine warfare. (No longer in use.)
Dirty up Direction from the final controller to the pilot to lower his hook, wheels, and flaps, preparatory to land.
Dixie Station The carrier station in the Gulf of Tonkin located off the coast of South Vietnam, fifty to seventy-five miles southeast of Saigon. The station was used to conduct close air support and interdiction against targets in the southern theater.
DLC Direct lift control. A device located on the upper surface of a wing about midchord which spoils lift when extended. Used to make small vertical corrections to an airplane's altitude. Used only on final approach.
DME Distance measuring equipment. Feature of airborne navigation equipment which measures distance to a ground navigation station.

Echelon Two or more aircraft in a formation lined up with equal .spacing on the same line of bearing from the flight leader.
ECM Electronic countermeasures.
EMCON Emission control. A shipboard condition of electronic silence.
FAC Forward air controller.
FAGU Fleet Air Gunnery Unit, Pacific. An aerial weapons school in operation from the mid-1950s to the early 1960s.
FCLP Field carrier landing practice.
Feet wet Fighter direction brevity code used to report that a plane had left land ("feet dry") and was now over water.
Final control That part of approach control which leads to a landing.
FRS Fleet replacement squadron.
"G" Unit of force of gravity.
GLOC "G" loss of consciousness. Associated with high rate of "g" onset.
Gosport A "y" shaped rubber tube used by the rear seat instructor in early Navy trainer airplanes for rudimentary, one-way intercockpit communications.
HEI High explosive incendiary. Type of gun ammunition designed to explode on impact and cause secondary burning of combustible material.
Hypoxia A condition of insufficient oxygen supply to the brain. Symptoms are the same as anoxia except that the onset is slower and less severe.
Kneeboard A device strapped to a pilot's thigh which will hold maps, charts, and provide a writing surface for copying clearances, et al.
Link trainer Early training device used to teach instrument flight procedures.
LSO Landing signal officer.
Mainmount One of the main wheels on a tricycle gear airplane.
Marshal A designated point in space relative to the carrier, described in nautical miles, feet of elevation, and degrees of magnetic bearing from the carrier from which an approach is begun.
Meatball Term for circular ball of light in the optical landing system reflected up the glide slope. Also "ball."
NATOPS Naval Aviation Operations Procedures system. System for standardization of procedures.
NORDO Designation for an aircraft with an inoperative radio.
OLF Outlying landing field.
Op order Operations order, a document written to outline the conduct of a naval operation, containing a detailed description of events, procedures, and responsibilities.
PIM Position of intended movement. A plan for the intended movement of an aircraft carrier which is given to carrier pilots prior to launch to aid in their subsequent recovery.
PLAT Pilot landing aid television. A system which provides television coverage for all carrier landings and catapults. Coverage provided by cameras in the carrier's superstructure and also flush-mounted in the landing area centerline.
RDO Runway duty officer.
RESCAP Rescue combat air patrol.
RHAWS Radar homing and warning system. Warns pilot of enemy radars.
RIO Radar intercept officer.
Route package Arbitrary geographical division of North Vietnam into Roman numerical designations for strike planning.
'Sader Abbreviated form for Crusader.
SAM Surface-to-air missile.
SAR Search and rescue.
UHT Unit hydraulic tail. First used to describe the horizontal tail surface of the F-8 Crusader. A slab tail with no trailing edge moving surface. Pitching moment is achieved by displacement of the entire surface.
VGI Vertical gyro indicator. The primary attitude indicator for aircraft in instrument flight conditions.
Wave-off Direction to discontinue a landing approach and go around.
WOD Wind over the deck. Critical criterion for the launch and recovery of carrier aircraft.
Yankee Station A modified location for U.S. Navy aircraft carriers off the coast of North Vietnam for the purpose of conducting offensive air

APPENDIX IV:
U.S. CARRIER FORCE LEVELS 1940-1975

Type	1940	1941	1942	1943	1944	1945	1946	1950	1952	1964	1968	1970	1975
CV/CVB	6	6	5	10	17	20	14	8	14				5
CVA										15	15	15	8
CVL				9	8	8	1	3	5				
CVE		1	2	19	63	70	10	4	10				
CVS										9	8	4	
Total	6	7	7	38	88	98	25	15	29	24	23	19	13

APPENDIX V:
F-14 MODEL NUMBERS

CURRENT MODEL	MODEL SEQ.#	SHIP NO.	BUREAU	DD-250 DATE	DD-251 BLOCK	CURRENT MODEL	MODEL SEQ.#	SHIP NO.	BUREAU	DD-250 DATE	DD-251 BLOCK
A	12	001	157980	09/02/71	55	A	49	049	158988	12/18/73	70
A	2	002	157981	05/27/71	5	A	50	050	158989	12/21/73	70
A	3	003	157982	01/04/72	10	A	51	051	158990	12/17/73	70
A	4	004	157983	10/26/71	15	A	52	052	158991	12/21/73	70
A	5	005	157984	12/03/71	20	A	53	053	158992	12/21/73	70
A	6	006	157985	12/18/71	25	A	54	054	158993	12/20/73	70
A(+) FSD	7	007	157986	09/19/73	30	A	55	055	158994	02/21/74	70
A	8	008	157987	01/14/72	35	A	56	056	158995	01/30/74	70
A	9	009	157988	12/29/71	40	A	57	057	158996	02/12/74	70
A	10	010	157989	02/29/72	45	A	58	058	158997	02/15/74	70
A	11	011	157990	03/17/72	50	A	59	059	158998	02/20/74	70
A	1	012	157991			A	60	060	158999	03/12/74	70
A	13	013	158612	05/12/72	60	A	61	061	159000	03/18/74	70
A	14	014	158613	06/09/72	60	A	62	062	159001	03/14/74	70
A TARPS	15	015	158614	08/31/72	60	A	63	063	159002	03/18/74	70
A	16	016	158615	09/27/72	60	A	64	064	159003	04/25/74	70
A	17	017	158616	11/14/72	60	A	65	065	159004	04/26/74	70
A	18	018	158617	10/06/72	60	A	66	066	159005	12/06/74	70
A	19	019	158618	10/31/72	60	A	67	067	159006	04/15/74	70
A	20	020	158619	12/15/72	60	A	68	068	159007	03/22/74	75
A TARPS	21	021	158620	12/31/72	65	A	69	069	159008	03/18/74	75
A	22	022	158621	01/19/73	65	A	70	070	159009	04/05/74	75
A	23	023	158622	03/24/73	65	A	71	071	159010	04/19/74	75
A	24	024	158623	04/14/73	65	A	72	072	159011	04/24/74	75
A	25	025	158624	04/19/73	65	A	73	073	159012	04/19/74	75
A	26	026	158625	04/24/73	65	A	74	074	159013	05/17/74	75
A	27	027	158626	05/02/73	65	A	75	075	159014	05/30/74	75
A	28	028	158627	06/05/73	65	A	76	076	159015	05/22/74	75
A	29	029	158628	07/07/73	65	A	77	077	159016	06/10/74	75
A	30	030	158629	06/27/73	65	A	78	078	159017	06/08/74	75
A	31	031	158630	09/30/73	65	A	79	079	159018	06/17/74	75
A	32	032	158631	08/20/73	65	A	80	080	159019	06/11/74	75
A	33	033	158632	08/28/73	65	A	81	081	159020	07/12/74	75
A	34	034	158633	08/31/73	65	A	82	082	159021	06/30/74	75
A	35	035	158634	09/14/73	65	A	83	083	159022	07/15/74	75
A	36	036	158635	10/15/73	65	A	84	084	159023	07/19/74	75
A	37	037	158636	10/13/73	65	A	85	085	159024	08/19/74	75
A TARPS	38	038	158637	10/12/73	65	A	86	086	159025	07/31/74	75
A TARPS	39	039	158978	10/14/73	70	A	87	087	159421	08/09/74	75
A	40	040	158979	10/31/73	70	A	88	088	159422	09/19/74	75
A	41	041	158980	11/13/73	70	A	89	089	159423	09/04/74	75
A	42	042	158981	11/30/73	70	A	90	090	159424	08/21/74	75
A	43	043	158982	12/11/73	70	A	91	091	159425	10/06/74	75
A	44	044	158983	11/23/73	70	A	92	092	159426	09/18/74	75
A	45	045	158984	11/28/73	70	A	93	093	159427	10/06/74	75
A	46	046	158985	12/17/73	70	A	94	094	159428	10/04/74	75
A	47	047	158986	11/30/73	70	A	95	095	159429	10/05/74	75
A	48	048	158987	12/21/73	70	A	96	096	159430	10/07/74	80

APPENDIX V: F-14 MODEL NUMBERS

CURRENT MODEL	MODEL SEQ.#	SHIP NO.	BUREAU	DD-250 DATE	DD-251 BLOCK	CURRENT MODEL	MODEL SEQ.#	SHIP NO.	BUREAU	DD-250 DATE	DD-251 BLOCK
A	97	097	159431	10/18/74	80	A	154	154	159607	08/07/75	85
A	98	098	159432	11/10/74	80	A	155	155	159608	08/11/75	85
A	99	099	159433	11/07/74	80	A	156	156	159609	08/18/75	85
A	100	100	159434	11/05/74	80	D(R)	2	157	159610	08/19/75	85DR
A	101	101	159435	10/26/74	80	A	158	158	159611	09/04/75	85
A	102	102	159436	11/14/74	80	A TARPS	159	159	159612	08/22/75	85
A	103	103	159437	11/21/74	80	D(R)	4	160	159613	09/17/75	85DR
A	104	104	159438	12/09/74	80	A	161	161	159614	09/15/75	85
A	105	105	159439	11/11/74	80	A	162	162	159615	09/30/75	85
A	106	106	159440	12/06/74	80	A	163	163	159616	09/09/75	85
A	107	107	159441	11/30/74	80	A	164	164	159617	09/18/75	85
A	108	108	159442	11/30/74	80	D(R)	17	165	159618	10/22/75	85DR
A	109	109	159443	12/16/74	80	D(R)	9	166	159619	10/22/75	85DR
A	110	110	159444	12/06/74	80	A	167	167	159620	11/07/75	85
A	111	111	159445	12/12/74	80	A	168	168	159621	10/22/75	85
A	112	112	159446	12/11/74	80	A	169	169	159622	10/27/75	85
A	113	113	159447	12/19/74	80	A	170	170	159623	11/08/75	85
A	114	114	159448	12/19/74	80	A	171	171	159624	11/26/75	85
A	115	115	159449	01/13/75	80	A	172	172	159625	11/21/75	85
A	116	116	159450	01/31/75	80	A	173	173	159626	11/19/75	85
A	117	117	159451	03/06/75	80	A	174	174	159627	11/13/75	85
A	118	118	159452	02/27/75	80	D(R)	8	175	159628	11/18/75	85DR
A	119	119	159453	03/04/75	80	D(R)	7	176	159629	12/04/75	85DR
A	120	120	159454	03/11/75	80	D(R)	18	177	159630	11/26/75	85DR
A	121	121	159455	03/10/75	80	A	178	178	159631	12/13/75	85
A	122	122	159456	02/10/75	80	A	179	179	159632	12/06/75	85
A	123	123	159457	03/26/75	80	D(R)	16	180	159633	12/10/75	85DR
A	124	124	159458	03/13/75	80	A	181	181	159634	12/18/75	85
A	125	125	159459	04/17/75	80	D(R)	15	182	159635	12/20/75	85DR
A	126	126	159460	04/02/75	80	A	183	183	159636	12/11/75	85
A	127	127	159461	03/31/75	80	A	184	184	159637	12/16/75	85
A	128	128	159462	04/18/75	80	A	185	185	159825	01/13/76	90
A	129	129	159463	04/18/75	80	A	186	186	159826	02/13/76	90
A	130	130	159464	04/03/75	80	A	187	187	159827	01/29/76	90
A	131	131	159465	04/25/75	80	A	188	188	159828	02/19/76	90
A	132	132	159466	04/18/75	80	A	189	189	159829	02/26/76	90
A	133	133	159467	04/24/75	80	A	190	190	159830	02/18/76	90
A	134	134	159468	04/30/75	80	A	191	191	159831	02/18/76	90
A	135	135	159588	05/23/75	85	A	192	192	159832	03/08/76	90
A	136	136	159589	05/29/75	85	A	193	193	159833	03/22/76	90
A	137	137	159590	05/29/75	85	A	194	194	159834	03/04/76	90
A TARPS	138	138	159591	05/29/75	85	A	195	195	159835	03/17/76	90
D(R)	10	139	159592	05/31/75	85DR	A	196	196	159836	03/29/76	90
A	140	140	159593	05/31/75	85	A	197	197	159837	03/30/76	90
A	141	141	159594	06/13/75	85	A	198	198	159838	03/30/76	90
D(R)	12	142	159595	06/24/75	85DR	A	199	199	159839	04/01/76	90
A	143	143	159596	06/09/75	85	A	200	200	159840	04/16/76	90
A	144	144	159597	07/16/75	85	A	201	201	159841	05/04/76	90
A	145	145	159598	06/24/75	85	A	202	202	159842	05/11/76	90
A	146	146	159599	07/16/75	85	A	203	203	159843	05/11/76	90
D(R)	5	147	159600	07/16/75	85DR	A	204	204	159844	05/28/76	90
A	148	148	159601	07/16/75	85	A	205	205	159845	05/28/76	90
A	149	149	159602	06/24/75	85	A	206	206	159846	05/11/76	90
D(R)	14	150	159603	07/18/75	85DR	A	207	207	159847	06/17/76	90
A	151	151	159604	07/24/75	85	A	208	208	159848	06/30/76	90
A	152	152	159605	07/29/75	85	A	209	209	159849	06/04/76	90
A TARPS	153	153	159606	08/01/75	85	A	210	210	159850	06/15/76	90

APPENDIX V: F-14 MODEL NUMBERS

CURRENT MODEL	MODEL SEQ.#	SHIP NO.	BUREAU	DD-250 DATE	DD-251 BLOCK	CURRENT MODEL	MODEL SEQ.#	SHIP NO.	BUREAU	DD-250 DATE	DD-251 BLOCK
A	211	211	159851	07/31/76	90	A	268	268	160412	12/01/77	95
A	212	212	159852	07/09/76	90	A	269	269	160413	12/05/77	95
A	213	213	159853	07/09/76	90	A	270	270	160414	12/21/77	95
A	214	214	159854	08/18/76	90	A	271	271	160652	12/23/77	100
A	215	215	159855	08/18/76	90	A	172	272	160653	01/06/78	100
A	216	216	159856	08/18/76	90	A	273	273	160654	01/13/78	100
A	217	217	159857	08/20/76	90	A	274	274	160655	02/04/78	100
A	218	218	159858	08/27/76	90	A	275	275	160656	02/22/78	100
A	219	219	159859	09/10/76	90	A	276	276	160657	02/23/78	100
A	220	220	159860	09/14/76	90	A	277	277	160658	03/08/78	100
A	221	221	159861	09/28/76	90	A	278	278	160659	03/28/78	100
A	222	222	159862	09/22/76	90	A	279	279	160660	03/31/78	100
A	223	223	159863	10/07/76	90	A	280	280	160661	04/21/78	100
A	224	224	159864	10/30/76	90	A	281	281	160662	04/18/78	100
A	225	225	159865	10/09/76	90	A	282	282	160663	05/04/78	100
A	226	226	159866	10/27/76	90	A	283	283	160664	05/17/78	100
A	227	227	159867	10/27/76	90	A	284	284	160665	06/15/78	100
A	228	228	159868	11/10/76	90	A	285	285	160666	06/15/78	100
A	229	229	159869	10/29/76	90	A	286	286	160667	07/01/78	100
A	230	230	159870	11/10/76	90	A	287	287	160668	07/11/78	100
A	231	231	159871	11/11/76	90	A	288	288	160669	09/21/78	100
A	232	232	159872	11/18/76	90	A	289	289	160670	08/01/78	100
A	233	233	159873	12/09/76	90	A	290	290	160671	07/31/78	100
A	234	234	159874	12/01/76	90	A	291	291	160672	10/02/78	100
A	235	235	160379	01/04/77	95	A	292	292	160673	09/22/78	100
A	236	236	160380	01/07/77	95	A	293	293	160674	09/23/78	100
A	237	237	160381	01/14/77	95	A	294	294	160675	09/21/78	100
A	238	238	160382	02/01/77	95	A	295	295	160676	09/21/78	100
A	239	239	160383	04/18/77	95	A	296	296	160677	09/22/78	100
A	240	240	160384	02/10/77	95	A	297	297	160678	10/19/78	100
A	241	241	160385	03/04/77	95	A	298	298	160679	10/29/78	100
A	242	242	160386	03/04/77	95	A	299	299	160680	10/25/78	100
A	243	243	160387	03/01/77	95	A	300	300	160681	10/30/78	100
A	244	244	160388	03/24/77	95	A	301	301	160682	11/15/78	100
A	245	245	160389	03/24/77	95	A	302	302	160683	12/12/78	100
A	246	246	160390	03/24/77	95	A	303	303	160684	12/08/78	100
A	247	247	160391	05/02/77	95	A	304	304	160685	11/22/78	100
A	248	248	160392	05/02/77	95	A	305	305	160686	11/29/78	100
A	249	249	160393	05/04/77	95	A	306	306	160687	12/08/78	100
A	250	250	160394	05/04/77	95	A	307	307	160688	01/04/79	100
A	251	251	160395	05/17/77	95	A	308	308	160689	01/08/79	100
A	252	252	160396	05/23/77	95	A	309	309	160690	01/12/79	100
A	253	253	160397	06/15/77	95	A	310	310	160691	02/06/79	100
A	254	254	160398	06/29/77	95	A	311	311	160692	02/01/79	100
A	255	255	160399	07/11/77	95	A	312	312	160693	02/27/79	100
A	256	256	160400	08/01/77	95	A	313	313	160694	03/06/79	100
A	257	257	160401	08/02/77	95	A	314	314	160695	03/20/79	100
A	258	258	160402	09/01/77	95	A TARPS	315	315	160696	06/13/79	100
A	259	259	160403	08/26/77	95	A	316	316	160887	04/24/79	105
A	260	260	160404	09/14/77	95	A	317	317	160888	04/27/79	105
A	261	261	160405	09/23/77	95	A	318	318	160889	04/26/79	105
A	262	262	160406	10/26/77	95	A	319	319	160890	05/17/79	105
A	263	263	160407	10/26/77	95	A	320	320	160891	05/09/79	105
A	264	264	160408	10/26/77	95	A	321	321	160892	05/03/79	105
A	265	265	160409	11/11/77	95	A	322	322	160893	06/07/79	105
A	266	266	160410	11/01/77	95	A	323	323	160894	06/14/79	105
A	267	267	160411	11/08/77	95	A	324	324	160895	06/15/79	105

APPENDIX V: F-14 MODEL NUMBERS

CURRENT MODEL	MODEL SEQ.#	SHIP NO.	BUREAU	DD-250 DATE	DD-251 BLOCK	CURRENT MODEL	MODEL SEQ.#	SHIP NO.	BUREAU	DD-250 DATE	DD-251 BLOCK
A	325	325	160896	07/02/79	105	A TARPS	382	382	161155	11/06/80	110
A	326	326	160897	07/09/79	105	A TARPS	383	383	161156	11/13/80	110
A	327	327	160898	07/11/79	105	A	384	384	161157	12/02/80	110
A	328	328	160899	08/31/79	105	D(R)	3	385	161158	12/12/80	110DR
A	329	329	160900	08/31/79	105	D(R)	1	386	161159	12/15/80	110DR
A	330	330	160901	08/31/79	105	A	387	387	161160	01/21/81	110
A	331	331	160902	09/27/79	105	A TARPS	388	388	161161	01/21/81	110
A	332	332	160903	09/27/79	105	A TARPS	389	389	161162	01/28/81	110
A	333	333	160904	10/16/79	105	D(R)	11	390	161163	02/19/81	110DR
A	334	334	160905	09/27/79	105	A TARPS	391	391	161164	02/23/81	110
A	335	335	160906	10/16/79	105	A TARPS	392	392	161165	02/28/81	110
A	336	336	160907	10/16/79	105	D(R)	6	393	161116	03/14/81	110DR
A	337	337	160908	11/20/79	105	A TARPS	394	394	161167	03/18/81	110
A	338	338	160909	11/20/79	105	A TARPS	395	395	161168	03/31/81	110
A TARPS	339	339	160910	11/21/79	105	A TARPS	396	396	161270	04/22/81	115
A TARPS	340	340	160911	11/21/79	105	A TARPS	397	397	161271	04/15/81	115
A	341	341	160912	12/03/79	105	A TARPS	398	398	161272	05/09/81	115
A	342	342	160913	12/05/79	105	A TARPS	399	399	161273	05/12/81	115
A TARPS	343	343	160914	12/03/79	105	A	400	400	161274	05/27/81	115
A TARPS	344	344	160915	12/10/79	105	A TARPS	401	401	161275	06/03/81	115
A TARPS	345	345	160916	01/04/80	105	A TARPS	402	402	161276	06/18/81	115
A	346	346	160917	01/04/80	105	A TARPS	403	403	161277	07/01/81	115
A	347	347	160918	01/11/80	105	A TARPS	404	404	161278		115
A	348	348	160919	01/25/80	105	A	405	405	161279	07/29/81	115
A TARPS	349	349	160920	01/23/80	105	A TARPS	406	406	161280	08/21/81	115
A TARPS	350	350	160921	02/06/80	105	A TARPS	407	407	161281	08/17/81	115
A	351	351	160922	02/04/80	105	A TARPS	408	408	161282	09/22/81	115
A	352	352	160923	02/11/80	105	A TARPS	409	409	161283	09/29/81	115
A	353	353	160924	02/12/80	105	A	410	410	161284	09/25/81	115
A TARPS	354	354	160925	02/29/80	105	A TARPS	411	411	161285	10/21/81	115
A TARPS	355	355	160926	03/05/80	105	A TARPS	412	412	161286	10/26/81	115
A	356	356	160927	03/14/80	105	A(+)KB	5	413	161287	11/11/81	115KB
A	357	357	160928	03/27/80	105	A	414	414	161288	11/11/81	115
A	358	358	160929	03/19/80	105	A	415	415	161289	11/25/81	115
A TARPS	359	359	160930	03/31/80	105	A	416	416	161290	01/04/82	115
A	360	360	161133	04/30/80	110	A	417	417	161291	12/14/81	115
A TARPS	361	361	161134	04/30/80	110	A	418	418	161292	12/18/81	115
A TARPS	362	362	161135	04/30/80	110	A	419	419	161293	01/19/82	115
A	363	363	161136	05/22/80	110	A	420	420	161294	01/28/82	115
A TARPS	364	364	161137	05/22/80	110	A	421	421	161295	02/05/82	115
A TARPS	365	365	161138	05/22/80	110	A	422	422	161296	03/04/82	115
A	366	366	161139	06/12/80	110	A	423	423	161297	02/25/82	115
A TARPS	367	367	161140	06/16/80	110	A	424	424	161298	03/30/82	115
A TARPS	368	368	161141	06/26/80	110	A	425	425	161299	03/25/82	115
A	369	369	161142	07/15/80	110	A(+)KB T	13	426	161416	04/05/82	120KB
A TARPS	370	370	161143	07/03/80	110	A(+)KB T	8	427	161417	04/26/82	120KB
A TARPS	371	371	161144	07/31/80	110	A(+)KB	4	428	161418	05/04/82	120KB
A	372	372	161145	08/11/80	110	A(+)KB	9	429	161419	05/12/82	120KB
A TARPS	373	373	161146	08/15/80	110	A	430	430	161420	05/12/82	120
A TARPS	374	374	161147	08/29/80	110	A(+)KB	17	431	161421	06/01/82	120KB
A	375	375	161148	09/22/80	110	A(+)KB T	18	432	161422	07/01/82	120KB
A TARPS	376	376	161149	09/15/80	110	A	433	433	161423	06/21/82	120
A TARPS	377	377	161150	09/23/80	110	A(+)KB T	1	434	161424	07/01/82	120KB
A	378	378	161151	10/07/80	110	A(+)KB	19	435	161425	07/13/82	120KB
A TARPS	379	379	161152	10/01/80	110	A(+)KB	2	436	161426	08/02/82	120KB
A TARPS	380	380	161153	10/01/80	110	A(+)KB	12	437	161427	08/02/82	120KB
D(R)	13	381	161154	11/06/80	110DR	A(+)KB T	6	438	161428	09/01/82	120KB

APPENDIX V: F-14 MODEL NUMBERS

CURRENT MODEL	MODEL SEQ.#	SHIP NO.	BUREAU	DD-250 DATE	DD-251 BLOCK	CURRENT MODEL	MODEL SEQ.#	SHIP NO.	BUREAU	DD-250 DATE	DD-251 BLOCK
A(+)KB T	3	439	161429	09/01/82	120KB	A	496	496	161860	11/02/84	130
A(+)KB T	22	440	161430	09/03/82	120KB	A	497	497	161861	11/02/84	130
A	441	441	161431	10/01/82	120	A	498	498	161862	11/02/84	130
A(+)KB	24	442	161432	10/01/82	120KB	A	499	499	161863	11/02/84	130
A(+)KB	7	443	161433	11/01/82	120KB	A TARPS	500	500	161864	11/28/84	130
A(+)KB	25	444	161434	11/01/82	120KB	D FSD PA	1	501	161865	11/30/84	130
A(+)KB	26	445	161435	11/10/82	120KB	A TARPS	502	502	161866	12/19/84	130
A	446	446	161436	12/01/82	120	D FSD PA	2	503	161867	12/14/84	130
A(+)KB	15	447	161437	01/24/83	120KB	A TARPS	504	504	161868	01/24/85	130
A(+)KB	27	448	161438	01/12/83	120KB	A	505	505	161869	01/30/85	130
A	449	449	161439	01/22/83	120	A(+)KB	31	506	161870	02/15/85	130KB
A(+)KB	10	450	161440	01/19/83	120KB	A(+)KB	29	507	161871	02/21/85	130KB
A(+)KB T	16	451	161441	02/10/83	120KB	A	508	508	161872	03/15/85	130
A(+)KB	14	452	161442	02/15/83	120KB	A(+)KB	32	509	161873	03/30/85	130KB
A	453	453	161443	03/24/83	120	A	510	510	162588	04/17/85	135
A(+)KB	11	454	161444	03/17/83	120KB	A	511	511	162589	11/20/85	135
A	455	455	161445	03/29/83	120	A	512	512	162590	11/20/85	135
A	456	456	161597	04/18/83	125	A	513	513	162591	12/13/85	135
A	457	457	161598	04/29/83	125	A	514	514	162592	01/22/86	135
A(+)KB T	20	458	161599	05/27/83	125KB	A	515	515	162593	01/13/86	135
A	459	459	161600	05/26/83	125	A	516	516	162594	01/23/86	135
A(+)KB T	21	460	161601	05/15/83	125KB	D FSD PA	3	517	162595	10/31/85	135
A	461	461	161602	06/09/83	125	A	518	518	162596	10/31/85	135
A	462	462	161603	06/27/83	125	A	519	519	162597	10/31/85	135
A TARPS	463	463	161604	07/05/83	125	A	520	520	162598	11/02/85	135
A TARPS	464	464	161605	07/13/83	125	A	521	521	162599	11/04/85	135
A	465	465	161606	07/19/83	125	A	522	522	162600	11/23/85	135
A	466	466	161607	08/10/83	125	A	523	523	162601	11/15/85	135
A(+)KB T	23	467	161608	08/15/83	125KB	A	524	524	162602	11/27/85	135
A	468	468	161609	09/01/83	125	A	525	525	162603	12/16/85	135
A(+)KB T	30	469	161610	09/15/83	125KB	A	526	526	162604	12/19/85	135
A TARPS	470	470	161611	10/27/83	125	A	527	527	162605	01/31/86	135
A	471	471	161612	09/27/83	125	A	528	528	162606	12/14/85	135
A	472	472	161613	10/31/83	125	A	529	529	162607	01/30/86	135
A	473	473	161614	11/05/83	125	A	530	530	162608	02/21/86	135
A	474	474	161615	11/29/83	125	A	531	531	162609	02/24/86	135
A	475	475	161616	11/30/83	125	A	532	532	162610	03/25/86	135
A	476	476	161617	12/19/83	125	A	533	533	162611	03/25/86	135
A	477	477	161618	12/17/83	125	A	534	534	162688	05/20/86	140
A	478	478	161619	01/23/84	125	A	535	535	162689	04/23/86	140
A TARPS	479	479	161620	01/27/84	125	A	536	536	162690	05/29/86	140
A TARPS	480	480	161621	01/23/84	125	A	537	537	162691	05/30/86	140
A TARPS	481	481	161622	02/07/84	125	A	538	538	162692	06/30/86	140
D FSD PA	4	482	161623	02/29/84	125	A	539	539	162693	06/30/86	140
A TARPS	483	483	161624	03/23/84	125	A	540	540	162694	07/30/86	140
A TARPS	484	484	161625	03/29/84	125	A	541	541	162695	08/14/86	140
A TARPS	485	485	161626	03/28/84	125	A	542	542	162696	07/30/86	140
A	486	486	161850	04/19/84	130	A	543	543	162697	08/29/86	140
A(+)KB	28	487	161851	04/24/84	130KB	A	544	544	162698	09/19/86	140
A	488	488	161852	05/25/84	130	A	545	545	162699	10/10/86	140
A	489	489	161853	05/22/84	130	A	546	546	162700	10/20/86	140
A	490	490	161854	06/05/84	130	A	547	547	162701	10/29/86	140
A	491	491	161855	06/14/84	130	A	548	548	162702	11/19/86	140
A	492	492	161856	07/02/84	130	A	549	549	162703	12/03/86	140
A	493	493	161857	07/26/84	130	A	550	550	162704	12/11/86	140
A	494	494	161858	08/16/84	130	A	551	551	162705	12/19/86	140
A	495	495	161859	08/17/84	130	A	552	552	162706	01/13/87	140

APPENDIX V: F-14 MODEL NUMBERS

CURRENT MODEL	MODEL SEQ.#	SHIP NO.	BUREAU	DD-250 DATE	DD-251 BLOCK	CURRENT MODEL	MODEL SEQ.#	SHIP NO.	BUREAU	DD-250 DATE	DD-251 BLOCK
A	553	553	162707	01/28/87	140	A(+)PROD	593	593	163409	12/13/89	155B
A	554	554	162708	02/28/87	140	A(+)PROD	594	594	163410	01/17/90	155B
A	555	555	162709	02/25/87	140	A(+)PROD	595	595	163411	02/20/90	155B
A	556	556	162710	03/25/87	140	D PROD	1	596	163412	05/23/90	160D
A	557	557	162711	03/31/87	140	D PROD	2	597	163413	05/31/90	160D
A(+)PROD	558	558	162910	11/14/87	145B	D PROD	3	598	163414	06/14/90	160D
A(+)PROD	559	559	162911	12/23/87	145B	D PROD	4	599	163415	07/13/90	160D
A(+)PROD	560	560	162912	02/10/88	145B	D PROD	5	600	163416	08/07/90	160D
A(+)PROD	561	561	162913	03/17/88	145B	D PROD	6	601	163417	08/31/90	160D
A(+)PROD	562	562	162914	03/31/88	145B	D PROD	7	602	163418	10/05/90	160D
A(+)PROD	563	563	162915	04/20/88	145B	D PROD	8	603	163893	08/31/90	165D
A(+)PROD	564	564	162916	04/29/88	145B	D PROD	9	604	163894	09/30/90	165D
A(+)PROD	565	565	162917	05/31/88	145B	D PROD	10	605	163895	10/31/90	165D
A(+)PROD	566	566	162918	06/30/88	145B	D PROD	11	606	163896	11/30/90	165D
A(+)PROD	567	567	162919	07/06/88	145B	D PROD	12	607	163897	12/12/90	165D
A(+)PROD	568	568	162920	08/08/88	145B	D PROD	13	608	163898	12/12/90	165D
A(+)PROO	569	569	162921	08/25/88	145B	D PROD	14	609	163899	01/25/91	165D
A(+)PROD	570	570	162922	09/15/88	145B	D PROD	15	610	163900	03/22/91	165D
A(+)PROD	571	571	162923	09/29/88	145B	D PROD	16	611	163901	03/27/91	165D
A(+)PROD	572	572	162924	10/14/88	145B	D PROD	17	612	163902	04/09/91	165D
A(+)PROD	573	573	162925	11/02/88	145B	D PROD	18	613	163903	05/31/91	165D
A(+)PROD	574	574	162926	11/14/88	145B	D PROD	19	614	163904	05/31/91	165D
A(+)PROD	575	575	162927	11/22/88	145B	D PROD	20	615	164340	06/28/91	170D
A(+)PROD	576	576	163215	12/08/88	150B	D PROD	21	616	164341	07/18/91	170D
A(+)PROD	577	577	163216	01/27/89	150B	D PROD	22	617	164342	08/22/91	170D
A(+)PROD	578	578	163217	01/31/89	150B	D PROD	23	618	164343	09/19/91	170D
A(+)PROD	579	579	163218	02/15/89	150B	D PROD	24	619	164344	10/11/91	170D
A(+)PROD	580	580	163219	03/14/89	150B	D PROD	25	620	164345	11/09/91	170D
A(+)PROD	581	581	163220	03/24/89	150B	D PROD	26	621	164346	02/28/92	170D
A(+)PROD	582	582	163221	04/21/89	150B	D PROD	27	622	164347	12/12/91	170D
A(+)PROD	583	583	163222	05/23/89	150B	D PROD	28	623	164348	12/20/91	170D
A(+)PROD	584	584	163223	05/13/89	150B	D PROD	29	624	164349	01/31/92	170D
A(+)PROD	585	585	163224	06/14/89	150B	D PROD	30	625	164350	02/07/92	170D
A(+)PROD	586	586	163225	07/13/89	150B	D PROD	31	626	164351	03/24/92	170D
A(+)PROD	587	587	163226	07/19/89	150B	D PROD	32	627	164599	04/24/92	170D
A(+)PROD	588	588	163227	08/25/89	150B	D PROD	33	628	164600	03/31/92	170D
A(+)PROD	589	589	163228	09/30/89	150B	D PROD	34	629	164601	04/17/92	170D
A(+)PROD	590	590	163229	09/30/89	150B	D PROD	35	630	164602	05/01/92	170D
A(+)PROD	591	591	163407	10/31/89	155B	D PROD	36	631	164603	05/29/92	170D
A(+)PROD	592	592	163408	11/14/89	155B	D PROD	37	632	164604	07/10/92	170D

VF-103 F-14A near Fallon NAS, Nevada.

SOURCES

The format of the bibliography will be a description of interviews which I had with the principal players in the story of the Tomcat. This is because those interviews constitute most of the primary source material of this book. In several chapters, the interviewee provided all of the material in the chapter. In most chapters, however, more than one person provided the sources. Any detail contained in this book in which there was a substantive disagreement between sources was resolved with the persons interviewed. There are several chapters for which the author is the primary reference source. They are identified; and a brief biographical note is inserted to qualify me in those instances. Aside from my own flight logbook, I used only a handful of other documents in the writing of this book, *The United States Navy in Desert Shield/Desert Storm*; Department of the Navy; Office of the Chief of Naval Operations, Washington, D.C., 15 May 1991 being one of them. This official Navy report was used principally as a reference to get the dates and locations of carrier operations precise. Among interviewees I found small differences in times and dates of carrier operations from one to another. This official report was the arbiter. Other sources are identified below.

Chapter 1: The Blooding

The description of the 1980 shoot down of the two Libyan SU-22s in the Gulf of Sidra came principally from Captain "Hank" Kleeman (to whose memory this book is dedicated). In a series of conversations with him when he served as the F-14 program coordinator in the Pentagon, he detailed to me the events of that particular flight. It is interesting to note that at the time of those conversations I had no intention of writing this book. As a consequence, many hours have been spent reconstructing those conversations. To help me along in that reconstruction process I interviewed "Hank's" wing commander, now Rear Admiral "Bad Fred" Lewis, Commander Carrier Group FOUR, a battle group commander. Those interviews helped me to recall details of my informal conversations with "Hank" who remains my primary source for this chapter. As the lead pilot in the flight, he remains the principal witness.

Chapter 2: The Admiral's Revolt

To be sure, there have been numerous verbal recountings of Vice Admiral "Tom" Connolly's famous testimony to the Senate Armed Service Committee. The edition of the Congressional Record, pages are the formal accounting of his famous remark. However, as anyone who has ever testified on Capitol Hill knows, what appears in the congressional record is not always a verbatim account of what was really said. Testifiers are usually accorded the courtesy of reviewing the record before the material goes to the printers. In other words, they always asked the question of me; "Is this what you really meant to say, Admiral?" Nevertheless, the accounting of all of the events leading up to that statement should properly be attributed to the man who said it. Therefore, my principal source for this chapter is Vice Admiral T.F. Connolly, USN (ret.). My account in the chapter is derived from several interviews during which the subject of the "Tomcat" came up casually. When, I finally decided to write this book, I went back to his office, declared a formal interview was in progress and turned on the tape recorder. As expected, he rose to the occasion and unburdened himself one more time. This time, however, it was a little different. Probably because he knew his words would appear in print, he tried to remember them more carefully. He also threw in more particulars which had perhaps escaped me in earlier conversations. Whatever the circumstances, that tape recording, as well as the notes I scribbled down are the heart of the source material for this chapter. Furthermore, this interview benefitted from the mellowing effect of reflection over the events of so many intervening years.

Chapter 3: The Requirement

Having spent my entire thirty-three year naval career either flying or supporting the U S Navy's maritime air superiority mission from a desk in the Pentagon, I assigned myself as the principal source for this chapter. However, as immodest as that may sound, it includes a whole retinue of giant intellects who helped, advised me, criticized me, directed me, instructed me and finally guided me in deciding exactly what the battle force commander's "real" requirement was, and still is today, for maritime air superiority. These dignitaries include Admiral "Ike" Kidd, USN (ret.) whose role as Chief of Naval Materiel was critical in the definition stage of the "Tomcat's" development as well as in the early testing. Another giant intellect is George Spangenberg, who at the time was the head design engineer at the Naval Air Systems Command. My interview with him at his retirement home in McLean, Virginia was very revealing. His perceptions were both enlightening and insightful in the writing of this chapter. During my first tour of duty in the Pentagon in an office carrying the sign "Air Warfare Analysis", I was sent over to the Navy Annex for ninety days to act as a fighter expert on the Navy Fighter Study, whose charter was to define the requirements of the F-14. People such as Rear Admiral "Whitey" Feightner USN (ret.), Rear Admiral "Tom" Cassidy USN (ret.), Captain "Gerry" O'Rourke, USN (ret.), Captain Boyd Muncie, USN (ret.), Captain J.R.C. Mitchell USN (ret.) and a host of other naval fighter aviation legends all were contributors in the process of inculcating me with a true understanding of U.S. Navy fighter requirements. I know that I have left out some names, and hope I have not offended anyone by the omission. There are so many that an accounting of them all would be a mere recitation of leaders of naval fighter aviation from the 1960s through the 1980s . . . a virtual hall of fame.

Chapter 4: The Concept

As in the previous chapter, the number of people who contributed is also too numerous to render a complete accounting. But there are some principal contributors. The principal person responsible for the F-14's design is Bob Kress, Vice President, Advance Design, Grumman Aircraft Systems Division. More than any other single person, he is the one who came up with the unique combination of elements; the AWG-9 weapons system, the variable geometry wing design, the twin turbo fan engines and the unique tandem seat airframe design. Certainly, there were others including Captain Joe Reese, USN (ret.), George Spangenberg, and Vice Admiral "Tom"

SOURCES

Connolly (ret.) who participated in the refinement of that design. My own interview with Bob Kress was initially difficult simply because he kept suggesting others who had a small part in the Concept. But after running down those people, I found all of them, to a man, pointing to Kress as "the man." Kress, then, became my principal source for the events that led to the F-14 design as well as the design process.

Chapter 5: The Acid Test

Rear Admiral John R. "Smoke" Wilson is the principal source of information in the writing of Chapter 5. That is because he, as a Commander, was the man in the front seat of the F-14 which conduct the big "six on six" air-to-air missile shoot which rendered the F-14 unique from any other fighter plane in the world. To be sure there were other people who helped, principally Rear Admiral John Weaver, USN (ret.) the former Phoenix program manager and now a Vice President for Hughes Aircraft Corporation. Wilson, now retired in Encinitas, California graciously provided me with several recorded interviews as well as a great deal of 8 millimeter film, photographs and memorabilia which helped me reconstruct the events of the 21st of November 1973. Particularly helpful were the efforts of "Mule" Holmberg, a former Marine and currently employed by Hughes, in getting me photography for this chapter and the chapter on Khatami.

Chapter 6: The Great Rebate

There were four people present the day Under Secretary of the Navy David Potter presented the fifty-two million dollar check to Deputy Defense Secretary Bill Clements. Mr. Bierworth, Grumman's President was the third and I was the fourth. Grumman was helpful in filling me in on the extra details which surrounded this interesting vignette in the history of the Tomcat . . . an Iranian bailout! History makes strange bedfellows!

Chapter 7: Selling the Shah

As in most earlier chapters, several key people played parts in providing me first hand primary source material. In this chapter Captain J.R.C. Mitchell, USN (ret.) played the principal role and provides the main primary source material. It took several taped interviews and two draft reviews before we were both satisfied with the account. Again, the Grumman Corporation helped with details. The principal purpose for including this particular event in this book is the conviction which I continue to have that the purchase of the F-14 by the Shah of Iran played a far greater role in the Tomcat's success story than most other observers give it credit for. Those too close to the acquisition process downplay its importance on the basis of an unjustified (my view) confidence in their ability to push through a program against heavy opposition. In most cases, I didn't share that act of faith then, nor do I now, in the warm glow of twenty-twenty vision. The description of the flight demonstrations of the F-14 and F-15 to the Shah at Andrews Air Force Base . . . a pivotal point in the history of the F-14 has been reviewed by Mr. Dennis Romano who was the radar intercept officer in the F-14 during the flight. The portion of this chapter dealing with the operation of the F-14 in the Imperial Iranian Air Force came from interviews with four gentlemen. The director of the Grumman/Hughes training team, Rear Admiral "Swoose" Snead, USN (Retired), arrived in Iran in early 1978 and was the driving force in the execution of the training plan. Mr. Chuck Zangas, a Grumman employee, was the aircrew training manager of the team and was present for the entire four years that the team was in country. Mr. "Mule" Holmberg, another Grumman employee, was one of the radar intercept officer instructors and was also there for the entire time. Finally, and most important, Lieutenant General Abdi Munispeher, formerly of the Imperial Iranian Air Force, was the tactical commander in charge of all Iranian fighter forces and especially of the F-14s at Shiraz and Khatami. His account of the combat performance of the Iranian F-14s against the Iraqi Air Force is the only reliable record of which I am aware on this subject which, until now, has been shrouded in secrecy.

Chapter 8: Khatami

The material which appears in this chapter is a distillation of the data gathered in four interviews. The most important of the interviewees is Major General Abdi Minuspeher, formerly of the Imperial Iranian Air Force. As the on-site commander of the Iranian F-14 fighter force at Khatami air base his input to this story has been essential especially in the manner in which it substantiated the information derived from the other three sources: Rear Admiral "Swoose" Snead, U.S.N. (Retired), Lieutenant Colonel E.B. "Mule" Holmberg, U.S.M.C. (Retired) and Mr. "Chuck" Zangas. Snead was the senior member of the Grumman/Hughes team in Iran and played a key role in the administration of the Grumman/Hughes employees; from pilots and RIOs to mechanics and ground school instructors who taught the Iranians how to fly, fight and maintain their F-14s. Holmberg was one of the radar interceptor instructors who taught their Iranian counterparts from the cockpit as well as the classroom. Chuck Zangas was the Grumman site manager at Khatami. Between the four of these fine gentlemen, I was able to get a fairly complete understanding of what it was like to carry out the mission of training the Iranians to operate the world's most sophisticated fighter plane.

Chapter 9: The Little Engine That Couldn't

I was one of the principal sources for portions of this chapter. As Director of the Priorities Analysis Group, I was an advisor to the Chief of Naval Operations on research and development matters from the vantage point of a staff (OP-00K) which reported directly to him. As a consequence I did not feel fettered by any intervening authority, and wrote several candid memoranda expressing my own personal views of the importance of the F-14 to the Navy at a time when it kept falling into developmental difficulties. Although I place no particular importance on the effect of any of those memos on the ultimate success of the program, they do establish my credibility as a witness in those early engine problems. That was in 1972 and 1973. Later, as head of the fighter wing in the Pacific fleet I had ample opportunity to rage at "those idiots in the Pentagon" for what was abominable engine performance in the F-14A. I had plenty of reason to complain for, despite extremely restrictive throttle movement limitations imposed on the aircrews, we were experiencing a little over one compressor stall per week in the fleet squadrons. A year or two later as, Director, Aviation Plans and Policy (OP-50) I initiated what came to be called the F-14D program. Although the program was advertised as a threefold improvement in engines, avionics and radar, the hidden agenda was really to fix the engines at all costs. My interview with Admiral Kidd, referred to earlier was particularly valuable to me for the insights into why the Navy waited so long not only to fix the engine problems, but also to initiate a newer model of what turned out to be such a successful airplane.

Chapter 10: NASA

The principal sources for the material which appears in this chapter came from a series of interviews with three people: Mr. Ed Schneider, a NASA test pilot, Mr. Joe Wilson, a NASA flight test engineer and Mr. Kurt Schroeder, Chief Test Pilot for Grumman. All three were extremely forthcoming in researching, finding and interpreting for me, all available NASA flight test data on the F-14.

Chapter 11: The First Tomcat Deployment

The sources for this chapter are Rear Admiral Lewis who, as a young pilot was in one of the first east coast F-14 squadrons. The other source is Captain Monroe "Hawk" Smith, USN, who was a young pilot in one of the first west coast F-14 squadrons.

Chapter 12: Fightertown, U.S.A.

As head of Fightertown, U.S.A. during the time in question, I am the principal source for this chapter. Much assistance was rendered by my former

SOURCES

supply officer, Captain Dick Scharff, USN (ret.) and my former Maintenance officer, Commander Ed Pryor, USN (ret.) in refreshing my memory on some of the finer details. My former Chief of Staff, Captain Keith Huisman, USN (ret.) has also reviewed the material in this chapter, along with my aide and radar intercept officer, Commander Frank Brown, USN. To all four of these fine gentlemen I owe a debt of gratitude for taking the time to review and amend as necessary for factual correctness.

Chapter 13: AIM/ACEVAL
The two sources for this chapter are Captain Monroe Smith who trained the Navy members of the "Red Force", and Captain "Boomer" Wilson who was the second in command of the Navy aircrews and then, after J.W. Taylor's departure, took over as officer-in-charge of the Navy aircrews in the tests.

Chapter 14: Television Camera System
Again, I have relied upon my own knowledge of the events in this chapter and again I sought the assistance of Commander Frank Brown in helping fill in details from his memory and personal records. This extremely important capability is unique in the F-14 and has proven to have enormous operational utility in the fleet. Assistance for technical detail was also provided by the Electro-mechanical Division of the Northrop Corporation, the producers of the television camera system.

Chapter 15: Fleet Aerial Reconnaissance
The Tactical Aircraft Reconnaissance Photographic System (TARPS) was introduced into the fleet to replace the ancient RF-8G photo Crusader. That venerable airplane had assumed the entire load of the fleet aerial reconnaissance after phase out of the RA-5C Vigilante. In 1988, with the phase out of the RF-8G, the F-14A with a TARPS pod suspended from an external stores station became the sole remaining carrier based photo reconnaissance airplane. TARPS was just phasing into the fleet replacement squadron at Miramar when I took over command of the functional wing. My own personal recollections of the TARPS introduction are related in this chapter. Assistance was provided by the Grumman Aircraft Systems Division in detailing information on the system.

Chapter 16: The Gunfighter
The primary source for the information contained in this chapter is the author. The background on fighter airplane gun requirements goes all the way back to my tour of duty as a weapons delivery instructor at the Fleet Air Gunnery Unit, Pacific in 1957. My combat experience in southeast Asia with the Crusader's guns add credence to the statement of requirements. Later, my personal experience with the Tomcat in the gunnery pattern and my experience as Director, Aviation Plans and Requirements in 1982-85 were called upon to articulate both the requirement and the gun capability of the Tomcat.

Chapter 17: The F-14B
The principal source for this chapter was Mr. Bob Kress, Vice President, Advanced Design at Grumman Aircraft Systems Division.

Chapter 18: The Future of the F-14
The primary sources for this chapter are Rear Admiral Dave Frost, USN who at the time was the F-14 program coordinator in OP-506 and the author who was Director, Aviation Plans and Programs. It took the two of us almost nine months to get the program legitimized in the Navy as an accepted program wending its way through the OPNAV wickets. It took another two years to get it officially approved by the Secretary of the Navy.

Chapter 19: The Blue Room
The principal sources for this chapter are Rear Admiral Lee Tillotson who relieved Dave Frost (previous chapter) as F-14 program coordinator, his successor Captain "Hank" Kleeman, USN and the author, still OP-50. After Frost's departure for bigger, and less painful duties, Tillotson took up the chore of getting the F-14 program through the wickets of the Navy secretariat . . . the staff. This process was more stultifying than getting it through the blue suiters of OPNAV. It was a slow, tough process and Tillotson also received orders to bigger and better things, having been relieved by Kleeman. It was "Hank's" chore to get the program brief through the final hurdle, the approval of the Secretary of the Navy in the Blue Room.

Chapter 20: The A-Plus
There were several sources for the material in this chapter. The two principal ones were Commander "Spike" Prendergast, Commanding Officer of Fighter Squadron Twenty-four. His squadron was one of the first to receive the F-14A Plus in the Pacific Fleet. "Spike" was one of the driving forces in advancing the employment of the A Plus in the air-to-ground (strike) role. The second source was (then) Captain Jack Snyder, F-14 Program Manager at the Naval Air Systems Command.

Chapter 21: Electronic Countermeasures
Three naval officers and a civilian provided the source material for this chapter. The first, Captain Larry "Hoss" Pearson, USN (ret.), provided a great deal of information during an interview I conducted while he was Commanding Officer of Naval Air Station, Miramar, California, "Fightertown, USA. The second source was Commander Frank Brown who fought the bureaucracy on several tours of duty in VX-4 and in Washington. Frank also appears in this story as my trusty radar intercept officer and aide when I was commanding the wing at Miramar. The third naval officer was Captain Jim Sherlock, USN who has been closely connected with the ECM woes of the F-14 almost since its inception. His incisive thoughts have been very helpful to me in interpreting the convoluted sequence of events which describe this bureaucratic disaster. The final source, a civilian, John Caffrey, is now the senior representative of the manufacturer, Grumman, at NAS Patuxent River, Maryland. John has been a key activist in enhancing the electronic countermeasures capability of the F-14 since its inception.

Chapter 22: The Reserves
Although there were several reservists who helped me to describe, briefly, the history of the introduction of the F-14 into their ranks and its performance since then, the greatest help came from Captain "Chuck" Long, USN currently working at the headquarters of Commander, Naval Reserve Forces in New Orleans.

Chapter 23: Off Lebanon
Rear Admiral "Bad Fred" Lewis, Commander Battle Group FOUR provided me with several interviews covering many other chapters in this story in addition to the description of the employment of the Tomcat in the aerial reconnaissance mission over Lebanon.

Chapter 24: Indian Ocean
Rear Admiral Lee Tillotson provided the bulk of the primary source material regarding the operational employment of the F-14 in the Indian Ocean. His association with the subject is quite broad. He commanded an F-14 squadron, then a carrier air wing, an aircraft carrier and finally a carrier battle group, all in the Indian Ocean.

SOURCES

Chapter 25: The Achille Lauro Incident
The principal source for this chapter was Rear Admiral "Bad Fred" Lewis who at the time was Commander Tactical Wings, Atlantic.

Chapter 26: Norwegian Sea
The primary source for this chapter was Captain J.R.C. Mitchell who commanded the *U.S.S. John F. Kennedy* during a deployment into the Norwegian Sea in 1976.

Chapter 27: Northwestern Pacific
Rear Admiral Chuck McGrail provided the material in this chapter as a battle group commander who took his carrier battle group into the Northwestern Pacific in 1986. The vignettes which he provided are particularly vivid. His prior experiences, particularly as Assistant Chief of Staff, Commander Task Force Seventy-seven and later as Commanding Officer of *U.S.S. Midway* give his testimony on Pacific theater operations great credibility. He provides several vignettes gleaned from these experiences which serve to highlight rather graphically how the F-14 performed in this neck of the ocean.

Chapter 28: "Navy Four, Libya Zero"
Rear Admiral "Snake" Morris gave me a sparkling interview as the battle group commander during this particular incident. The flight leader involved in the actual engagement also provided me with a very insightful interview. Sadly, he must remain nameless for security reasons.

Chapter 29: Persian Gulf
Vice Admiral Jerry Unruh, as a battle group commander in the Persian Gulf during hostilities there was my principal source of the material in this chapter. In addition, Commander J.J. Quinn as Commanding Officer of Fighter Squadron TWO (VF-2), the Bounty Hunters, participated in the first strike operations from the Persian Gulf from the deck of the *U.S.S. Ranger*. He provided useful insight at the squadron of how the F-14 was employed in the several phases of the war. Captain Lyle Bien, USN was the senior naval officer on General Schwarzkopf's staff in Riyahd. He provided a valuable perspective on the execution of the air war as well as the employment of the F-14 in that conflict.

Chapter 30: Red Sea
Rear Admiral Riley Mixon, as the battle force commander in the Red Sea during hostilities there in 1991 provided material for this chapter. Another valuable source was Lieutenant Commander Jerry Beaman, USN who was assigned to Captain Bien's section of the staff at Riyadh. His insights from the squadron level were invaluable because he flew combat missions in the F-14 not only from carriers in the Persian Gulf but also from carriers in the Red Sea. Jerry is now the Operations Officer at the Navy Fighter Weapons School, "Topgun."

Chapter 31: F-14D "Super Tomcat"
The author is the primary source of this chapter by virtue of his direct involvement in the program as Director, Aviation Plans and Programs from 1982 to 1984. Rear Admiral Phil Anselmo, as the functional wing commander at Miramar had the responsibility for fleet introduction of the Super Tomcat. In his next tour of duty as Director, Aviations Plans and Programs (OP-50), Phil had the unpleasant task of implementing the cancellation of the F-14D program by a badly misled Navy leadership.

Chapter 32: "Tomcat 21"
The author is the primary source for the material contained in this chapter and was assisted by Bob Kress, Vice President for Advanced Design at the Grumman Aircraft Systems Division in Bethpage, Long Island.

Chapter 33: The Advanced Strike Fighter
The author is the primary source for this chapter. It represents the distillation of thirty-three years of hands on involvement in Navy tactical aviation. Some of the views expressed in this chapter are at variance with positions taken by Navy leadership at the time this book went to press. The author is solely responsible for the thoughts articulated in this and in the final two chapters.

Chapter 34: The Little Fighter That Can't
The author is the primary source for this chapter for the reasons stated in the chapter above.

Part VIII: "Quo Vadis?, Naval Aviation"
The author was the primary source for the material contained in this chapter for the same reasons stated in the previous chapter.

Appendix I
Data provided by Navy Fighter Weapons School, the F-14 program office of NAVAIRSYSCOM and the Grumman Corporation.

Appendix II
Data provided by F-14 program office and NAVAIRSYSCOM.

Appendix IV
Data provided by CNA study, 1968.

Appendix V
Data provided by the Grumman Corporation.

Also from the publisher

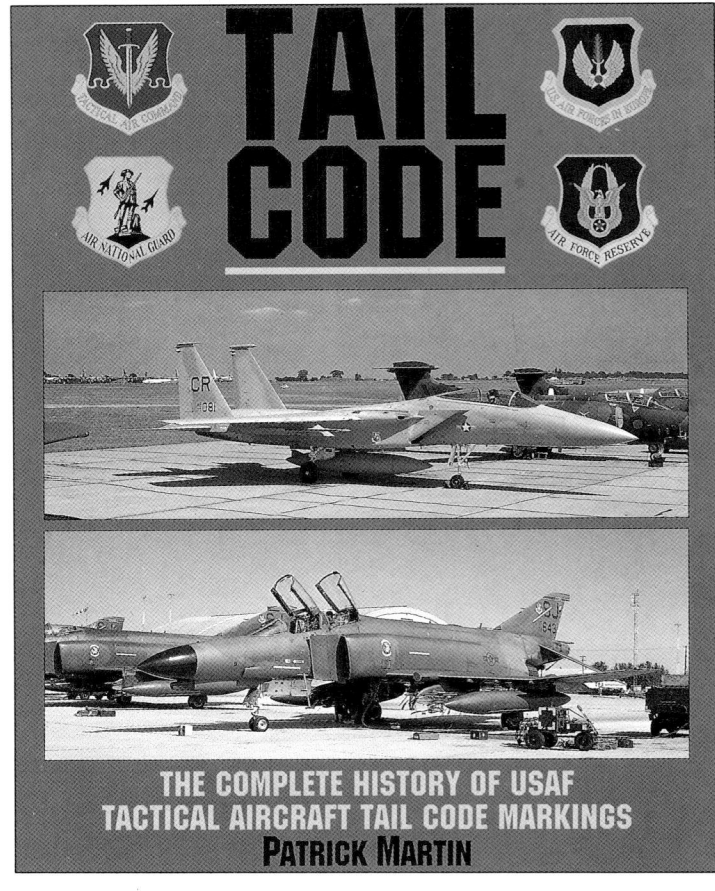

VF-124
GUNFIGHTERS

VF-142
GHOSTRIDERS

VF-143
PUKIN' DOGS

VF-154
BLACK KNIGHTS

VF-191
SATAN'S KITTENS

VF-194
RED LIGHTNINGS

VF-201
HUNTERS

VF-202
SUPERHEATS

VF-211
CHECKMATES